341/500

Suzanne

WHOLEHEARTEDLY

The One You Want To Find Is You

HOLLY RUTH FINIGAN

Thank you for your heart

[illegible]

For information about speaking engagements or purchasing book in quantity or for any other book related inquiries, please email hollyruthfinigan@gmail.com or visit hollyruthfinigan.com

Cover & Branding by Michael Molloy & Jasmine Takanikos
Interior Design & Layout by Sara Feather Farley
Flowcode & Flowpage Consulting by Katie Norton
Photos of Holly Ruth Finigan by Georgie Morley

Published in the United States of America by Holly Ruth Finigan
ISBN: 979-8-9874321-0-5
First Printing 2023

For Ruth
For Jack
For Christina
For Sanna
For Teri
For Steve
For Jackson
For Brendan
For Anthony
For Courtney
For Nina
For Amie
For Family
Always. . .
And In All Ways.

We're going on a

Part One

FINIGAN'S EXISTENCE

Part Two

RUTH'S CONSCIOUSNESS

treasure hunt...

...and the one you want to find is you.

Part Three

HOLLY'S BLISS

Part Four

I AM

"The truth is like a lion;
you don't have to defend it.
Let it loose;
it will defend itself."

— AUGUSTINE OF HIPPO
(supposedly)

Dear Reader,

We write this to you from the other side.

We are home. We are free.

This book is a treasure hunt to Self and with that knowledge, we want you to remember that you can read this story however you choose. While we somewhat recommend the old fashioned way—you know, from the beginning to the end—we can also inspire you to pick a page, any page, and see if that story, chapter header or question at the end resounds with your heart.

After all, this book is simply telling you once again what everyone has been telling us for lifetimes before:

We begin by going out and end coming home within.

For all these winding roads lead back to the same one path.

And what is the path's name?

Well . . . sounds like it's time to start reading.

Are you ready?

The Truth is, if you are holding this book right now, you are ready.

So we wish you well, dear reader.

We wish you courage on this journey with peace in your heart and a smile in your eyes.

Now take a deep breath in . . .

Exhale . . .

. . . and begin again.

Wholeheartedly,

Holly Ruth

How the Story Begins

April 7th, 2014

I could hardly look at her when I walked into that room. Her room. Where she used to savor the afternoons on her king-sized bed while doing a crossword puzzle. A twenty-minute snooze would follow, the paper on her chest, a pillow covering her eyes.

But now I barely recognized her, sitting straight up in that rented hospital bed, her brown doe eyes protruding out of swollen dark sockets. Her short salt-and-pepper hair looked wiry and wild; it needed to be brushed, and desperately needed a wash. She was thin—hell, she always had been thin—but now she was borderline skeletal. Her smooth Italian skin had weathered and yellowed, and she had lost the ability to close her jaw.

Without making eye contact she called me in. "Holly? Holly?" she cried out.

"It's me. I'm right here," I said. It took everything I had in me to put a smile on my face; my heart had been breaking for months.

"Holly, did you write something?" She couldn't focus. Her gaze darted around the room.

"What? Mom, I just got here," I told her. "I just drove up from Nantucket."

Her eyes stopped moving around and settled on my face. Sounding both clear and frustrated, she repeated herself. "Holly, did you write something?"

Mute, shaking my head, I just looked at her. We locked eyes as she said her last four words to me, *"Don't worry, you will."*

PART I

Finigan's Existence

1.

The Dreamer

Grey Lady
Summer 2005

A mermaid and her little black book: this is where we begin.

I am a writer. My life is filled with countless journals in which I share deep dark truths and lighthearted stories.

Everyone told me being a writer wouldn't pay me any money. So, I became a real-life bartender who was quick with a joke or a light for your smoke, but, as Billy Joel said, there was some place that I'd rather be. For me, that was sitting on a beach with music in the background, a felt-tip pen and a black journal with unlined pages close at hand. I am a color-outside-of-the-lines kinda gal: I have never been interested in keeping things perfectly straight and narrow.

I would bartend at night, then awaken late in the morning, grab a bagel and coffee, and go straight to the sandy shores of Madaket. I prefer that these beach days be enjoyed solo in a serene spot with no cell service. My first boss on the island showed me a secret beach on the west end of the island, a place where if you saw four cars, you'd turn around, as it was too crowded.

"Don't tell anyone about this spot, and you're welcome," he said with a wink, as we set up chairs to savor the sunshine before another crazy Saturday at his restaurant, Schooners.

I would literally and spiritually find myself back at this beach for the next seventeen years, just me and my little black book. Rarely did I bring anyone to this place: something had to be all mine. As a bartender, I gave so much of myself to serve others at night that, during the day, I had to figure out a way to recharge.

Let's go back and talk about how I even got here, to this little island thirty miles out to sea off the coast of Cape Cod in the state of Massachusetts. It is called Nantucket

I didn't grow up here: I didn't summer here. I didn't have a family home here, or any family that lived here, unless you count my "big sister" in my sorority at the University of New Hampshire. She grew up here; she went to high school here; and she had a family home here. And since we were about to graduate from our lives in the Granite State, she invited me to come live with her family for the summer and tend bar on the island.

I had worked at an Irish pub in college, and had minored in binge drinking with a major in journalism. In June of 2005, I thought to hell with news writing. I felt that the world of journalism had failed to mention that a degree in that art form translated loosely to a life behind bars. Choosing to sling drinks instead of write stories, I decided that I would spend one more summer avoiding the "real world" on this island whose nickname is The Grey

Lady. I threw my diploma in the back of my Altima, packed up my party dresses, and boarded a ferry to an island whose name translates to "faraway land."

Nantucket was a place you could get to only by ferry or by flight. It was home to Moby Dick, and to flip-flop wearing billionaires with deep pockets for good causes. Many year-round residents and natives had deep roots in the early nineteenth century whaling era, which had made Nantucket a familiar name around the world; some could trace their roots back to the first English settlers. But what they call me (the locals, that is) is a wash-ashore. That is the name for those of us who weren't born on Nantucket. Regardless of whether you washed-ashore, flew here, or grew up here, this place was not easy to get to . . .

. . . and that's exactly why I liked it.

My Life, Your Vacation

Summer 2008

By the end of my first three summers on Nantucket, I had become an excellent eavesdropper with an incredible memory. This combination gave me the ears of a skilled listener and my days off to write and process what I had heard.

So began my first blog: www.Hollyblackbook.blogspot.com. Don't even try to look it up: it doesn't exist anymore, for a plethora of reasons. By day I wrote, and by night I lived to serve you. During our family-style meal before opening, I would read from one of my little black books quotes that I'd overheard at the bar, like, *"Islands are for finding yourself or losing yourself. Unfortunately, too many people lose themselves here on Nantucket."* Then my co-workers and I would start work and get people drunk. Then we'd get drunk, with a giant wad of cash in our back pockets.

Think of the bar like a spirited travel agency. You pay me to get intoxicated, and I listen to whatever you want to share while the cocktails kick in. You ask me what you should do, and you listen to what I say. Then you do what I tell you to do.

See, I only tell you to do the things that I would do, and I have spent the last three years savoring the island's social scene. I spend the summers living it up, and the winters chasing summers.

"Holly Finigan is living the dream. Always." That is what my Skype "away" message says. Because this is the dream, right?

My mom disagrees. She believes I'm living in a fantasy world. She calls Nantucket Birdland. She calls me Mermaid, and she often calls me out for this late-night lifestyle that I have made my norm. "Writers write, Mermaid," she'd preach. I'd feel bad, thinking that she is judging me—telling me to get out from behind the bar.

"But writers don't make any money, Mom. Everybody knows that." And as for me? I know I am in the right place for a college journalism major. Because the news around this rock is that I am not just a bartender . . . I am a Startender.

And if this was a dream? I say do me a favor, and don't wake me up.

What Do You Want?

Fall 2009

"You bartenders," the old man observed, while clutching a glass of Kettle One in one hand and holding a handkerchief in the other, "You're like high-end therapists. And if you're a good bartender, let me tell you, you can be anything in this world.

He was a well-loved and respected Nantucket restaurateur who had owned and operated one of the most iconic restaurants here from the '70s through the '90s. He had seen island life through its ebbs and flows. He wasn't there to chat me up; he was about five decades too old for me. But his words stuck in my mind throughout my last years behind the bar. Being a bartender was like being a therapist, but, to me, it was more like being a personal concierge.

My bartender buddy says the job is 10 percent pouring drinks and 90 percent knowing how to deal with people. My father says life is all about relationships. I believe there is something very intimate about the way Nantucketers, visitors and natives alike, perch upon barstools. I spent the majority of my first decade "on island" standing behind the bar, telling people how to sip, shop, and stay on Nantucket. And when I got tired of that, I would invite friends and family down to live out the tales I was telling, and to check out the restaurants, retail, and real estate scene with me in person. I always had a stack of cash and felt the need to overserve my friends who took the time to come visit. I was like a tour guide, taking them on bar crawls, shopping sprees, and finishing every night with live music and dancing at the legendary Chicken Box, although most of those nights, I would have to bartend from 4:00 p.m. to midnight.

Friends would sit at my bar, sip and nosh while they got stellar service, and then I got paid to have my pals hang out with me. It sounds like fun, but there was a real issue at hand. The problem was that my hands were doing the work at night, but by day all I wanted was some peace and quiet and space to write. Tending the bar was all a performance—a means to get paid so that I could start being who I really was.

A writer.

One local that summer gave me another great quote: "Ya gotta do what ya gotta do, to do what you want to do." That was his life's motto.

But what did I want to do with my writing? I was never quite sure. No one ever had asked me what I wanted; that, as a bartender, was my job.

Xennial

Winter 2012

Can anyone always and forever keep a secret? Never tell anyone?

I don't believe so as secrets were created for sharing. So where did this secret come from?

My boyfriend (BF) told me once that my blog could be so much more. He always stood up for me and my writing. Although he had started as my barback, he knew my talents went way beyond remembering an eight-top's drink order in my head. He was first my friend and then my boyfriend: he had known me, the real me, from the get-go. And he knew where I was happiest: writing in little black books on beaches. In December of 2011, after a year of hardship and struggle with family sickness, months spent in hospitals, and leaving one island gig for a "sneaky" bar in another iconic Nantucket building, BF told me to slow down and take my blog and writing to another level. "Make your black book into an online magazine," he suggested, "a place where people can go to find out what is happening on Nantucket when they can't pick up a copy of the local newspaper or N Magazine."

BF and I are what they call *Xennials*, a micro-generation born between 1975 and 1985, who grew up with the internet and also deeply remember a life without it. We saw the great opportunity that the wild, wild west of the internet generation brought. We knew how to use social media for fun and business, and at this point in 2012, Facebook was becoming an emerging marketing platform in itself.

Plus, it was free. And while I was fake rich in the summer, I was dirt poor in the winter, a condition that causes creatives like me to get a little scrappy. So, I turned the blog into **The blACKbook**, *Nantucket's online lifestyle guide to all things hip and fresh*. I would tell readers all the things they heard from me behind the bar, but now give those summer people a new sense of ACK-cessibility. (ACK is Nantucket Airport's code, another way to say Nantucket that only insiders would know.)

"There is just one thing," BF stressed. "Until you launch, you're going to have to keep this a secret."

I nodded; I promised.

I have always been good at keeping secrets.

Just ask my mom.

Blog-tender

Summer 2012

I knew I wanted to get out from behind the bar eventually, but how? Writers don't make money, yet for some reason I thought my muse could. Maybe these little black books were my way out. At first, I could bartend and blog, then eventually blog and not bartend.

However, things don't shift as quickly as we might want them to. During my first few years launching blACKbook, I still bartended three nights a week while running the website. It was an insane schedule, and it went something like this:

Work from 4:00 p.m. to 2:00 a.m.; tell everyone about the blACKbook all night; try not to get so drunk that I can't drive home.

Get home; blog from 2:00 a.m. to 4:00 a.m.; try to stay awake after the buzz wears off, and sleep from 4:00 a.m. to 7:00 a.m.

Wake up to launch my blog post on Facebook at 7:00 a.m., since algorithms have not come in yet, then go back to sleep for two hours.

Head to the beach to write again; gear up for the next launch.

Go back to work.

Rinse and repeat.

And then in 2012, I was asked to help with marketing the Nantucket Book Festival. What I really wanted was to have a book in the festival, and not just post on Facebook about it. But these years were for paying my dues, and this year my job was to organize the "Authors Behind Bars" event. And who better to do that than a blogger-bartender-wannabe Carrie Bradshaw of *Sex and the City* fame?

There I was, getting the writers of this book festival buzzed, as fans would shake the hands of those who wrote their favorite books. It felt bittersweet to me, as I poured glasses of champagne and made weird drinks only an obscure writer might order. While waiting in line for the bathroom that night, I heard a girl whisper to her friend, "That's my favorite blogger!" and she pointed at me.

I smiled, feeling a bit elated that I'd been recognized, but quickly brought myself back to reality—there was no Bloggers Behind Bars event; that was just my life.

The It Girl

Winter 2013

When I had conceptualized the blACKbook, my goals were two: I wanted to be an "it girl" on island with whom everyone wanted to work, and I wanted to create the cheapest and best advertising platform on Nantucket. After my first full year with the platform, I didn't know this, but what I was called in the media world was a "disrupter." I was moving into a very established marketing business and shaking things up without ever realizing how powerful I was becoming. I was working at such an unsustainably fast internet pace that there was no time for me to stop and see what I was creating. I was only concerned about keeping my head above water while my followers continued to watch me with excitement.

I was becoming Nantucket's most "liked" page on Facebook, with the most followers on Twitter. I took a deep dive into Google Analytics and loved seeing the spikes in web page views after I launched new pieces on the top five sneaky bars, or the top four ways to celebrate July 4th, or the top ten places to have drunch (a drinking lunch).

I was all about the list and the numbers, but the real numbers that I needed, the cost to advertise with other platforms—places like the local newspaper, the magazines, the weekly newsletter, and flyers—I didn't know how to ask for. I had nothing to compare my own offerings to, and none of the others would talk to me about my new social media business. They made fun of my marketing, while I sneaked around, trying to find out their advertising rates. And when I did get them, I just made my ads cost less, with a firm stamp of return on investment.

I was better, and I was cheaper: that was my business model. But this model came with a high price of no one taking me seriously. Right around the holidays, some guys from a local internet marketing company contacted me to try to persuade me to raise my rates. I was too cheap, they claimed, and because I was so good and so inexpensive, they couldn't monetize their own platform and leverage their following in the way that they knew it was worth. They said all this with good intentions, but it fell on my deaf ears.

I thought that they were competitors, not realizing they were, in fact, coming to show me that I was in the deep end. I was in with the rest of the local marketing sharks, and I was just as good as they were, so it would benefit me to see myself and honor my fin. But here I was, playing myself down like a dolphin, always just wanting everyone to "like" me, and yet going to sleep with this quote next to my bed:

"First they ignore you, then they laugh at you, then they fight you, then you win."

Social Media Marketing

Summer 2013

"There is a gift for you on the bar," my manager said. It was an oversized box that read Jimmy Choo: it had a big red ribbon around it.

It was the summer of 2013, and I was at the height of my bartending career. I had even named this bar, a private room on the second floor of the restaurant, after me: "Holly's House." I would host dinner parties that ended as dance parties with loud music and people swinging from the rafters. I dressed the part in sparkly mini dresses, chandelier earrings and knee-high boots. I was a good hostess, setting flowers on the tables and writing names on place cards so everyone in this four-seater bar knew where they were welcomed, while others understood that the spots were reserved. Then I made upwards of a thousand dollars a night.

In some very odd way, I had formed my own nightclub here on the second floor, in the quietest of three-hundred-square-foot dining rooms. It held a max of twelve people, though I would often pack in at least twenty.

When the present arrived during our pre-meal, my co-workers watched me unwrap it as though it were Christmas in July. A Santa-like friend had gifted me a green leather, oversized Jimmy Choo bag that I had bid on during the silent auction at one of her events. While I did not win it that night, I had won her heart by covering that event on mental health through my social media platforms. This gift was her gratitude.

The Jimmy Choo bag wasn't the only box to come for me that summer. That same week, I arrived home to find a package that said Bose on it. Inside were a portable speaker and two sets of headphones. They arrived thanks to the Bose marketing exec, who had been a big fan of my bar and my blog. She told me just to enjoy the gifts; inside there was a card that read, #bosespeakers.

I couldn't believe my luck. Designer handbags! State-of-the-art technology! And all I had to do was cover events and Instagram products on blACKbook?

Dream job.

Happy Place

Winter 2014

"Ahoy from my Happy Place!" the postcards from my mom read. Bronzing and buzzing in the Bahamian sun on a little island called Eleuthera, she probably would have been enjoying a rum and pineapple juice while she wrote them.

My mom loved this island for the white sand beaches and the turquoise waters and for the freshly caught grouper that they bought daily at 3:00 p.m. She loved Eleuthera for its utter simplicity: lunch at Tippy's, followed by a favorite fish dinner in their two-bedroom beach cottage. She had gone to this island with her family as a child. She had watched her parents kick back and truly relax from their bustling Long Island life as they enjoyed this casual island life. Like many things that happened as kids, my mom felt herself stepping back in time every time her feet stepped off that little jumper plane from Nassau.

As an adult, after every cancer treatment, she gifted herself a trip to Eleuthera for persevering; it was her present to herself for making it through. In 2002, it was a full hysterectomy, which meant Christmas in Eleuthera for everyone. In 2008, she celebrated being cancer-free for half a decade with Steve (her husband) and my older sister Christina, on Ten Bay. In 2010, after having had three-quarters of her right lung taken out, it was her December birthday trip to the Bahamas that went through New Year's. And in 2011, 2012, and 2013, there were two-week trips to commemorate tiny tumors being removed.

But in February of 2014, after enduring months of a fever of unknown origin, her winter break to her happy place was canceled. Although her doctor had stressed that the vacation would do her good, her body had different orders. She didn't have a lot of happy thoughts: there were to be no more piña coladas and no more walks on Ten Bay. She was now bedside at Dartmouth Hitchcock Medical Center in New Hampshire. She was beginning Day One of her final ten-night stay. And all I could think was, my mom's not going to send me any more postcards.

And a hospital? Well, that felt like more of a crappy place than a happy one.

#MyLifeYourVacation

Summer 2015

Tis the season to be Holly.

It's the summer of 2015, and I've now traded up bartending for full-time digital marketing. I am a woman about town, and the "it girl" in the know. I no longer read out of a little black book. Now I blog on the blACKbook, Nantucket's ultimate online guide built on advocacy over advertising.

I dress the part. I show up at all the parties and have all my martinis dirty, with blue cheese olives. People keep calling me an "influencer" which is so weird, because I really loathe that word, but I love getting all this swag, and I'm unboxing new presents every week: #gifted.

My digital business revolves around doing what I did behind the bar. Except this time, I sit in front of the bar and have trade dollars at all the hottest restaurants. I borrow all my clothes from the chicest boutiques, and I sport new outfits nightly, as though I were Marie Antoinette. Instead of letting them eat cake, I use my phone screen to show them what this cake job of an "influencer" looks like. I get into all the high-end events, and never have to pay for a ticket. I showcase multimillion-dollar homes, and Insta-tour how the other half lives. I spend my winters gallivanting around the globe to feature comped #luxuryvacations, and I spend my summers as the island's premiere social media star.

All I have to do is document my every move and share it on a multitude of online platforms. All I have to do is take hundreds of photos; filter the perfect one, and then upload it, using different wording, on Facebook, Twitter, Instagram, and my blog. Oh, and maybe I'll Pin it later too.

All I have to do is be everywhere, while never really being anywhere.

People always come up to me and say, "I just don't know how you're doing all this." And I smile, while looking down at my phone. Because, honestly, I'm broke; my heart's broken; and I'll do anything not to feel what's really going on.

So what happened to me?

Well, that's quite the tale.

So let's begin again,

Where we all do.

2.

The Parents

Mother

Literally attached to her hip.

That's how my mother said I spent my first six months out of the womb. She then prided herself on learning how to do everything with one hand. A one-armed mother of two, and three years later, of three. Crazy to think of all the things we can overcome and ways we can adapt.

While my mother remembers me beginning my days on earth that way, I distinctly remember how she began every day with me.

"Good morning, I'm heeee-rrrrre!" she would say, the here being four seconds long. This was a line from Pee-wee's Big Adventure, which we were all so oddly fascinated with. The way that Pee Wee looked at his bike every morning was the way that our mother looked at each of us.

She also "slipavinned" in my room just about every morning, too. That is what she called a fart. I think she helped me understand that there is nothing more important than announcing to the world that you are here every day. That and the fact that there is no happiness quite like a regular bowel movement as soon as you get up.

My mother's name was Ruth, which is also my middle name. My mom was by far one of the most beautiful women I have ever seen, and yet she was always talking about the need to start a diet or that something about her appearance was not right. One time I told her that a kid named Pat said I had the prettiest mother in the whole school. She replied quickly, "Pat needs glasses."

Sometimes I wished that she had a pair.

My mother taught us at a young age her three rules of life:

1. You don't ask people how much they weigh.

2. You don't ask people who they vote for.

3. You don't ask people how much money they make.

I never asked her why. I don't even know who gave these rules to her. But that's the real problem with my mother's ever present unspoken fourth rule.

4. Do as I say and not as I do.

Father

My father has always been the fun guy. The handsome guy. The great at golf guy. The AM Sports Radio all day guy. The guy who always knows a guy as he loves to help out other guys. My father grew up as one of six kids and was the fifth child, the first boy, and the long awaited legacy, named John Bernard Finigan Jr, nicknamed Jack. He was raised in an upper middle class suburb of Boston and thus did all the traditional New Englander stuff. Like summered on the Cape. Played golf and swam at a Country Club. He enjoys every season and has literally lived in his hometown for all of his sixty-six years. Growing up we didn't spend nearly as much time with him as we did our mom. So when I asked my father what his first memory of me was. . . he said it was from when I was two. Apparently it was one morning, when he found me awake and alert, standing in my crib admiring my first piece of work as I had smeared the poop from my diaper all along the wall behind me.

Art imitates life and in 1985, my parents' marriage could be described as a shitshow.

Maybe the Poo-casso in me was me desperately trying to get someone's attention. See, I may have been just a toddler but I believe I was wise beyond my years. My art translated to: *Good Morning. I am here. And there's a lot of shit around me. Someone might want to take care of this.*

Divorce

I learned at a very young age how to escape hardship by going on a European vacation.

I was shipped to Italy in June of 1988, when my parents sent me on my first big trip across the pond to be with my mom's sister, Aunt Nina. From Boston to Rome with a layover in Brussels, I was leavin' on a jet plane wearing a sash that said, "unaccompanied minor," which loosely translates to modern-day "kidnap me." I guess I should have felt safe, as I was traveling with my older sister, Christina, and she was six. Our younger sister, Sanna, was only two at the time, so she didn't get to go on the big journey abroad. (Probably because they hadn't made unaccompanied minor sashes in her size yet.) When we touched down, my Aunt met us at the arrivals to which I looked at her, squeamish, and cried, "I have to go tissy real bad."

Tissy was what our mom called peeing. Apparently I never went to the bathroom once during that entire trip on the plane.

I turned five while in Italy with this favorite aunt, who was also a middle child. During my stay, I began a lifelong habit of eating pizza for breakfast. I met my first foreign boyfriend, Fabio, and discovered a love of foreign men.

And when my sister and I returned to the States that July, we found out that our father had moved out of our house and our parents were officially divorcing.

Suddenly it was just us girls, soon to be moving from Massachusetts to New Hampshire to be closer to my mother's parents. When I asked my mom why they got divorced, all she said was that she'd tell me when I was older. During this time of transition, I learned a toxic coping mechanism: you can run away from your problems. You can make them go away by going on vacation. And if you come home and things feel unsettled? You can forget about them some more by moving away and starting over somewhere else.

Remarriage: Mother – Part I

The first time my mom got remarried it was August of 1991 and I was eight. She married a man who had been in our lives for about six months, and they had gotten engaged after just six weeks. This guy was very much the opposite of our preppy father as he was ten years older than our thirty-one-year-old mother, had salt-and-pepper hair, a thick mustache, rode a motorcycle, wore cowboy boots, and had a two-door red BMW.

Even now I don't know that much about him, but looking back, I guess I understood this: With a Harley and a sports car, he wasn't looking to become part of a family of five.

That and his name means bad in French.

Remarriage: Father

My dad got remarried when I was a month shy of my tenth birthday. We were at our extended family's Cape Cod house on Memorial Day weekend of 1993. My mom had gotten remarried two years before, so this would be the second wedding party I would be in without first being asked whether I wanted to participate.

My father was marrying a blonde bombshell named Teri—a Michigan native and beautiful bartender with a big smile and a bit of a belly, as she was four months pregnant. If you want to get your judgment out, you might be wrong: my dad and Teri have been married almost thirty years now and the longest relationship I have consistently watched. Although it may sound cliché, this is the real deal and love.

I wondered if any kids in my fourth-grade class were going to be in a wedding that weekend. I thought I was probably the only one watching their dad get remarried. I remembered my mom saying she would tell me why she and my dad got divorced when I was older and now, I was older. My dad was starting another marriage, and I didn't have a clue how or why the first marriage had fallen apart.

I put my nautical junior bridesmaid dress on a bit early that day and then ran amok around the bunk house with my cousins. The side of the dress got caught on a nail on a shingle and ripped at the waist, above my underwear line and right at my hip. Now there was a flap hanging off in the front, a bit too large to pretend the tear never happened.

No one was particularly thrilled (or surprised) at this development. My aunt sewed the dress back together as I sat there feeling ashamed, that oh-so-selfish kid feeling that I had already almost ruined the day and it hadn't even started.

I didn't really know anything, but somehow, I sensed that everything was changing faster than I could understand. As a kid, when life seems to be both standing still and spinning quicker than you can imagine, I found myself just trying not to make a scene. Just trying not to wreck my dress. Or someone else's big day.

Remarriage: Mother – Part II

The second time I watched my mom get married, I was eighteen. It was July 4th, 2001, and I had just graduated from high school and was working as a chambermaid at an inn in Rhode Island. I drove up from the smallest state to the Green Mountain state to watch my mother marry her beau, Steve, who'd been with us for the last six years. They got married in front of the log cabin that Steve had built with about twenty people in attendance.

My mother's engagement ring was a solid emerald in between two big diamonds. Her dress was a purple frock instead of a white gown. She didn't have her hair or makeup done. There was no wedding party or even much to do after the "I dos." It was her day, her way. It didn't feel like a wedding and didn't feel like Independence Day either. It just felt like something my mom needed to do for herself. And I could accept this. Because I was finally old enough to wear whatever I wanted to a wedding and I began to realize that, for my mom, if you had a man you had a plan.

Her Womb

The first time I ever understood mortality, I was nineteen. My mother had asked us all to come home for a July weekend. I was still spending the summer months down on the coast of Rhode Island, so coming home to New Hampshire without a car was no easy feat. But I made the trek. I could sense something was going on, but I didn't even stop to think about what it was. That should have been the first sign. If it was something so big that it needed to be told in person, I should have realized it was serious. But when you're nineteen, and so wrapped up in your own life, you become somewhat blinded to everyone else's.

My mom and younger sister were living in a condo complex in Hanover. By the time I had turned off exit 18, I decided that I knew the news: we were set to move again. My sister was about to be a junior in high school, and my elder sister was a senior at Syracuse. I would soon be a sophomore at University of New Hampshire and none of us spent much time in the three-bedroom unit. It didn't really make much sense to live here. Especially since my mom and Steve had gotten married the summer before.

You know when you realize that your parents only stayed in a place for you? To keep something in your life consistent? That's what began to settle in. My mom had loved Hanover for us. But her life was about to start as soon as we graduated. Empty nesters, that's what they call them, right? I figured my mom was ready to step into a new phase. I couldn't blame her. She had become a mom at just twenty one years old and we had moved six times during my K-12 days in Hanover. And when you move around as much as I did as a kid, you become so used to change that home is not a place. Home was just where my mom was.

My sister and I arrived home that weekend, and we walked around our picturesque Ivy League hometown. Over the past eight years, I had not spent one summer there. It felt like a ghost town to me. Like I already knew this place was a part of my past. I was grateful that I got to use the word Hanover when I was at UNH as it seemed to come with some clout—like I was smart and wealthy, which were two things that were constantly debatable in my mind.

When we got back to the house, Mom sat us down in the living room, on the couch that Steve used to sleep on before they got married (even though I was sure that he sneaked into her bedroom every night).

"I have cancer," she said.

Not good. Not good at all. That C-word. That word that belonged in Lifetime TV movies. Not my life. She tried not to cry. It's always like that, right? The one going through the trauma is the strong one.

As soon as she said it, I ran upstairs to my high school bedroom and slammed the door in defiance like a teenager. Sobbing, I face-planted on my bed. I didn't even understand the name of her cancer. Leiomyosarcoma? What the hell kind of cancer was that?

Later that weekend, I would learn it was a soft tissue cancer. It was in her uterus and she would be having a full hysterectomy. It would take me another two decades to fully comprehend it. And it would take my mother numerous surgeries and a dozen years to fight it. Yet, on that summer's eve, I decided it was a losing battle as soon as my head hit that pillow.

It was the first time I realized my mother was going to die. There was no set date, no details, just the truth that everyone dies. And when it's 2002 and you hear the word cancer, you understand one part of your mother's life has ended and a new chapter (that may also end soon) is about to begin.

I wasn't ready for this book. I wasn't prepared.

But that's the thing. No one ever is.

My mother's cancer was very powerful.

But what I didn't realize then, was that so was she.

Our mothers are the first real-life superheroes we get to meet.

3.

The Matriarchy

Grandmothers

My maternal grandmother's name is Dorothy, which was also the name of her mother. We called my great-grandmother Grandma Wyman, yet called my actual grandmother Amie. I loved her name because it rhymes with Mommy, but Amie was also our friend, just like the word means in French.

Amie was originally the eldest of three girls, the epitome of a lady and a product of the Great Depression. She dressed like a Kennedy, scratch-cooked scrumptious meals (where we were taught to finish every morsel) and read the likes of Old Yeller and Grimm's Fairy Tales to us at night. She always kept a prim and proper face for the masses and would hold her bathrobe all the way to her neck, as to never expose an inch of chest or skin. Amie is the type of person who writes a thank-you note to someone for writing her a thank-you note and she says sorry so often, you'd think that everything in the world was her fault.

My sister Christina was born on Amie's fiftieth birthday: September 4th, 1981. Everyone was quite lit that night at Amie's party so when the call came in, someone cried out, "Ruth finally had her baby! It's a girl! She weighs 9 pounds and 17 ounces!" Of course, there are only 16 ounces in a pound. What they meant was that Christina was born at 9:17 p.m.

Amie's early life was no walk in the park. By the time she was five, her three-year-old sister Polly had been hit by a car and died. Soon after her parents got a divorce. Unlike me, Amie wasn't sent off to Italy—she was sent off to an orphanage. I always thought it was strange that her younger sister went to live with other family members, yet Amie was shipped off to strangers. The fact that Amie was named after her mother never sat right with me either. I always suspected there was something more to this tale. Something deeper that was left unsaid.

Daughters

One of my most distinct memories from childhood is a very simple one. I think that's the thing with all our biggest life-changing moments as kids. They aren't terribly earth shattering or super long-drawn-out stories that take forever to tell. Because as kids, things are simple. It's those adults who make everything seem so much more complicated.

My epiphany happened on the playground while watching two boys nut tap each other. *OH MY GOD*, I thought. *I could have been a boy!*

So, when I got home from school, I sat my mom down and prepared myself for some exciting truth.

"Mom, if I was a boy, what was my name going to be?" Expecting the adult story hour about the trials and tribulations of coming up with the name for her potential unborn son, I kicked back and readied myself for a good old tale about the day that everything could have been different. But my mother was not interested in story hour for this one. That is because this was the shortest story known to this wo-man.

"Your name would have been John Bernard Finigan the Third," she said. "Your sisters and you would have all had that name."

Well, that's not that interesting, I thought. And I am glad that I am not a John. There are like ten in my grade already! But that wasn't really what sank in. What percolated was the follow-up. The sisters. The lack of men. The name that still loomed large. For that boy's name was not just any name. That name was set to be a legacy.

And because I was a girl, I wasn't holy enough to receive the name of my father as his son, who at this point was still a ghost. The phantom JBF III.

Sisters

"Someday, you and your sisters will be best friends," our mom preached to us, right after I had thrown a hairbrush at Christina and Sanna had punched her in the back, while chucking a clog at me from across the hallway.

With tears streaming down our faces, tongues stuck out at each other, and the three of us vehemently shaking our heads, our sign language said we begged to differ.

For all the things we couldn't talk about . . . we would fight about. Of course we did this because that's what was what was all around us from a young age. Fights about money. Arguments around what time to meet on every other weekend. Our parents fought constantly. So . . . so did we. Us girls have been three warriors from the start.

But I also think we all kind of wanted to be like each other. Christina has always been the trendsetter, and I would steal her gray, long-sleeved, button-down Gap shirt with the white collar and sneakily wear it to middle school while she was in high school. Sanna always wanted to be included so she would lay like a corpse under my bed while I talked to my Bestie on the phone, eavesdropping on my conversation until she got claustrophobic and couldn't take it anymore. I have always had a bit of a chip on my bony shoulder as Sanna has always been known as the pretty one. One time, when Sanna came to my bar, the maitre'd at my restaurant said, "Oh my God, I just met your sister. She is beautiful! You guys don't really look alike."

On the surface level, we would come through for one another, but deep down, we all kept it in and never talked about the hard stuff growing up.

We may be blood related, yet we are still three very different women, and we all have our own strengths. When I asked my mom later in life to describe us in two words, she gave me this: "Christina is good and strong. Sanna is motivated and resilient. And you? You are sunny and funny."

Author Elizabeth Fishel has said, "Your sister is both your mirror and your opposite."

But to me, my two sisters and I were more like the Three Musketeers. In one word play, it could be because we all had a major sweet tooth and ate an ungodly amount of candy and chocolate. . . And in another reference, we were also that trio because whether we realized it or not, we were all for one, and one for all.

Because what happened to one of us . . . happened to all of us.

Aunts

I was six when I first felt the *shiverees*. We were at our family's Cape house. It was the first community home I can remember, and the place, named the "Irish Mist," was a six-bedroom home on the water in North Falmouth—and a Summerland paradise. My father is one of six children, and each one of those kids had a lot of kids, so the Irish Mist was always packed with tons of action and spirited afternoons of cocktails on the water. It remains the home that will live in infamy: *Oh, why did we ever sell it?* But let's not focus on that. Let's focus on my Aunt Courtney.

Courtney was dating my dad's only brother, and she was the coolest of the cool. She had long, permed brown hair, always half up in a scrunchie, and she wore acid-washed jean shorts and oversized cropped neon sweatshirts. She was tall and had the biggest smile and the kindest full belly laugh. She had manicured brightly painted oval-shaped nails. All my girl cousins and I looked up to this '80s goddess because she loved to play with us—and as a kid that's all you ever want from a cool adult. Just some attention. In the evening, after a tub or an outdoor shower, which was after corn on the cob and burgers, where my father would salt all my food including the baked beans, we would get our jammies on and line up next to the wicker couch in the living room for the Treasure Hunt with Courtney. It was a time to calm down this rowdy bunch of cousins who were sunburned and jacked up on Fun Dip and Skittles from the Tea Room, a nearby beach snack shack. To do so, Courtney would pull our nightshirts up and use her nails to take us to a far-off land with a treasure hunt on our backs.

"We're going on a treasure hunt, X marks the spot. With a *dash, dash, dash* and a *dot dot dot* and a great big question mark." She'd draw the X, the commas, the periods, and the question mark perfectly. It felt like a stairway to heaven, and then the real fun would come. "Shrills go up, shrills go down. Shrills go all around." Her nails would lightly run up and down our back and then tickle our side. "Crack and egg, let it fall." She'd gently knock our noggin and then run her hands down our hair like yoke sliding down our manes. "Ocean breeze and a squeeze!" A quick blow on the back of the neck and a short massage on our shoulders. She'd laugh and give us a hug from behind as she'd whisper, "Now you've got the shiverees."

My body would get goosebumps and it felt like the best damn connection to an adult that I can remember. As soon as it was over, I'd yell, "AGAIN! AGAIN!" Because we come from such a large family, there'd be eight other wee ones next in line, waiting like good eggs, and I'd have to get back in line to wait another turn. My cousins and I would try our best to remember the directions to the treasure hunt and try it on each other while we waited. But it never was the same.

I loved the idea of life being a treasure hunt. I loved how fun aunts were. But mostly, I just loved the way my body felt when I got the *shiverees*.

Aunt Flo

I don't remember exactly when I got my period. I just know that I really, really, really wanted it in sixth grade when all the other girls started talking about it, and one or two of the more well-developed ones had gotten theirs. I was not well, nor developed, when it came to being conscious of what this period thing really was, but I did know that I was impatient. I wanted to get this thing so I could just be like everyone else . . . and maybe even be a little ahead of this game and be an early adapter.

But listen, I was a late bloomer. I am pretty sure the back brace I'd been wearing since I was eight was stunting any growth that would have been considered "boobs." At this point mine just looked like a couple of nipples that could have belonged to a boy if you kept my jeans on and chopped my head off. And when it came to my period, that was nonexistent . . . but I was persistent. Every time I would go to the bathroom, I would look down at my cotton Hanes briefs and think . . . anything? And every time I would get back into that same disappointment of nothing . . . yet.

Nothing was happening to me . . . so I decided to happen to it.

One day, I wiped my bum really hard and when I looked down at the toilet paper, there were two dots of bright red blood. I thought, *I'm pretty sure the period doesn't come out of the butt, but no one else can see if I got this right now, and this was blood.* So, I high-fived myself for being able to shortcut my way to the Red Tent. The next day, I stole a pad from my mom (one of those Always with Wings that was the size of a seat cushion and no, of course I didn't tell her because that would require more information and evidence—two things of which I had none). I put that pad in my brief and went to school with a sly grin all day as I awkwardly waddled around from social studies to study hall. I was so sure that everyone knew that I had my period. I think I even wore light-colored pants, just to see if this period would be so heavy that I would leak out of this woman-made diaper and have true evidence with a big rouge stain on my butt.

You can imagine my surprise when I went to the bathroom and the pad was a blank canvas, like my briefs always were. Once again, there I was trying so hard to be "one of them" and faking it. Even though I didn't even know what *IT* was. No one ever really taught me about what it meant to bleed every month. One hard wipe, and I thought I was a lady. Then one clean pad and I was back to being a pubescent fraud. Ah, the trials and tribulations and the lack of education on how one becomes a woman.

Listener

The first time I went to therapy I was twenty-nine. I had spent an entire lunch with my dear friend telling her about all the issues I had with my father. It was December of 2013, and I was fueling my stomach with hot toddies and red wine, and the sun wasn't even close to being down yet. Once something cracked open in me about all the ways my dad had disappointed me over the years, it was a total free-for-all. My friend did like any good friend does. She listened. And she listened so intently that she realized that someone else probably needed to hear this too. Someone who didn't know me as well as she did. So, she gave me her therapist's number. My therapist listened to me talk about the anger and resentment I had toward my father for a few months. Until February, when it was time to talk about something else.

Something I never wanted to talk about.

And that was the fact that my mother was dying.

Mentor

"You could really benefit from a meditation practice," my Mentor told me, sitting crossed-legged on the couch of her cottage while sipping on tea. It was 3:00 p.m. on a Friday in January of 2016. She had landed on Nantucket from New York City for the Entrepreneur Escapes, a retreat weekend we put on for the community. And retreat is what she did first.

She checked into the hotel, shed her travel clothes, and immediately got grounded into her space. She was in her living room, wearing a robe and lathered in coconut oil as she had just taken a bath while relaxing into the $1,500 per night wharfside paradise. She had just arrived and the first thing she did was treat herself like a queen. *Taking a bath?* I thought.

Who has time to do that during the day? And tea? Why are you drinking tea? Are you sick?

I had no idea that this was the way one could enter into a working vacation. I thought about asking my Mentor if she wanted some coffee and Adderall so she could perform for the dinner party tonight. I was so enamored by her coming that I would have done *anything* for her. It was like when you're a kid, and you ask the coolest girl to come and sleep over at your house, and when she says yes you start to go completely insane when you get home, rearranging everything, hiding anything that would make you look like a baby, and also trying to get a new family in the process.

My Mentor had come to Nantucket that January to talk about what she'd told me at her Brand*Human* workshop a few months earlier. But this time, it would be in front of more than thirty Nantucket entrepreneurs. I wanted them to hear exactly what I did. I wanted them to see the value of social media and hear about better boundaries and why the internet is where it is at. We paid her $3,000 and covered her travel and lodging. I spent four months with three other local entrepreneurs on the weekend, and we lost money on the venture. But I never cared about the money. I cared about the message. The trust economy. That was the money. I just needed these people to agree. And then, I needed them to start really paying me.

And wait, what did she mean, benefit from meditation? To sit and not do anything?

I definitely didn't have time for that.

Women's Circle

"I went to school for journalism, which basically means career bartending. They just failed to mention that in Newswriting 101," I said to anyone who asked what I studied in college. I felt a deep need to discuss that my major was a major disservice, especially since everyone I knew who was really making it in the world went to college for things like Econ and Entrepreneurship.

I didn't know what either of those words meant until my late twenties. And because I still didn't understand how a business profits, I basically ran my business of blACKbook like it was a nonprofit. Not like the kind where you give back a bunch of money to underprivileged kids, but like I never turned a profit. My net was gross. I just felt so weird charging for my services. So, I just tried my best to make ends meet.

That's what I watched my mom do growing up. She would balance her checkbook to the penny. Mine was more like I just had a grand left on a credit card until April. I was always subconsciously thinking about my mom, but especially when I drove up I-89 in January of

2016. I had started to think about moving off island.

No, no, not forever, just like most people, for the off season. They say Nantucket is amazing in the winter as long as you spend it in the Caribbean. I thought about switching up my seaside island for Stowe and truly contemplated moving to Vermont. It's important to say I was in a relationship at this point, and BF had no interest in a winter up in the Green Mountains. This was me in one of Tony Robbins's classic five relationship styles.

I was in the fourth one . . . plotting my escape.

It began with a girls' getaway to Stowe. I was to showcase a new hotel property, and had connected with the sage, savvy owner of the chicest boutique in the mountain town. I partnered with various local businesses to show these girls how to sip, shop, and stay. The first night of the getaway I did what I do on Nantucket, have a girls' night out at a wine bar with just enough food to make you full and maybe a little bit more spirit than many women may need. Two of the girls who signed up for the getaway were new to me, but they had followed blACKbook for years and bought their tickets through my Instagram.

Although most of us went home that night after the wine bar, a few stayed out a little later. When I awoke the next morning, we went snowshoeing at the von Trapp lodge and even though a couple of the women seemed a little bleary-eyed, we all appeared happy for the crisp air. As I was checking my email in between posts and tweets and rushing from one event to the next, I got a message from the chief inspiration officer of the hotel group, saying there was video of one of the young women from the retreat, very drunk and trying to get into the hotel by using a stone to break a window. There had been hundreds of dollars of damage and the girl was going to have to pay for it. She was sorry to start my days with this, but it was a brand-new hotel and videos don't lie.

I was shocked, as that same young woman had been snowshoeing acting like nothing had happened the night prior. So that afternoon, alongside my co-host and my Mentor, I went to her room, and I politely told her that she would not be able to come sit with us in circle at the Yoga Barn. That she would have to pay for her damage and that this retreat was finished for her.

I felt bad telling her this. Spirits make you do weird things, and if anyone knew that it was me with my degree in career bartending.

Pushing forward, that afternoon we all sat in circle, a special moment where we had twenty women talking about health, love, and what they really wanted in life. When it got to me, much to my surprise, I broke down.

"I don't want people to see me as the party girl anymore," I cried. "I don't want to think it is okay to just get drunk and act like things don't happen." As I was in that cocoon of a circle, with my younger sister in attendance, I felt like our mom's presence was there too. I was beginning to share my truth with all of these women. There was something about those words, though.

Something about getting drunk and pretending that things didn't happen.

But I wasn't ready. Not yet.

4.

The Words

Copycat

The first memory I have of school is from kindergarten. We were in a circle, telling each other what we did for Thanksgiving. Sam said he went to his Cape Cod summer house, climbed the jetties, and played with his cousins. When it was my turn, I told everyone that I went to my Cape Cod summer house, climbed the jetties, and played with my cousins.

My teacher said that I needed to come up with my own story and not just copy Sam's.

But that's the thing.

I didn't copy Sam's story.

We are cousins. His mom and my dad are siblings, and we vacation at the same Cape house, often at the same time.

I guess this was where I should have been more honest about my family from the get-go. Or maybe this was the place where I began to second guess all my stories from the start.

Pain

The first time I broke a bone I was seven. I had gotten into a fight with a neighbor who lived up the street. This girl came from a much physically stronger group of women, so when I called her fat, she pushed me down the Carter Street hill. Turns out, when you are skinny and gangly you can run fast, but when someone bigger than you catches up, you're screwed. Or in my case, pummeled. To the ground, right outside of my own house. I got up quickly, thinking I was okay and not wanting to tell my mom what happened. I was embarrassed. I knew if we got to the heart of the matter, she'd know that I had "started it." So, I didn't tell my mom.

I didn't tell anyone.

A few days later, I was down at my dad's for the "every other weekend" visit. We were all sleeping in his waterbed, and I couldn't get comfortable. Turns out I had a broken collarbone from where my neighbor had shoved me. It was the first time I remember staying in my pain body for way longer than I needed to.

Curse

The first time I underestimated the power of the written word, I was on the bus. We were riding H4 to school one Friday morning when I decided to write FUCK YOU on a Post-it and pass it to my neighbor. I don't know why I did it. It was not very neighborly of me. I don't even recall the first time I heard that word. It was probably during a fight between my mom and dad.

I passed the note without any true reflection into what I was doing. My Neighbor, that little rat, took the Post-it and proudly announced he was going to give it to my mom when he got into class, because at this point, my mother was working as an elementary school teacher's aide. I'm pretty sure my first reaction was that I sharted. When the initial body reaction wore off, I stared at him, flabbergasted. I couldn't believe he wouldn't give it back.

"I didn't mean it!" I told him. "That's why I wrote it down! Please Neighbor! Give it back! I am sorry. I am so sorry!" But the damage had been done. He had the note. It was my words, my handwriting, and when my mom found out, it was going to be my ass.

Naturally, I did the only thing that I knew how to do in third grade. I had real-life diarrhea at school, faked a terrible stomach bug to the nurse, and was sent home by snack. Amie picked me up, and I tried to enjoy *The Price Is Right* and talk shows like *Sally Jessi Raphael* that I had no business watching, while scared shitless about what was going down at school. The good news was it was Friday, and every other weekend we went down to Concord to be with my dad. I thought between leaving school and leaving Hanover, I could leave this little Post-it situation behind me.

I was wrong. My Neighbor had followed through with his bus promise and given my mom the note that morning. Words, it turns out, are very powerful. I can't remember what happened to me when my mom got home. I think she was mad. Especially for lying about the fake illness. I think she grounded me, but being grounded never bothered me. I loved being in my bedroom away from everyone and as a middle child I would happily play by myself.

My mother realized that sending me to my room and exiling me was more of a present than a punishment. Always one to live and learn, I started to be a bit more careful with my words and switched up Post-its for long-format writing and began a lifetime of love letters to myself by writing in a diary.

Lies

The first time I remember really lying was to my dad, and I was in third grade. We were at his condo for the weekend, and he ordered our Friday faithful from Dino's, but this time he didn't order my go-to cheese pizza. He ordered Italian subs—one for each of us. And let me state for the record, I may have loved my Italian aunt, but I loathed Italian subs. We ate in front of the television, and in order to keep watching, I had to finish this sub. I was obsessed with Friday night television. TGIF wasn't just a saying to this kid. It was a religion. We started with *Family Matters*, lived vicariously through the three sisters in *Full House*, got a weird vibe from that bizarre bromance of *Perfect Strangers*, then if we were lucky, we got to finish the night with *Step by Step*—a mixed-up family that made me feel like my divorced parents were more normal.

I knew I had to somehow finish this monster of a sandwich. So while my dad was in the kitchen, I wrapped that sub up in a few napkins and snuck upstairs. I entered the one full bathroom in the house, stood over the porcelain god, said farewell to that hot mess of a sandwich, and flushed the entire thing down the toilet. By the time I made it back downstairs, my father was impressed and a bit bewildered that I had eaten the whole sub. I lied and said I was sorry, and it was actually really good and I actually like Italian subs. He gave me a Klondike bar as a treat for finishing it. (Which was perfect, because I was starving.)

We watched *TGIF*, hung out with him on the couch, and in that moment, all was right in the world.

That was until about 2:00 a.m., when I heard a shout . . . a warning signal coming from the bathroom. "Oh, you gotta be shittin' me," my dad said. I wasn't too sure of the pun in the saying, but turns out, when something large and unnatural goes down the toilet, it ultimately comes back up. And in the middle of the night, I walked into the bathroom to see shredded lettuce, rinds of a tomato, marble-sized black olives, slices of pepperoni, and a sprinkling of pepperoncini all swirling in the bowl, only to be completely taken up by a sub roll that had now expanded into the size of a small log.

I was mortified. Who knew that a full footlong sub couldn't really be flushed down the toilet? I should have broken it up into pieces. A few in the toilet. A few in the trash. A few out the window. Oh, how I wish I could have gone back and done it differently. That sub made me realize if I was going to hide something, I should become better about how I'm holding that information down and not let it come up so easily.

Encee

The first time I used a tampon I was nine, and by no means anywhere near getting my period. Growing up Irish Catholic meant I had a few older cousins and lots of aunts who shared bathrooms in our Cape house and yet no one really talked about all their toiletries in the washroom or their women troubles over dinner. I just remember seeing my eldest girl cousin in the fetal position on the bed one afternoon crying about something called cramps. (Which I had only heard about from eating too fast and then swimming too quickly after.) Bored, inquisitive, and exploring the bathroom one day, I found a box of Tampax on the back seat of the toilet. I briefly read the directions and tried to follow the process of the tampon to the vagina. Curious, yet very, very naive, I had lots of interest but no real intellect about the physical anatomy of the female body.

What I knew was this: my mom didn't really call any of the things down there, well, what other people did. She called the vagina an *encee*, she called the pee hole where you *tissy* from and the poop hole where you *ish* from. And since the eye could gauge that this super Tampon definitely couldn't go up the tissy hole, I took a deep breath and began to put it up my butt. I got about a half an inch in before I realized I was by no means prepared for this type of pain. I would have to just wait for that period thing that all the ladies and my cousin complained about.

No need to rush this one, I decided.

Looking back, I now know two more things. First, there is a third hole in your encee between the tissy hole and ish hole that only women have where babies come out of, and tampons are put into. And second, super tampons and anything resembling that shape and size should never, ever go up your butt unless you've prepared yourself and/or are into that kind of thing.

Secret

The first time I was told to keep a secret, I was in fourth grade. It was winter and everything in that A-frame house was so gray. For some reason we were allowed to stay home from school. Mom seemed really scared, but she also finally bought us a Super Nintendo from KB Toys. I don't remember much else from that day, just this: our mom's Second Husband had done something wrong and we had to keep it a secret, especially from our father.

So, we did as we were told.

Ugly

The first time I heard I was ugly, I was in middle school. And let's be honest, sixth, seventh, and eighth grades are often an ugly time with a lot of mean kids. My favorite cousin Meghan and I are about three months apart, and we were hanging out and doing what kids did during this time. We called boys on landlines and passed the phone back and forth chatting about stupid stuff in life. It was like the '90s version of Snapchat without any visuals.

Or so I thought.

Meghan and I were talking to two boys in her class at Sanborn Middle School. I can't think of their names to save my life. But while I was in between a conversation trying to sound so independent with how much I hated Sunday School with the first one and trying desperately to think of something cool to say to dude #2, dude #1 passed the phone to his friend and said, "Here you go." His friend, in a muffled voice said, "Who is this girl again?"

And dude #1 said, "Meghan's cousin. Her name is Holly. She sounds ugly."

Well, he was right on the name and relation . . . but on me? How could he tell from this cordless phone that I was ugly? Sure, I had an eye tooth coming in completely wrong and didn't have great clothes on, mostly because a lot of them didn't fit over my back brace. But seriously . . . boys can already tell that I'm ugly just from my voice?

I realized again that words have a lot of power. And maybe I wouldn't use my voice to talk to boys I don't know as much. Maybe it was time to just write stuff down and keep quiet. At least till this eye tooth settles in. And I get real braces. And I get boobs. And have cooler clothes. And finally get my period. And can put on makeup.

Then I'll look cooler. And then I'll be pretty . . . and boys will know that, even just from a phone call.

Right?

Smart

The first time I believed I was smart, I was fourteen. Although I was a pretty decent student and excelled in English, I struggled heavily in math and science. Methods in Science, as this ninth-grade class was called, was one of those intro classes that all the freshmen took. My science teacher rocked turtlenecks, a vest, and pleated khakis. Kind of like a taller Tina Fey in *Mean Girls.* The one thing that really bothered me about my teacher was that she always paired me with the kids in class who didn't try. Who didn't talk. Who didn't contribute. We called a lot of them Lobby Bobbies because they hung out in the entrance waiting for school to be done, like a caged animal waiting for release.

But I did try in this class. This was one of those classes in high school where we were all equal. My friend who took college math was in this class, as well as the gamut of smart kids I grew up with. Most of us had Ivy League-itis—from growing up in a town with one of the best universities at our doorstep. It was easy to think that we all had to attend a big 12, or top 20, or whatever overrated and overpaid university, after high school.

I was ingrained to think that I had to be better than my upbringing. That I had something to prove. I was often struggling and feeling inadequate. Maybe it was living with a single mom. Or having to babysit to get the clothes that I wanted. Or the fact that every other weekend I had to go down and hang out with my dad, who by now had another child and a whole other family going on. Being a middle child had something to do with it too. Even with friends, I didn't know where I stood. I was nice to everyone but didn't really fit in with any group. I wasn't pretty enough to be popular. I wasn't smart enough to be a nerd. I was too chatty to be a wallflower. And because of my back brace, I'd never been able to play sports unless you wanted to count me as a varsity piano player. I guess a lot of us kids fit in by not fitting in.

But back to 1998, when Donna Martin was graduating, and teen movies were huge, and Brit Brit was about to make school girls cool, I went to my science teacher to ask her a serious question: "Why, oh why, couldn't you pair me with one of the smart kids?" I wanted to do less work, and I wanted to be around someone who would chat with me. I didn't want to be sitting next to someone who didn't pull their weight. All I wanted was some partner's intelligence to rub off on me during this Methods in Mad Science.

My teacher looked at me with kind eyes in a somewhat exasperated way, as so many saintly teachers probably look at an insecure student. "Oh Holly," she sighed. "I can't pair you with a smart kid because *you already are one of the smart kids*. I need you to help other students who can learn from you."

My mouth dropped. *I am a smart kid? Are you sure??* I didn't want to question her because I felt so elated that someone had recognized this. Someone other than my mom and dad. This was real and true and a pivotal moment in my life. Regardless of whether my science teacher told that to every kid who came to see her, or solely told it to me, all I know is that that sentence changed my life.

To have someone believe in you is a mega powerful thing.

Weed

The first time I ever smoked weed I was a senior in high school at a house party. Someone had a bong and asked if I wanted to take a hit. Having no idea what that meant, unless it involved a physical fight with my sister, I didn't want to seem like a loser, so I of course said yes. I watched somebody do it. Didn't get it. Didn't ask for another lesson, just put my mouth over the glass tube, held my breath for what seemed to be five minutes, and watched someone light this little hole with what looked like oregano in it.

By the time the thing was burning, the guy with the lighter said, "Okay go go go," and I got scared. I really needed to exhale so I blew in the bong and ruined the entire stash. I learned a valuable lesson that apparently you suck a bong. I also learned that in high school, oregano weed is super hard to find, so I was not invited back to another house party until after graduation.

Rejection

The first time I got rejected, I was seventeen. This is the type of rejection that runs so rampant during spring at high schools around the country that it may well be considered a mass epidemic. It's unavoidable. It arrives in the mail. It causes teenagers to question their worth, parents in their driveways to slam their fists against the steering wheel, and legacies everywhere to pick up the phone and call their adversaries and scream obscenities like a terrorized English soccer fan. Of course, we're talking about getting rejected from college. For me, there was no escaping it.

Back in the early 2000s, there were many things that gave away the college rejection letter. A paper-thin envelope with that first uninspiring sentence of the letter ("we regret to inform you . . .") might as well have just read NOT HAPPENING. But what was hardest for me wasn't the four waitlist letters and one rejection, it was the fact that the first letter I received was an acceptance to college. A glowing acceptance in a thick brown envelope that came for me in March of 2001. It arrived, and I opened it and barely even noticed the news before I threw the contents into the pile of junk mail and bills for my mother. Then I left the house to go workout at the River Valley Club and sit in the hot tub with my Bestie as we tried not to make eye contact with our nude teachers who were just there to decompress.

But let's not get sidetracked with nude teachers. Let's start with who I was as a student at this point in my life. I got above average on my SATs. I was sporadically on honor roll. I was treasurer of the Student Council. I was the editor of the yearbook. I spent four years on the Class Committee. I volunteered with Students in Action. I was part of the French Club. I was friends with the librarian, and seriously good buddies with the school receptionist. In fact, I was way tighter with the adults than the kids, as I hoped those admissions officers reading my letters of recommendation could tell.

When I started to think about going to college, I daydreamed of places like a bride getting ready for her honeymoon. Instead of Saint Barths, it was Saint anywhere warmer than New England. I wanted to go far south and get the hell out of the North East. I applied to six colleges and did as my college adviser told me. One or two reach schools. One or two most likely schools. And one or two safety schools. Reach. Likely. Safety.

I visited the schools my dad could take me to. Figured out Virginia is for Lovers and set my sights on University of Virginia and the University of Richmond. One reach. One likely. I added in Villanova 'cause my dad thought that would be a good one. I put Wake Forest down because I read somewhere that it was like the Ivy League of the Tar Heel State. And for a safety, and because everyone looked really attractive on their marketing, I added Clemson in South Carolina.

I wanted to go to the University of Richmond because I liked the weather the day I visited—it reminded me of a warmer Dartmouth. I wanted to apply to one Catholic university to say that I did, just like I said that I went to confession once in a while. I wanted to go to North Carolina or South Carolina because they were far away and that was the goal. And finally, I really wanted to go to UVA because I liked the prestige that came with the name. Getting into that reach school would show that I did it. I was enough. Also, I wanted to go to UVA because my most beautiful summer friend went there. She was the coolest person I had ever become "friends" with, and I thought that getting into that school would magically make me turn into her as well. That is the power of acceptance.

I wrote my essays diligently and asked my favorite teachers for recommendations as my mother filled out the financial aid side and cringed at the costs per application as a single mom. Then I waited. My friends at Hanover had applied early decision, and one had already gotten into Harvard, another to Yale, and a third would be going to Cornell. They had been spared from Ivy League-itis. Although I wasn't naive enough to apply to all Ivy Leagues, I knew that my UVA and vast array of Southern Charm schools would show people that I could be the Holly of the Ivy of the South.

But, of course, you know that this is not how this story unfolds. The story unfolds with me unwrapping thin envelopes over and over again like Bill Murray in Groundhog Day. First Villanova. WAITLISTED. Oh well, God damn it, I didn't want to go there anyway. Next up was Wake Forest. WAITLISTED. This was fine because I never visited and never even knew why I applied there. But then Clemson arrived. WAITLISTED. The tears came fast, and I was furious. When the University of Richmond waitlisted me too, I knew it was over. It was a rejection in the form of a waitlist. I knew it didn't matter about UVA. Oh, how quickly our sky-high college confidence nose dives by these crushing blows. If I couldn't get into my likely school, I knew my reach was so far out of reach of ever accepting me.

By then, the real tough part wasn't the four waitlists or the one big fat UVA rejection. It was the first letter, the acceptance letter, from the one school where I was actually a legacy, as my great-grandmother Wyman had been an English major at this university in the late 1920s. The only place that said yes to me was the one college that I had said a hard no to during all four years of high school.

That one place was the University of New Hampshire.

My own state school.

Oh the irony. For the only place that wanted me, was the one place I told myself I would never go.

And that's exactly where I went.

Fear

Did you know that almost half the world is afraid of snakes? This includes my manly stepdad, Steve, who I like to joke was born with a cigarette and a gun. Steve is a 6'2, husky built, football playing, deer hunting, big truck driving, well-loved plumber. He jokes that in his hometown in Vermont, people may not know his name at two in the afternoon, but by God, they sure as hell know his name at two in the morning if something in their toilet overflows.

While we were growing up, Steve often had to use his plumbing skills to clear out the drain of the shower that we shared with our mom. Lots of long hair, shaving cream, and extra thick

Bath and Body Works shower gel made it so our tubs would backup on the monthly. He would do something called snaking the drain where he would put some contraption down the pipe and come up with a disgusting looking, rusty, soapy hair ball that would make your knees weak. Ask any woman with long hair if she has withstood a shower that has turned into a half tub, and she'll know what I am talking about.

Steve was an expert with the drain snaking, but he HATED actual snakes. He feared them beyond belief. I once heard him tell a story that he saw a small garden snake in his backyard, took a rock, smashed the thing and proceeded to puke immediately afterwards.

My fear has never been snakes, but was what Steve did . . . throw up.

I grew up petrified of letting the gross stuff out of me.

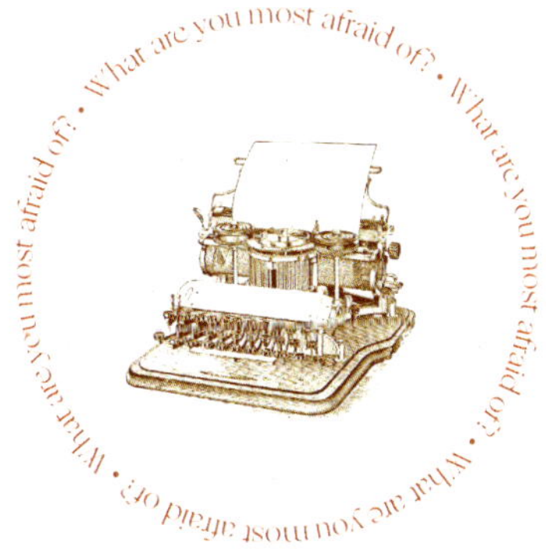

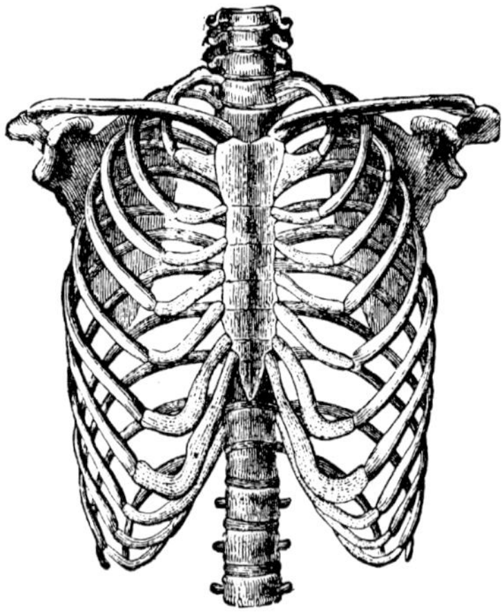

5.

The Body

Heart

On my first half birthday, my parents found out that my two-year-old sister, Christina, had a heart problem called Marfan Syndrome. It was Christmas Eve of 1983, and I am assuming it wasn't a very merry one.

Gut

When I was a toddler, my mother took me to a pediatrician to talk about my eating habits—or apparently, my lack of good ones. I was first attached to my mom's breast, and then to her hip. I was a big fan of this woman and her milk. I have to mention that at this point I had just turned three. My mom was on to kid number three and now nursing my baby sister, Sanna. Perhaps I was jealous of my new sibling, and maybe I decided to show it by going on a hunger strike.

As this story is told, the doctor listened to my mother's worries and calmed them quickly. He asked, "Does she like to drink juice?"

"Yes," my mother responded, as I was a big fan of Mott's Apple.

"Then just keep feeding her that," he told her.

And there it was . . . my first juice cleanse. I guess I've always been a bit ahead of my time.

Spine

My party trick growing up was that my body rivaled Gumby's: I was made of elastic and completely double-jointed. I can bend my pinky all the way back and my knees, when extended, looked like the aliens from The Arrival. Yet, my really big show came from demonstrating to people how I could "jump rope" with my arms. I'd connect my hands behind my back, then bring my arms over my head while my left shoulder joint popped out of its socket. Then, with a big grin on my face after hearing a good "ewww" from someone in attendance, I'd find my arms back in front of my stomach without ever breaking my clasp. However, no matter how bendy my arms were, there was one part of my body that was bent out of shape, and not in a talent show way. That was my spine.

In 1991, a back doctor told me that my scoliosis was severe enough that I would have to wear a back brace full time. I was eight and didn't have a clue what this meant. The afternoon I got fitted for the brace I realized fixing this part of my body would be way different from the sling I got for the broken collarbone. Wearing Hanes undies and a piece of cotton resembling a tube top that went from my now fixed collarbone to my nonexistent hips, I was taken into a room where a man wrapped me in plaster. I remember my mom crying, but I don't ever remember shedding a tear.

One day I was a normal third grader in jeans, and the next I was a normal third grader wearing elastic-waist corduroys with a big white cast around my midsection. That's the best part about being a kid: adapting and accepting are a hell of a lot easier. Plus, I had no concept of time, and no one made me aware of the fact that I would be wearing a back brace for the next 2,500 nights.

Stitches

The first time I hosted a party I didn't get to enjoy, I was ten. It was my double-digit birthday bash, and I was hosting a dozen friends at my favorite town hangout called Storrs Pond. We would have a pool party complete with cannonballs off the deep end and pencil jumps with our noses plugged off the high dive. We would run around the pond area and walk into the freezing cold water while trying our best not to get stuck in the mud and roots as we noisily splashed our way in. We would swim out to the raft and lie our long, lean bods down on the floating dock, then play rock-paper-scissors, who can get closest to the edge without falling in, and the inevitable game of truth or dare.

I was feeling pretty good about this party. I had started to realize that a summer birthday was where it's at, even though I didn't get to have cupcakes and happy birthday sung to me in the classroom. I realized that June 24th was the perfect time for a birthday; it was six months from Christmas Eve, so I spread out my presents evenly. Thank you, Mom and Dad.

I was also feeling extra fly because this was the first birthday party at which I didn't have to wear my back brace. On my ninth birthday, I was still wearing the brace twenty-three out of twenty-four hours, but by my tenth birthday, I had to wear it for only twelve hours at night. Hell, yes.

I awoke on the big day, jumped on my brand-new neon orange Huffy bike, and went cruising. I loved the freedom a bike gave me. I decided for my birthday I would start the day with an everything bagel with butter from the Bagel Basement. (I was a simple eater, and bread and butter would have satisfied me for decades. I like to think I could do well in captivity.) I savored the four sides of that perfectly toasted bagel and then hopped back on my new bike to cruise home and get ready for my big bash.

About ten minutes from my house, I had to maneuver around a rather large woman on the sidewalk. I should have just gotten off the bike and walked it around her, but this was a hot orange boy's Huffy. This thing had power, so I decided I would just swerve on the grass and then back onto the sidewalk when I had cleared the woman.

Unfortunately, this is not the way it worked out.

I swerved onto the grass and did a bit of a reverse C around the woman. "Excuse me," I said as I passed her, but in my mind it was more like, "Watch this, lady . . . you've got a real treat in store for you when I pop this wheelie on my way back up the sidewalk right in front of you!" Of course, my ramped-up imagination was always two steps ahead of reality, and when I stood up and went to pop that wheelie, the front wheel didn't make it to the lip of the sidewalk. My standing power thrust caused the handlebars to slam down on my knee, right above my kneecap. A screw made a miraculous incision in my leg.

I saw a large walnut-sized hole above my right knee. It was so deep that I could see what looked like little white circles. There wasn't even blood, just a weird light pink in a hole that made its way deep, like, to the bone. The woman I was trying to avoid was now very much in my life: she was my saving grace as I lay there, entangled in my orange Huffy and beginning to wail, not because of the pain—that would come later—but from the fact that I knew my birthday party wasn't going to be what I had envisioned.

Upon seeing the hole in my leg, the woman flagged down a truck, and they loaded my bike in the truck bed, put me in the back seat, and drove me home. My mom ran to the front yard, took one look at the knee, rushed me into her Jeep, and we were off to Dartmouth Hitchcock Medical Center. I needed stitches—ten of them—to match my birthday. But the real gut punch didn't happen with the stitches. It came when the doctor told me that I couldn't go into the water for two weeks.

"WHAT?! Two weeks? What about my party today? I am having a pool and pond party!!"

"You can go to it," the kind Doctor said. "You just can't go into the water."

My mother tried to console me, telling me that it would be okay: I could still have the party. I would just have to watch everyone else from the sidelines.

That day, I realized it wasn't about the stitches . . . but about my sight, as I began to understand how important my perspective was going to be at this party called life. I can't go in the water, but I can still watch others enjoy it? That was a tough lesson to learn, especially on my tenth birthday.

Bruises

By fifth grade, all I wanted was to be seen as cool. I wanted to be one of the popular kids and have all the girls and all the boys like me. I always wanted to stand out, but I felt like I was never properly seen.

My dad was remarried and had just had his first baby in seven years. My mom was single again, and she was set up on dates with people who had kids in my sister's grade. I was tossed back and forth between Hanover and Concord. I was constantly hoping that friends would invite me over to their houses so I could see what a normal family looked like, maybe to watch a dad and mom in the kitchen making dinner. I evolved into the friend who would clean up the playroom or make my friend's bed or talk extra-long with the mom in hopes that I would be invited over again (and potentially adopted). Eventually, I would become the babysitter who became like a second daughter.

I got into a bit of a boyish stage, changing my style from floral dresses and pink corduroys to stirrup black leggings and B.U.M. Equipment maroon sweatshirts with a white turtleneck and a San Jose Sharks hat, half of my hair pulled out in front of one ear and the other half behind my pierced ear.

In my New Hampshire hometown, "SKs"—short for shit kickers—were popular with the boys and also with some of the tomboyish gals. These are the tan boots with gold laces and leather tops with steel toes. They're what construction workers wear—the type of heavy shoe that you wear doing manual labor.

One day during recess, the cutest boy in our class was playing wall ball with us. He wore jeans that were slouchy, a bit too big. He was constantly pulling them up after hitting the ball against the wall.

I thought this was a great time to make my presence known, to be one of the guys in my hockey hat with a team I didn't even know, and these SKs that I didn't know why I was wearing. I was in line and half-joked to the Cutest Boy, "You should get a rope and use it as a belt so your pants would stop falling down."

That got the Cutest Boy's attention. He walked straight over to me and took his own SK-clad foot and kicked me with all his ten-year-old force in the middle of my left shin. The pain was excruciating. I didn't want to be the girl kicked by the Cutest Boy. No, I wanted to be the girl who one day got kissed by a boy like that! I looked down at my legging and there was a dirt footprint where he had kicked me. After recess I went back into class knowing there was a new type of heartthrob in my lower leg. When I ran my trembling palm over the spot, it was like cupping a lemon: I was very grateful that I was wearing stirrup pants, so I didn't have to see what this looked like.

When I got home, I skipped my normal after-school routine of watching a television special with a box of Cheez-Its. I wasn't feeling hungry, and I was safe now, so I could stop pretending I wasn't hurt. I sat on the floor of my room and cautiously took off my leggings, trying not to puke when I saw my leg—a bruise the color and size of a small plum was in the middle of my shin. This was not good. I always had bruises all over my legs from my own clumsiness and lack of nutrients, but this was not anything that could blend in. It was mammoth, and it scared me.

I finally cried, letting all those tears flow, knowing that something bad had happened to me, and once again, I couldn't talk about it. I didn't want to get the Cutest Boy in trouble. I had told him to get a belt for his pants. If I hadn't said that, he never would have kicked me. This was my fault, me and my big mouth.

My mother came into my room while I was sitting on the floor with my legs outstretched. She took one look at me and asked what was wrong. I quickly tried to hide my leg, but it hurt too much to try to sit on it, so I just yelled at her and told her to get out, which was very out of character for me. She knew something was not right, and when she saw me covering my leg, she took one horrified look at the bruise and demanded that I tell her what had happened.

I didn't want to, but a mother's nurturing has a way of opening up a closed-off kid. So, when she asked, "How did this happen?" (with a tone that conveyed *I love you, you are important to me, I am listening*) I unfolded the story about wall ball and the SKs and belts and the Cutest Boy. It came out completely out of order, but the details ultimately connected when she hugged me and told me that I was going to be okay. She put a big bag of ice wrapped in a dish cloth on the bruise and sat on the bed with me as I tried to calm down. She told me that it was never okay for someone to kick me. That it was never okay for someone to hurt me—thank God the shin wasn't actually fractured—and that we would have to tell the teacher and the principal about this.

No, no no. I wanted to do what I knew she had done when a man had done something bad: *Let's just pretend this didn't happen*. But she wouldn't let me do that to myself. She forced me to go to the principal the next day, where the Cutest Boy and our SKs sat to talk about keeping our hands (and feet) on our own bodies and keeping kindness in our words.

Clitoris

The first time I remember consciously masturbating I like to believe I was in middle school. I write this with some hesitation because as a child of the church, I have faith that it was a puberty thing and not that I was an early sex addict. I feel a little dirty writing this, as I was still going to Mass every other Sunday. During most of that time (that literally stood still), I often thought about the complete damnation of my solo sex acts, wondering if a self-given massage was worthy of a confession. But as I delve into the truth of it, what's so bad about pleasuring oneself? I think we should all be a little more honest about this subject from the get-go.

My experience of sex education at school was hearing information that boys get wet dreams, and we're allowed to talk about that, but you never hear about girls' wet dreams. Maybe it's because we're a lot better about our "mess" and, like most things, we have been silenced on this subject for too long. Looking back, my first time masturbating might as well have been a wet dream from what I was experiencing. I was in a pool, solo. I do have to mention that I was always on a solo mission during these middle school times, as the back brace, rogue eye tooth, and a double-jointed, gangly body weren't necessarily putting me at the top of anyone's Seven Minutes in Heaven list.

But if we're going here (and yes, we're going here), the true first time I really remember something down there tingling was from watching a *Punky Brewster* episode on television. Punky and her cute blonde buddy were racing turtles and I was in my nightgown, on my stomach with my hands under my chin, completely mesmerized by the television and unaware of how this scratchy carpet was leaving deep imprints in my exposed knees and thighs. So, the two of them (Punky and the blonde) must have somehow realized they liked each other because during that moment, I realized that something in me liked watching them like each other. Next thing you know, I was gyrating my cotton-covered pelvis against that itchy carpet like two sticks trying to make a fire, while a feeling of electricity took over my body. I don't remember what happened after that, but I'm pretty sure whatever I was doing looked like what a dog does in heat, so I probably wasn't fooling anybody around me. I was only five and with a strong Irish Catholic heritage (i.e., a hundred cousins and no one who uses birth control), so no one seemed too into addressing this kindergartener and her self-massage on the carpet.

Where I actually got off was in the water. In the summertime, when I would spend two weeks with my dad (according to the divorce orders), I would leisurely enjoy "reading by the pool." By this, I mean I would put my paperback of *Sweet Valley High* right on the concrete above where the jet was in the shallower side and then I would pretend to be absorbed in the stories of these gorgeous blonde twin sisters who always had boy problems (probably fantasizing that I was one of them and we were in some situation that was more Penthouse Forum than high school). I'd then slide my Speedo one-piece over to the side of my right thigh with just enough open skin to have my vulva penetrated by a ferocious jet stream for a few pages until I couldn't take it, and would have to dunk my head in the pool to let out a scream, which, unbeknownst to me then, was apparently an orgasm.

And then I did what any twelve-year-old would do: with a sly smile on my face, I would pretend that nothing had happened. I would get right back into the correct position and do it again. And again. And again. Crazy, the stamina of a pubescent teen.

Booze *a.k.a.* Spirits

I was sixteen when I got drunk for the first time. I was nannying for my Favorite Family at their summer house in Weekapaug, Rhode Island. I loved this spot because it felt like camp, but for adults. There was less archery and arts and crafts and more beaches and BBQs. I had finally gotten both my braces off, and I was coming into myself a bit more. I was babysitting for two sweet little blonde girls who became like my little sisters. We made up dances to Backstreet Boys and sang along to Abba and watched Never Been Kissed and Spice World on repeat.

I loved being a girl, and, even more, I loved being an unassuming role model to the kids. Luckily for me, the girls' parents were part of the cool group of adults who reigned over this May to-October summer community. They were friends with a lot of other parents who had teenagers my age, and I'm pretty sure they asked their friends to ask their kids to hang out with me. I didn't care. Being associated with my Favorite Family meant I had the Willy Wonka golden ticket into the cool kids of this summer community, and these teens were in a league of their own. Over the course of a few weeks, I had quietly made my way into their nightly meet-ups, trading flashlight tag with the little kids for fake IDs and beer runs with the big kids.

Every summer there was always one big party that the cool kids talked about all year long. It was a themed party in a friendly rival town. Normally they played these kids in a weekly wiffleball tournament, but for one night a summer, they'd get totally wasted in the back of one of the kid's houses. It was the summer of 1999, and they were about to party like that, but throwing the theme back to the 1970s. I didn't know what to expect, but I did know that the woman I babysat for had lived through that decade and that she would know how to dress for it. She loaned me a gorgeous black sequined miniskirt that I paired with my least-washed black halter and a pair of way-too-high black wedges that I could barely walk in. I think I had on some aviators. I think the mom helped me put on black eyeliner and mascara. I think I put my hair in a half ponytail. I was so excited for this night and couldn't wait to finally go to a party: I had finally made it.

When I arrived for this disco bash, I remember all the girls loving the sequined skirt, putting their hands on the piece like it was a work of fashion art. The guys gave me approving looks and head nods. I felt like I finally fit in, as we took a group shot with my disposable camera—everyone in their '70s glittery getups. That photo would prove it: I was one of them.

When we arrived at the party, we found that a quintessential summer cottage had been turned into a frat house. Each room had its own drink theme. One of the rooms was covered with tin foil, top to bottom. There was a disco ball in the middle of the ceiling, and the teens who created the room showcased it to the Weekapaug girls like it was a masterpiece. There were beers and drinks in every room, and Dave Matthews Band and OAR pumped out of every stereo.

Everyone looked so fresh and cool, and the night showed so much promise. I was feeling electric, so much so that I agreed to do something called "the luge" as soon as I was asked. A luge? Sign me up! Is it a waterslide? Is it that Olympic sport that the Cool Runnings guys did? Was this a relay team thing? I tried to think of which girl I should grab as my partner when they showed me this luge . . . but, apparently, it's a singles sport. I saw the leader of our pack, at the top of this thing that resembled a block of ice. There was a carving in the ice block that looked like a trail, and next to the table were a couple of plastic handles of cheap liquor and a jug filled with something red. "Just go to the bottom, kneel, and put your mouth on the bottom of the luge," someone directed me.

This seemed a little off to me, so I watched one of the girls I was friends with do it first. The Leader poured the red stuff down the ice block and the liquid made a swirl and ended in my friend's mouth, some of it dribbling down the side as she quickly tried to salvage her white tank top by holding her hands in the form of a cup under her chin. "Too much, asshole!" she yelled, as she walked around the block to punch the Leader in the arm.

"Your turn, Holly," the Leader said, looking my way. I tried to remember what my friend had just done, but I was concerned about the sequined miniskirt and about exposing my white Victoria Secret brief. I was already so unsteady in those wedges, and to sit on my heels felt even more shaky, but I figured it out. I balanced my hands on the dining room table and put my mouth to the ice. I thought of the kid in *A Christmas Story* who got his tongue stuck to the pole and prayed that that wouldn't happen to me. I tried desperately not to think about my undies showing, or even worse, a plumber's crack exposed to the people behind me. I wondered what this red stuff even was.

Before I could think of anything else, a surge of what initially tasted like fruit punch began burning its way down my esophagus. It was a rush, and if I had been a little more prepared, I probably would have taken a deep breath in from my nose. Instead, most of the liquid went down the side of my top and skirt. Luckily for me, everything I was wearing was black; I just dusted myself off, pulled myself up, and put on a really big fake smile. I was hoping I had something in my bag to take the taste of this disgusting juice out of my mouth. "So good," I lied.

I rushed back into the house to find the other girls. I had that disposable camera with me and took photos throughout the night. I would find Weekapaug girls in various rooms and we would press the button for the flash and get together and do our best Posh Spice imitation. I would find guys who I thought were so cute and ask them to take a photo with me; I felt even more on top of the world when they accepted. A few more red Solo cups of juice and booze and I was feeling steadier on my toes and ready for that ice luge again. The second time I did it, I was way more prepared. The breath through my nose helped, as did the fat buzz that had been accumulating. More photos. More Solo cups. More dancing . . . like the way I made up dances with the girls I was nannying.

The third time at the luge was the last one I remember. The fruit juice was all gone, but no one took that as any reason to stop; they took that as the message to take this party to the next level. That's when I apparently did a luge of grain alcohol.

Everything after that went a little blurry. I remember walking through the luge room to the tin foil room, out to the garage and I finally made it to the grass. All that fruit punch made its way up my throat and spewed out of my mouth like hot lava. (My fear had always been throwing up—puking in a public place.) Luckily, a few kind adults, who may have been there as drunk lifeguards, escorted me from the manicured lawns to a nautical-themed bathroom. I took one step into that washroom, tripped on those ridiculously high heels and fell nose first into the toilet. I was throwing up and bleeding out of my nose, which sent the word around the party that I was throwing up blood. By the time I had emptied my luge-filled stomach, it was decided that I should be taken home.

And then I woke up.

My head. Where am I? Through the blurriness the room came into view. I saw the TV where the *Spice World* DVD sat; I recognized the white blanket over me with its eyelet floral detail. I made out the curtains with the sliding door that led out to my Favorite Family's lawn. Oh, thank God: I was home. Well, my home for the summer. I sat up . . . I was wearing a men's St. Paul's lacrosse sweatshirt that had McLaughlin embroidered on the chest and my white Victoria's Secret underwear. There was a familiar bucket next to the bed just like one that kids used to catch crabs at the Jetties. Inside that bucket was no marine life, but what I assume was my own puke and bile.

I got up to go to the bathroom. I turned on the shower and sat in the tub and let the water run over me. I could not put the puzzle pieces together yet; I just knew that I never wanted to feel like this again.

By the time I managed to stand up, mostly because the hot water had run out, I half-dried myself off and went to brush my teeth at the sink to try to get rid of the vomit that seemed stuck under my tongue. That's when the steam rolled off the mirror and the reflection became confusingly clear, showing purple makeup on my nose. Did I have eyeshadow on my face? Had I been tagged? Did I pass out and everyone wrote on my face and drew dicks on my cheeks like I saw in *10 Things I Hate About You*? No . . . no: this was far worse. This was a silver-dollar-sized bruise that encompassed most of the tip of my nose and the skin surrounding it. Damn! And double damn! It was from my fall into the toilet and it was going to be my drunk tattoo for the week to come.

How could I explain this to my Favorite Family? I had never gotten drunk before. I didn't even know what happened or how to explain it. I had no idea how I got home, but whoever had brought me had to drive on the shell driveway, and that would wake up anyone. I pulled the sequined skirt up off the floor and checked for spots of puke and grass stains. The thing was a warrior: not a missing thread on it. I decided this was a good sign, and I could go up to the mother and return it to her and try not to look her in the eyes for four to seven days. Her husband was away at work, so this was also a bonus. I believed I could just pretend that this didn't happen and get back to making up a dance to "I Want It That Way" by lunchtime.

The mother, no stranger to the summer nights lifestyle, took a compassionate look at me and said nothing while saying everything. She asked me if I wanted to go to the doughnut shop with her. I obliged, as the girls weren't up yet, and I thought I could use something sweet to coat my empty stomach. She was beyond kind on the ride when she asked me what happened last night. She had been woken up when I was being carried into the house.

"Did I wake the girls?" I asked. She said no. Phew. I couldn't face them either, even though I would have to face them with this bruise by the time we arrived home.

"Holly, this is just so out of character for you," she said. She was right. I didn't know who that girl was last night. I was trying to play this cool girl and, clearly, I didn't play the role well. I started to cry, and she comforted me at the drive-through.

"It happens to everyone," she told me, passing a doughnut. "And it will all be okay. Just try to be more careful next time."

I was so elated after this moment, as the sugar and her words made me temporarily feel better. I figured I could get back into this day and begin life again and pretend that night never happened.

That was until she played tough love.

"We're going to have to tell your mom about this," she said.

"Oh. Yeah. Okay, you can tell her," I said.

"Oh no," she said. "You are going to call her and tell her." *Damn it! Why can't you just take one for the team for me?*

I had spent my teens quietly running away from my own home to avoid having to tell the truth.

Breath *a.k.a.* Spirit

I was nineteen the first time I had a panic attack. I was still in Weekapaug, but now I worked at the Inn instead of as a nanny. It was July, the sun was shining, the weather was fine, and I had acclimated in this summer-job-sweet-spot as a jack of all trades: I was a part-time chambermaid, waitress, and kids' camp counselor. Life was pretty damn easy, looking back on my days there. I simply had to wake up, work as a waitress, go to the beach, go back for lunch, go back to the beach, then work dinner, and then drink on the beach. It was not a tough schedule, and I did truly enjoy moving up the ladder from the chambermaid to the waitress rounds.

My friends in the summer community had jobs that were a little more, let's say, upscale. One was a tennis coach. One was a sailing instructor. One had an internship. And the others? Well, they were able to do whatever they pleased, as most were pretty financially stable: living at their parents' house made for "cruisey" summers of sun and fun. I had to work a bit harder to get my bunions in the door, but I wasn't afraid of that work hard/party hard lifestyle.

I had really come into my prime of burning the candle at both ends. After my freshman year at UNH, and even a semester of living at my sorority house, I thought this would be the summer that I really came out of my shell. After a full year of living in a triple, the summer gods blessed me with my first time living in a dorm in my very own room. Sure, I had the smallest single in the place, but I didn't care. I was basically an upperclassman, it being my second summer at the Inn, and, if you also counted my years of nannying, I was a fifth-year senior. I thought I was just about as high up on the cool ladder as anyone could be.

Speaking of high, I was never really into smoking weed. I was still feeling a bit traumatized from that first try at a bong during high school, and was worried about showing my true green colors when people saw what a novice I was.

But weed is one of those drugs you have to prepare yourself for. The one thing that you weren't supposed to do was overthink about it. You weren't supposed to give it too much brain time, just give it a quick puff puff pass. I wasn't really ready for the "smoke weed every day" mentality that I had heard on Dr. Dre's song lyrics, but I was less afraid of it being around me. If a joint came in my direction during college, I'd just go to the bathroom or pretend to be chugging a bottle of booze so it was clear that I wasn't really trying to get high: I was trying to get drunk. I was constantly trying to avoid having to say, "No thanks. Not for me. Not tonight." But for some reason I always had a hard time saying a hard no. I would always skirt around the issue, and try to change up one vice for another to show that I was cool.

One night on the dunes of a Weekapaug beach with a few locals and my best Inn friend, I decided without much thought that I would smoke a joint. I had been smoking cigarettes for most of my freshman year, so I was no stranger to inhaling a filter wrapped with a substance that would make me cough but also feel cool. When the joint got passed around in our party of five, I took a hit and passed it around again. Then it came back around with the bowl. The bowl was such an awkward thing to try to smoke out of—worse than the bong, if you asked me.

Sitting in this circle, I desperately tried to pry open my high eyes and watch the others do the bowl smoke. Always too much in my head when the bowl came to me, I fumbled with my fingers. Which one goes over the hole? How can I light this with one finger in the hole, and why is my thumb always just about to get completely burned off because I can't get the Bic to stay lit? Am I a righty or a lefty? By this time my thumb was burning, and I looked like I was playing a flute. I sucked in some puffs of resin, hoping no one noticed that the weed never got truly burned. I tried to light a cigarette to show that I did know how to smoke one thing properly. That's what's so crazy about growing up—who actually knows how to smoke weed? Who taught you the proper way to light a bowl? To roll a joint? To know when you've smoked enough? To understand what "high" feels like? It was all trial and error for me with this drug. After the puff puff, cough cough, smoke smoke, pass pass, my friend and I got up to go home. It was very late, and we had to work breakfast the next morning.

Breakfast. Oh, how food all of a sudden sounded so completely appealing. We raced back from the beach, bobbing from side to side, and sneaked into the staff kitchen to gorge on whatever we could find. For me, it was awkward handfuls of granola out of a glass jar matched with a spoonful of peanut butter from an industrial-sized tub. I couldn't get enough into my stomach; I'm pretty sure I didn't even chew anything. I just put it in my mouth and tried to wash it down with whatever weed-tasting saliva I could manage. After leaving behind what probably looked as though two rodents had bum-rushed the kitchen, we tiptoed back into our dorm rooms and said a hilarious good night to each other. I slammed my body down on the mattress where the heaviness of my quiet room set in.

"Breathe," I said aloud, startling myself with the command that seemed to come from nowhere. I did as I asked, even though the peanut butter felt like a glue that kept closing my esophagus.

"Breathe." I said it again. This time doing exactly what I did the first time: in from the mouth and out through the mouth.

"Breathe." I started to breathe in faster and faster, my heart racing and a panting coming out of my chest.

"Breathe," I said standing up, looking in the one mirror over my dresser. *Wait*, I looked at myself completely confused. *Why am I telling myself to breathe?* My body wasn't functioning without me telling it to do something? *Breathe*. The breathing got shorter and more forceful. My mind began to race and my heart was pounding. *I am going to die here! And it's all because I can never say no fully to things I don't want to do!*

I must have fallen since my friend heard something and rushed into my room.

"I have to keep telling myself to breathe," I managed to get out.

Trying not to laugh, my friend asked, "Want me to take you to the hospital?"

"YES," I silently mouthed, my face flushed with panic.

By the time we got to the bright overhead lights of the hospital, I realized that this was it. I was going to die here tonight from weed. I had once heard that no one could overdose on weed, but I also knew I was a special breed so perhaps I would be the very first and make it into public news and shame my family and put my Weekapaug friends' names in the news.

I worried for my friend. She went to Georgetown and had so much ahead of her. I was about to ruin it all.

When I sat down for admittance, I was inhaling and exhaling with the sound of a mule tied up by its neck. I looked around at the handful of elderly souls in the waiting room and couldn't believe that this was to be my last spot. I was to die with these people on this night next to the pizza place that I loved to go to with the kids I used to babysit. Oh my God, and when they find out about this, that their babysitter died of chronic weed and became the cautionary tale, my legacy would be ruined. It was all coming to an end. The sharp breathing could not stop.

No air was getting in, but by the way I was gasping, the sounds of my breathing must have been really annoying to the receptionist. And, since my friend wasn't kin and no one was around to console (or shush) me, I was jumped to the top of the patient line and put on a bed where they hooked up a heart monitor, took my blood pressure and my temperature—all while the breathing continued, completely out of control.

A doctor came over in a white coat; by this point, he was like an angel in my eyes since I had pronounced myself dead on arrival. He took one look at me and asked me if I had had anything to drink tonight. *Nooooo*, I silently screamed. It was the truth, and I was grateful he didn't ask me about drugs. He then asked if I was under any stress, any poor relationship? *Just with my lungs*, I thought, but shook my head as the bright lights kept me coming to.

"Everything is fine, Holly," he said kindly as he patted my shoulder and looked me squarely in the face. "All your vitals are normal. Your heart is just fine. Your temperature is normal. You are going to be okay." Those words brought the tears, which came fast and furious. *I was okay*. "You are having what is called a panic attack. Just breathe in through your nose and out through your mouth. Do it with me."

I followed him as my breathing took a serious detour into calmville, and I started to shift the direction of all the anxiety to focus on the breath for the first time—maybe ever.

In through the nose, out through the mouth. In through the nose, out through the mouth. In through the nose, out through the mouth.

"There, there," soothed the kind doctor, "do you feel better?"

I did. It was all chill, and back under my control. Everything else suddenly went silent. My mind had quieted, and my energy was all on this breath thing.

"No need for medication," the doctor assured me, "But you may want to try this technique before you go to bed on a nightly basis. You can check out now."

I got up quickly, with a lightness in me that matched my light head. I walked out feeling like a new woman, breathing in a completely different way. The breath? That was it? It wasn't the weed. The peanut butter. The nonexistent ailments I diagnosed myself with so quickly. Maybe there was something to this breath thing.

But first . . . sleep. And a good story for the morning.

All was well with that little ER visit—that is, until the mail came for my mom a few months later. As you may imagine the $400 Westerly Hospital bill didn't settle with her as quickly as it did with me. She was totally confused about why I had been there at 3:00 a.m. in the first place.

"I was stressed, that's why I went," I told her, and I apologized for not telling her sooner. "Too many days at work took a toll on me," I told her.

Oh, those big little lies . . . those were my specialty.

6.

The Home

Harry Cottage

Have you ever heard of that game on how to find your porn star name? You take your first pet's name followed by the first street you ever lived on. Our first pet was named Harry. He was a little black ball of fur that was kind of cute, although I've rarely had much interest in pets. One time Amie brushed Harry while she was watching *Masterpiece Theatre* on PBS. By the time the program was over, Amie looked down and gasped: Harry was now hairless. I learned two things that day: never brush a cat with a human hairbrush. And two, don't repeatedly touch someone with something unnatural.

The first street we lived on, well we have to go on a little detour for that. My mother was no stranger to moving homes over the course of my childhood. While we moved five times within Hanover, she and my father also moved twice within my first five years of being on this Earth. My mother never talked about that first house on Cottage Street. It was the house where I made that deep impression by smearing all my *ish* on the crib wall. I found out later that my father wasn't around very much during this time. A social butterfly with a love for horse tracks, he often left my mother alone and apprehensive. But, like I said, I found these things out later, because silence was the remedy for hard truths on Cottage Street.

Broken Home

When I was in fourth grade, we moved into a four-bedroom A-frame house on Dogford Road. (There were lots of Dogs and Fords on the road, so that is where the name came from. It was quite a simple place.) I really didn't like this house. It was dark, and my two sisters and I lived in the basement, which was also where the TV resided. The upstairs was too bright, with a big window that overlooked a deep wood. Mom and her Second Husband's room was a large loft that opened at the top of the triangle. It was oddly spacious up in their area—yet somehow this house felt so tight—like we didn't all fit comfortably in this place.

But back to other families, with whom I was becoming fascinated . . . I watched an ABC Afterschool Special about a mom getting beaten up by the dad. The kids saw it all happening, and together the children and the mom left the dad, and the mom got a divorce.

That evening I told Mom that I now knew why she and my dad got divorced. No need to worry about me anymore, I insisted, I am old enough to understand that it was domestic violence, and she took us and then divorced Dad.

This was not our story, so my mom had to tell me. "We divorced because we had financial issues," was what she said.

"I don't understand," I responded.

"Exactly," she said. "That's why I said I would tell you when you're older."

Ah, sometimes it's just so hard to be a kid.

Summer Camp - Part I

The first time I felt truly at home, I was ten, and it was August. I had never even set foot on these grounds, and I wasn't allowed to stay . . . but one late summer afternoon, my Amie took us to tour the sleepaway camp that she grew up going to. The place smelled of wood chips and pine cones, and I longed to jump in and join the kids kayaking in the lake. I watched two boys laugh and laugh while they beat the crap out of something called a tetherball. The nightly activities board displayed notices about things like square dances, storytelling, and Kangaroo Court. The girls' area opened up like a treasure chest: I couldn't believe that people got to live like this.

Every cabin felt like a mini-house and every bunk looked like a tiny bedroom. I gazed up at the cabin boards, and noted that they were covered with everyone's name and the year they arrived. There was even advice on the walls: *Men are like toilets. They're either taken or full of shit. Or there's a long waiting line.* I had no idea what that meant, but regardless of their gender, everyone I met looked so happy, so alive, and so free.

This sacred place was called Camp Billings on Lake Fairlee in the great state of Vermont. It was just thirty minutes from where we lived, and every time I rounded the lake's corner, I felt like I was stepping back into a magical land that was created just for me. From that August day, and for seven years after that, I spent every fall, winter and spring counting down the days till I could go back to Camp—counting the moments till I finally could go home.

Summer Camp - Part II

The first time I had sex, I was six days past my eighteenth birthday. By the standards of my peers at the time, I could be considered a late bloomer. But honestly, I had been so awkward and uncomfortable in my body during most of high school, that asking my first boyfriend to take off my back brace at night so we could make love like they do in the movies just didn't seem right. Besides, I didn't even have a boyfriend in high school to do that with. So, I did as you do: I watched a lot of *American Pie*, and I waited.

Everyone remembers their first time, right? It's like one of those vivid dreams that you barely believe actually happened and the story itself ultimately becomes some great Greek myth that you either embellish or exclude true details from. But alas, this is my book. My mom used to say that by being a writer, I have creative license. So, with that gift, I have the writer's license to take you on the drive of my first sex trip.

There once was this Inn, which was like *Dirty Dancing* of New England. An old, old, old-school inn that, when you talk about now, sounds like a dream, but I swear at one point it existed. The inn had forty rooms and none of them had locks on the doors, or any technology for that matter. They were just a living space with a bed, a mini-fridge, and a bathroom with a tub. There was no bar; instead, liquor cubbies where you kept your booze for the week were provided. There was a formal dining room where the waitresses were your servers for the entirety of your stay. They wore old-fashioned, super-unsexy, French maid-looking dresses that were seafoam color for breakfast and lunch, then those dresses became even less alluring but more formal (in black) at dinner. There were also chambermaids. Usually, the chambermaids were the less gregarious of the bunch. The summer I lost my V card, I was fortunate enough to find myself one of them.

Normally, the Inn did not hire any of the summer community kids. They liked creating their own little college summer camp with kids who had no preconceived notion of what summer life in this little town could feel like—probably so they would work more, party less, and feel more responsibility for the inn. I was hired, reluctantly, because my Favorite Family for whom I used to nanny was well connected with the owners and the parents vouched for me.

As a six-day-a-week chambermaid, I wore a starched, Pepto Bismol-colored frock that buttoned down the front. It was slightly see-through in the right morning light, and I would sport a white string bikini underneath: I couldn't wait to jump into the ocean after work and cleanse myself of the copious amounts of Clorox bleach, the occasional used condom I would find in beds, and the splashes of shit that rimmed the toilets that were part of my day. At work, I would usually unbutton the top button of the dress and let my breasts breathe; this thing felt like my back brace, except I got to make money while wearing it.

I learned how to make hospital corners and how to clean tubs in a way that would make my Virgo grandmother proud. I understood how to vacuum in a way that would leave lines on the carpet that said, "I have just been vacuumed." I never fully learned how to polish door knobs correctly, but what I really deeply understood was how to sleep off a hangover in the twin-style beds on the third floor, where no one ever checked for you if you went missing for a few hours.

The reason that this place truly felt like a set from *Dirty Dancing* was because the staff lived in two dorm buildings. The boys' dorm was the Elks; the girls were in the Pagoda. In between the buildings was a space called the Bomb Shelter, where the staff, after spending days catering to the guests, went to get buzzed (or bombed, once in a while too).

I arrived in this paradise on June 17th, 2001, just days after graduating from high school and ready for my first summer as a real worker. Normally I would have been in Weekapaug for a few weeks in August to nanny, but now I had two full months ready to unfold in front of me. I checked into what felt like a new version of the summer camp I had loved as a kid. There were eight singles and two doubles in the Pagoda, and because I was the youngest and newest employee, I would be part of the one-and-only triple. Since I didn't know any differently, I assumed a triple would be more fun. One of my roommates had yet to arrive, but the other roomie was very much making her presence known as I walked in and there she was. My first roommate.

This roommate was tiny, maybe a little over five feet, with a tanned, toned, and tight body. I knew this immediately, as she was lounging on her bed in a lime-green snakeskin bikini that looked like something I would have seen in the Frederick of Hollywood catalog. The bottom barely covered her butt and when she turned over, the top didn't have to cover much of her small breasts, but it did have to cover two things, and those were her nipple rings. She was smoking a Newport, while reading a star book that looked like something I would have found at that hippie store in Hanover. Between super-short, light orangey-red hair and a beautiful set of white teeth, her blue eyes pierced me when we made contact. She gave me a once-over. I was preppy and gangly, and wearing my favorite outfit that I had saved all my babysitting money to get: J. Crew khaki shorts with a drawstring and a short-sleeved, navy-striped tee.

She asked me one question: "When is your birthday?" I was taken aback as I thought she was actually going to ask me what my name was. I was about to turn eighteen the following week, while I was there with my new roommates, so I thought I must have exuded something of an adult-like presence as soon as I arrived.

"Funny you ask," I said. "My birthday is next Sunday, June 24th!" I walked toward my roommate expecting that she would hug me and rub her nipple rings against me, while congratulating me on the one thing that I really had no part in creating. But that's not how she responded—not at all. She actually inhaled her cigarette deeply as her eyes glazed over and her face showed disappointment.

"Cancer?" She exhaled a cloud of Newport in my direction. "I've always hated Cancers."

Me too, I thought, totally not realizing we were not talking about the same thing. As I would learn, my roommate was a budding astrologist. Her nickname became Star Search, and while we may have been the same age, she was studying the stars the way I had studied for the SATs. I had somehow enrolled in Astrology 101 that summer, and she taught me more about Capricorns and Cancers (the father and mother of all signs) than I ever could have imagined.

But what the stars were aligning for me that summer of 2001 wasn't a space odyssey. Soon after my eighteenth birthday, I finally became an adult in more ways than one.

Over the past two summers, I had become friends with the cool kids of this community. I had forever had a serious summer crush on a prep school lax-playing, Massachusetts native who was set to be my first, and just what I hoped for when it came to saying farewell to my V-card. He was cute, and played the cool guy card. This meant he didn't talk to me until he'd drunk enough, and at that point, whether he was slurring or swaying didn't make a negative impression on me. I was into it. To be honest, I was into any boy talking to me. While Hanover was a place where I felt stuck in my good girl, nice, nerdy girl role, I loved spending the summer reinventing myself. First it was sleepaway camp. Then it was Camp Weekapaug.

Very little about the night I lost my virginity has stuck with me. I didn't go out that night thinking *This Is It*. There were no rose petals; there was no courting or unwrapping my corset or turning the key to my chastity belt. Hell, I didn't even know I would be hooking up with My First that night. That was a crap shoot, depending on the amount of booze involved in the beach party.

It wasn't legendary; it wasn't anything for the books, and I can assure my former self that when they say "it gets better," that is a very true statement. That said, it was actually My First who had a problem with the night, not me.

It turns out, he found out it was my first time from his friends, who heard it from my friends the day after. My First was upset I didn't tell him, but I didn't think it was a big deal for him to know. Plus, if he did know, maybe he wouldn't have done it. And then I would have had to deal with more rejection and, after the fiasco over my college applications, I couldn't stand being waitlisted with my V-card too. Most of my friends had lost their virginity to high school boyfriends or summer flings. My mom never talked to us about sex, and since I had never had a beau in high school, there was no reason for her to bring up the sex topic. I talked about sex more with Salt & Peppa than I ever did with my own parents. I just knew that since My First used a condom, I had checked off the most important box: not becoming a teen mom. And I wouldn't be moving into my college years as a "prude."

Isn't that crazy, how we identify with our first time with sex? It's like, the older that we get and we're still a virgin, we are all trying to, Taylor Swift-style, shake it off. Looking back, I realize that I had put so little thought into it, and I was fine with that. It was the guy who wasn't, who realized that I probably deserved more—at least a couch over a car seat, or perhaps a conversation about what we were doing, instead of five minutes of me pretending to know what I was getting myself into.

But all I knew was how to keep secrets about things that may have seemed unbecoming, because that was the real cancer that followed my family around for decades.

Summer Camp - Part III

Once upon a time, on an island thirty miles out to sea, a summer community of Ivy League-educated, WASPy, tennis-playing, yacht-clubbing, Polo-wearing, Chardonnay-drinking, Range Rovering, *wait*, that's not what this chapter is about. Once upon a bar, on a crazy island in the middle of nowhere, lived a bevy of partying college kids, crazier postgrads, and a plethora of adults still attending the University of Nantucket.

Thanks to my sorority sister in college, I have arrived at a tiny island off the coast of Cape Cod, where Lilly is queen and Lacoste is king. A place where Defenders and Wagoneers rule the roads. This was a land where an iced coffee costs a cool five bucks and a martini on the beach costs you a twenty, plus tip.

I was twenty-two, a recent University of New Hampshire grad, and, much to my father's dismay, I was enthusiastically embarking on a new career as a waitress, hostess, barback, and one-day-a-week bartender. I felt like I had won the lottery every time I counted my tips after my shift; I couldn't believe people paid these prices for lunches and libations. I was young enough to be eager to work all the time and experienced enough to recover easily from hangovers by using Visine and taking a cold shower. I never grew up with this Nantucket lifestyle; my single mother used to say things to me like, "I have ten cents until next Thursday," and it seemed like she meant it.

But my mother referred to me as her Mermaid, referencing my happiest moments stretched out on the sand at the beach. It was no surprise to most of my family that I decided to take another endless summer after college and prolong my entrance into the real world for a few more months. Nantucket quickly seeped into my blood, and I was never the same. I loved the fact that there were no Wal-Marts, no Wendy's, plus there was no way off island after 10:00 p.m. The island's celebratory lifestyle enraptured my senses (and endangered my liver). Always one to make friends easily, I soon found myself in a land of a thousand drinking buddies and no best friends. I savored every second of it.

Never one to shy away from a good time, I spent most of my bar earnings on sparkly mini-dresses from Eye of the Needle and equally festive bottles of Veuve Clicquot. I went out as much as I could to over-tip bartenders the way that they once a week showed their love to me. The way to move to the top of the bar food chain was to spend all your money on Stoli cocktails and Fireball shots, then over-tip other bartenders to make sure your bar was on their radar during the next industry night.

But alas, like all good benders, there comes a time when the body wears itself out and there isn't enough cold water in that a.m. shower to drown out a bad night at the Chicken Box. This is what best-selling Nantucket author, Elin Hildebrand, commonly refers to as the eight weeks of August. It's a time when the island is so overrun with questionable tourists and unhappy wealthy campers that the hospitality industry takes its toll . . . and it sure did on this mermaid. I was all ready to move to Nantucket forever around July 4th, but after the third week in August, I was pleading the fifth, as to why I was so unhappy and just wanted to find an easy way out. So, I did what most college kids did. I had to leave to start my real life. I had to get health insurance. I had to make the leap into America. It was time for me to get away from the Grey Lady and move into the Real World.

It was the first time I really understood "you don't know a good thing until it's gone." After just one winter in the "real world" of Boston, I promptly got back on the slow boat to the far east that following April, and got ready to do this Nantucket thing all over again. And again. And again. For eighteen more years.

Settle Down

"Where would you like to live?" I was giving my mom the Proust Questionnaire one afternoon in late March of 2014. My time with her was coming to an end, yet I still had so many questions that needed answers. The queries continued:

"On what occasion do you lie?"

"What is your favorite journey?"

"Who is your hero in real life?"

"What is your greatest regret?"

These were the things I was trying to pry out of her before there wasn't a voice left to respond with. And of course, "Where would you like to live?"

This seemed like such an odd question to ask a woman on her death bed. Like there wasn't even going to be an option to switch locations or even shift vantage points in her own home. At this point she hadn't gone number two in weeks as her cancer had blocked her bowels. She needed help just to sit up while someone adjusted her pillows.

She answered: "Woodstock, Vermont."

I thought it was a strange choice, because she lived in South Royalton, and these Green Mountain towns were only two exits from each other. She already lived in the same county as Woodstock. Why would she need to upgrade to just a few miles away?

A year later, I found myself going to Stowe, Vermont, so I could drive by her exit, the aptly numbered #2. Driving long distances had become such a luxury, and I loved the ability to go more than 45 miles per hour (which is as fast as you can drive on Nantucket). I dreamed about starting over on the journey up. I'd cruise by all these tiny nondescript towns and secretly wish that I could go home there. I bought a VT sticker at a gas station and put it on the right bumper of my gray jeep. I don't have any tattoos, but those two letters were my type of ink job—a constant reminder of my mom in my car.

"Home is where your mom is" was written on a box that I gave to my mom for Christmas in 2006. So, what happens when your mom's no longer home? By now, you'd think Nantucket would have been home. I had spent almost ten years there and moved fifteen times on the island. In the winter I would pack my belongings and shuffle from Nantucket to 'Sconset. It was just seven miles down Milestone Road, but going to the only other "town" on the island felt like a world away to me.

Nantucket was my South Royalton. 'Sconset was my Woodstock.

I was paralyzed about committing fully to being in one place. Because, if I settled down, that meant I was settling . . . and I'd rather die than do that.

I think.

Escape

"I miss my travel agent," he said over breakfast at the Four Seasons in Boston.

It was October of 2014 and we were pitching this Bay State billionaire on the idea of combining travel and social media—sharing our world with the world at large. My partner and I had gone to college together; we'd even rushed the same sorority during our first week freshman year. Years after we graduated, we both fell in love on Nantucket—I with promoting the island, and she with the editor of Nantucket Magazine.

We knew we had something special, as we both could entertain a crowd effortlessly and keep people informed. For her, it was from years of being on TV and radio. Her fan base was primarily Boston, and her forte was the restaurant scene. My home was Nantucket, and my power was the internet and social resort marketing. We decided to combine forces and create a new platform that winter: modern day travel agents. We'd call ourselves City & Sand Escapes.

However, if I am being honest, what I really wanted to escape was my own life.

I didn't want to feel this year of firsts that I kept living after my mom died: Thanksgiving, my mom's birthday, and Christmas would soon be arriving. I didn't want to focus on all that, and since I didn't have the money to move, the answer was a working vacation.

So, we pitched this über successful entrepreneur on our travel concept. We'd go to resort destinations; tell the best ways to sip, shop, and stay, and we'd share it over Instagram, Facebook, email, and video. He enjoyed our enthusiasm and saw the potential of social media. He talked to us about the power of things going viral, then he made an angel investment and sent us on our way.

But just being given money doesn't make something succeed. Just ask any trust fund kid out there. As RuPaul would preach, "You Better Work." So, we took the funds and spread them out over four trips. We pitched an airline. Connected with a beloved resort destination. Got a videographer on board with the promise of a free vacation in turn for fresh footage. We took a leap and watched the hammocks appear. We had a lot of drive, a little money, and thousands and thousands of followers. But you can't put a price tag on influence . . . can you?

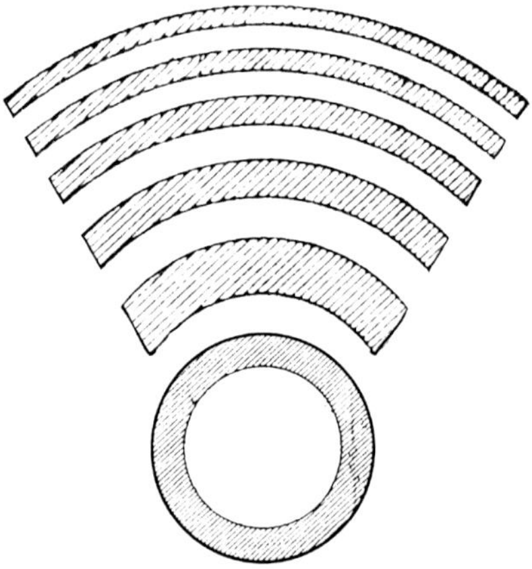

7.

The Internet

User

After a loved one dies, especially a mother, one may find oneself quite lost. Quite scared. Quite sad. And quite not ready to deal with any of those emotions. And that, my friends, is where the internet makes for one hell of a drug.

You can hide from the world and at the same time show everyone how you are living your best life from pretty photos and punny tweets. You can attend every festival: wine, film, yoga, comedy, dance, and every nonprofit event, like Dreamcatcher, August Fête, POPS on ACK, Summer Groove. You can show how you are giving back so much to this world, but your world, unbeknownst to most, could also be completely falling apart. And when you add champagne and Adderall to this equation, well, let me tell you, this is a recipe for a limitless and spirited productivity.

But every superhero needs to know her kryptonite. Mine was silence. So, I made sure I had none of that. Because when you get quiet, all those pesky problems start to show up. And when you start to go inward, you can't avoid the fact that you have a broken heart.

That sounds like a nice quote that I would have pinned during this time.

Branding

The first time I got on an internet chat room was thanks to a friend, whose father was an early tech adopter in the .NET scene. Somehow, in seventh grade, we had discovered a chatroom where you could talk to anyone and everyone in a very basic way. We coined our username, BlytheHolly, because those were our names, but no one would talk to us. We tried to insert ourselves into as many instant messages conversations as possible, yet responses were few and far between.

I think this is when my marketing brain turned on. No one was talking to us because our username looks like *BlyTheHolly*. "We need to switch this up," I told her. So, we did. We changed our name, and everyone started to talk to us. Two seventh graders with brown hair, and one of us with a back brace and massive middle school insecurity too, but no one on the internet had to know that. Our screen name was now *BarbieGirl16*—and everyone was interested in talking to that girl.

The Facebook

I was a senior in college when I heard about Facebook. My Bestie, who didn't need to "friend" me at twenty-one to have me care about her, told me there was this new thing on the internet called The Facebook, and I had to join. You got to pick your profile photo, could write on other people's walls, and had the opportunity to poke people. All online. She said I needed to look up the kids from our high school. It was like a high school reunion, a few years too early, and no one had actually done anything of merit yet, but you could see who gained the freshman fifteen, and still had it as a senior. "Jack even has his profile picture as Hillary Clinton," Bestie messaged me. "How hilarious is that?!"

Back then, I had no idea what this platform would do. How I would ultimately make a business out of this crazy thing that would be known as social media. It was just a classier version of hotornot.com that told me that it was this girl's birthday on December 10th, and I had no idea why I should have known that. By the time Facebook dropped the "the," I had graduated from college and the platform had become part of my days—whenever I could find that addictive thing called the internet.

It was the beginning of me realizing whether we "liked" it or not, we were all truly connected.

Miss blACKbook

I never went to school for social media; a class like that didn't exist when I was in college.

I learned social media through living it—the good, the bad, and the downright cancel-culture ugly that comes from being an early adapter. Even today, I don't think anyone honestly can say they are an expert at social media. There are people who know it deeply through experience, but the textbooks haven't been written yet. More time and research need to happen before we can understand the science behind this social science.

I deeply experienced each platform. Trial-by-fire and trial-by-error is how I learned. As soon as I learned how to use social media, I wanted to teach others how to use it as well.

During the winter of 2013, I created classes teaching Social Media 101, Email Marketing 202, and things like Pinstagram, that were so early in their social media wave, we combined Pinterest and Instagram together. I did this alongside another digitally savvy friend. We knew the platforms could be successful only if others understood how to tweet, post, and pin, too. While I didn't have a degree in social media, I taught knowing I had a diploma in the school of hard knocks. My co-teacher gave me the nickname of Miss blACKbook, and I embraced the title. I kind of felt like Miss Honey in Roald Dahl's *Matilda*, kindly doing my best to help students on social media to be the person that I needed.

I joined Facebook in November of 2004. I got on as a Blogger in January of 2008. I hopped on LinkedIn in 2012; signed up for Twitter that same summer, and downloaded Instagram by Thanksgiving. I got accounts on Pinterest and Mailchimp by 2013; started my first WordPress site in 2014, and even tried my hand at Snapchat the following spring. You name it, I've tried it. (*What up, Vine.*) Sure, they didn't all stick, but I have stuck with the big guy since he began.

Facebook has been life, and the rest was just sharing details. My persistence was the foundation; my consistency was the secret sauce. This has been a recipe whose final product is still a mystery to me. I had been baking something here for eighteen years without a clue of what I was cooking.

The Internet Unconscious

I did it. I told someone about the secret.

I couldn't help myself. It had been months of building out the blACKbook idea, and dozens of shifts behind the bar when people asked me what I was doing, and I lied and said nothing special. But this was special—the concept of this new online magazine, the blACKbook. It was going to take off. It was going to change the marketing scene. I knew it. And I just had to tell someone other than BF (who was a great sounding board, and an even better secret keeper). I had to tell someone other than my web developer. I had to tell someone other than those to whom I had been pitching the concept.

I had coffee with a local businesswoman who made me sign an NDA (Nondisclosure Agreement), and I thought, *Wait, is this what I am supposed to do? To make sure people don't take my idea? Should I create this one-page document that discusses the repercussions if someone copied my blACKbook?*

No, no, no. What I was supposed to do was tell no one about this. But alas, these loose lips were ready to sink ships, and a few weeks before I was about to launch the website, an older 'Sconset woman, who was all about locals and local community, sat at my bar on a quiet spring night and began to discuss the internet, the island, and the integrity of sharing thoughtful information.

We shared stories and my tales of blogging. I started one of the first island blogs in 2008. Now almost four years later, talking with this woman, I felt like I was on the same page with someone, even someone of another generation. She felt trustworthy, almost a bit maternal. I told her about the blACKbook. And my idea around a website of the island's hip and fresh scene.

She nodded and smiled. We were on the same webpage. She told me she was also about to launch her own site. One that was by Nantucketers, for Nantucketers.

Carl Jung coined the term "collective unconscious" in the 1920s—the idea that our minds are all connected, and there are no original thoughts. Right as I was planning and launching my website, there was a woman down Milestone Road doing the exact same thing. But I was still unconscious of the idea of a collective. Instead, I was focused on what I believed meant you were the best.

And that, was being the first to get it out there.

High Earners Not Rich YET

It was the holiday season far into my second year of blACKbook, and things were heating up: I was becoming a force on the internet. I had the likes, I had the followers, and I had an avid fan base of HENRYs (High Earners Not Rich Yet). *Yet* being the key word. I reached the digitally savvy pre-affluent, the young and the internet restless.

I thought Facebook, Instagram, Pinterest, Twitter, and my blog were enough to reach the masses . . . but then I got word from a millennial surf company that I was missing a key advertorial component. "You don't have an email list?" they asked me, somewhat shocked.

I thought I was cool with all the other social channels; I had no idea I would have to add one more networking platform to my already very full social plate. They wanted to advertise this holiday season, and wanted me to do it through my email list. Apparently, Mailchimp is where that holiday gift ROI (Return On Investment) is at.

But I had actually consciously decided not to start an email newsletter. There was already a prominent guy around town, who had begun an online newsletter eight years back, and he had been adamant that he did not want me to start an email newsletter: he was wary of my blACKbook from the get-go. I used to write for the guy. I had a column called "HollyWould" in his email newsletters, and even though I now wrote for myself, I didn't want to stir the competition's pot by adding in my own newsletters. But those surf boys wanted web-surfing traffic, and they told me that it came from smart email marketing.

Time to build up an email list. I was always good at beginnings. And how do you build an email list? You have to give to take. I created a contest where you could win a $75 gift card to a local restaurant if you gave me your email. Three hundred emails and one happy winner of a delicious meal later, and *blACKbook weekly* was born.

I believe your first email will always get the highest open rate, so you better make it a good one. But no HENRY had alerted me that you could use links to click over from email text and photos, so the opening blACKbook email had all the content but none of the click overs.

All that work for nothing. Or was it?

Almost Famous

Drew Barrymore's favorite Nantucket store is Current Vintage. Leonardo DiCaprio was at The Pearl last night. Edelman and Adriana were spotted walking down the Wharf. Gronk was guest-bartending at Cisco Brewers. Sharon Stone just arrived for the Dreamland Gala.

I had always been a fan of browsing the US Weekly section "Stars, they're just like us" while in line at the Stop & Shop. And all these Nantucket celebrity moments would flash up on my Twitter and I would think, *I should go get a shot. US Weekly could use this!*

But it never felt great trying to sneak around to get a photo of these "stars like us" on Nantucket. I don't know why I ever thought I would want to be associated with a gossip rag or a magazine that loves to highlight other people's private lives. I just knew that I was in the public eye, and that paparazzi didn't come to Nantucket. I mean, who wants to pay $800 a night to get a hotel to get a photo of a star on vacation while having a $60 dinner while you wait? There were no Dumpsters to hide behind or fenced-off areas for overly eager photographers.

That is the thing about Nantucket—this is not a place meant for being seen. It is a place that thrives on anonymity and being just like everyone else. The older your car is, the cooler you look bumping down the cobblestones. The more worn-in your Nantucket Reds, the more conversational they become. You can save those Manolos for Manhattan, as these streets aren't even high-heel friendly. The reason that this place has become a favorite of celebrities and the hyper-rich is simply because of its simplicity, its step back in time.

Life is slow here, and it isn't for everyone . . . and that is exactly why we like it

Vanity Fair Game

"Oh yes, I've heard about you. I read about you in *Vanity Fair*," the man at the bar said, drinking his second martini.

"Um, no sir, I think what you meant to say is *Nantucket Magazine*," I responded. "I write a monthly column for them."

The man shook his head. "No. It was *Vanity Fair*. They just did an article about Malibu and Nantucket erosion, and you're quoted in it."

My head was spinning. I was bartending, so I couldn't just stop serving this man to serve myself and get this magazine. I texted an intern who had been helping me and asked her to run down to The Hub to grab the August issue.

As I served the man strozzapreti with broccoli rabe and chicken sausage, I felt like a chicken with my own head cut off. How could I be quoted in *Vanity Fair*? No one had ever even interviewed me! And what do you mean, an article about erosion? I mean, I had spent the latest winter storm tracking around 'Sconset, and I had shown on social media how that house on Baxter Road had started to fall into the ocean. But where are they getting this information?

While I had no idea what had happened, something in me tingled, thinking this was my big break. The intern arrived with a somewhat scandalous cover photo of Kerry Washington in a white one-piece lying in a pool. But that wasn't what caught my eye—"Movie stars and billionaires vs. nature's wrath: the looming danger to America's super rich playgrounds."

I opened the magazine to page 100 to see in the article "From Coast to Toast," a visually alarming image of 'Sconset and its houses perched dangerously close to the bluff. The quote the man was talking about was this: "More than 3,000 miles to the east, Holly Finigan, the founder of The Nantucket blACKbook—THE 'it' guide connecting those on & off island with all things hip & fresh! Crazy for ACK—was tweeting her more than 3,000 followers: 'Word on Baxter [Road] is that this Bluff House only has a few more days . . . right?'"

Wait, what? Twitter? Quoted from Twitter? Now my brand, my words, and my business were part of a *Vanity Fair* article that I didn't even know about? How was it even possible to be quoted from Twitter?!

All that star tracking had paid off. Turns out, I didn't need to tweet photos of celebrities on Nantucket. In the end, a photo of a home falling into the ocean was more noteworthy than any star sipping poolside at The Summer House.

And wait . . .

Is social media the new journalism?

#blACKbookVaca

SBH is another airport code that doesn't scream its location and takes a little extra time to get to. This island is known for its photo-worthy runway, for its decadent six-hour champagne lunches, for its natural beauty, five-star hospitality, and mega-yachts.

It's not #Nantucket; it's very much its own island. And this Caribbean dream spot was the winter vacation of many blACKbook followers, so I knew I had to see it to believe it.

Bienvenue à Saint Barths.

We came for a week-long stay, and I quickly understood the reason why there was a popular tee shirt that said "ST. BARTH'S FUCKING PARADISE." The beaches, the decadence, the people-watching, the wealth: it was fascinating, like watching the Travel Channel come to life. I had not grown up with these types of vacations, so this was all new to me. And my fresh set of eyes couldn't wait to show up online with these images to share in the depths of a New England winter.

Sure, we did the Nikki Beach thing, the Le Ti thing, the La Plage thing, the Bagatelle thing. They were all just as fun, festive, and fabulous as I'd watched online. But the day that really made the trip was the one that I never posted. It was just BF and me. We rented an ATV, and picked up bottles of sparkling water, a baguette and cheese, and drove to the beach you could only get to if you hiked to it. The sand was so pristine, the shore so quiet, the hike so gratifying, and the sparkling water so refreshing. The whole day cost us $100. It was St Barth's paradise, alright, and it was the best afternoon of the vacation.

Because it was the one time that I was off my phone and *in my life.*

The Internet Generation

Got trolls?

As a child of the '90s, of course; we all did. Those plastic topless dolls with the neon-hued hair that stands straight up in colors you can see from a mile away? Sure, we all remember them. I mean, they originated way before this, though. They were actually born in 1959, the same year as my mom. But something my mom would never truly get to see as a Baby Boomer (1946-1964) is when a troll shifted from being an amusing toy to being a far from amusing human—from playing with them with our hands, to using those same hands on a keyboard to write things that would make your hair stand up on end. Things that you couldn't look away from. Messages that you would constantly refresh to see if they had gone away . . . or worse, to see if more of those faceless trolls had shown up.

But before we dive into the trolls, we have to dig into the tales.

I have a teacher of consciousness who shares a profound way to deal with uncomfortable stories and narratives that we don't want to keep following us around. Every time we retell a story that hurts us, we reopen that wound. So, she offered this three-step storytelling process. She taught that the first time you tell a story, it's to release it. The second time you say that same story, it's to understand it. And the third time, if you ever tell that story again, it's to gift it.

The problem that many of us have with this three-step formula is that we get stuck in a rinse and repeat of release to understand. We start "releasing" a narrative that hurts us to every person who will listen with understanding eyes and ears. And without rectifying the story's lesson (i.e., the *why* that it happened ***for us***), we get caught in a loop of telling the same story again and again of what happened ***to us***. And the only person who really gets hurt is the one doing the storytelling.

I want to talk about online bullying, something that I am grateful I didn't have to deal with as a young child. Unfortunately, I did have to deal with it as a guinea pig of the internet during my adult life. I feel for Generation Z kids (1996-2010), as they have grown up with technology and social media as a completely normal part of their childhood/teenage years. Thus many kids get bullied *twice* during puberty: once in person, and another time online. And since their parents (often Generation X, 1965-1980) didn't have to deal with that digital reality themselves, there were millions of kids out there who have had to parent themselves and learn the tough way how to deal with Finstagram (fake Instagram accounts), trolls (people who love to stir up drama online with things they probably would never say in person), and threads of Snapchats and direct messages that were "deleted"—but in the hearts and minds of these impressionable kids, they forever stayed.

I have compassion for all of us who grew up during this time, including us Millennials (1980-1996), who started using the internet without knowing what it really was. A very good thing can turn toxic, especially when it is used to connect in a hurtful way. I didn't have social media platforms to use and abuse as a teen, and didn't have to watch my kids go through that process, but I did have a type of child during this time: my baby was my business. I had started a blog that turned into a successful entrepreneurial venture—telling internet users how to enjoy the best of Nantucket. As an advocate (as opposed to an advertiser), I was a disrupter in the media and marketing field, so I had to endure the love and hate that comes with inevitable change. While it may help you to grow a thick skin, it can also seriously take its digital toll on a person.

It took me a long time to write this next part of my book, not because I don't remember it, but because I really didn't want to relive many of these painful moments. I felt that I had healed from them, but every time we open that Instagram post with hurtful comments, we are reopening Pandora's box and flooding ourselves with the emotions that come with reliving a difficult digital past. Nevertheless, I've committed at long last to finishing that loop, to releasing and understanding these moments, and finally to gifting the story.

Friends on Facebook

If we had eight mutual friends, I would automatically accept your "friend" request. That is the power of connection and trust when it comes to the wild world of Facebook. But as we all know, being friends on Facebook does not mean being besties in real life. This kind of friendship was just allowing some people a glimpse into whatever best life you wanted to showcase. And no one was better at showing and saying that they were "living my best life" than I was. I used Facebook as a way to gallivant around the globe and share my travels in the process.

My first blog was called *The Kiwi Chronicles*; it tracked four girls for three months in 2008, while we visited two islands, and made one crazy trip to the South Pacific when we spent a winter in New Zealand. The blog became a coming-of-age story, where I first shared stunning landscapes as well as my hangovers. By the end, I had fallen in love and shown the piece of my heart that I left Down Under after those three months were over.

That year, I came back to ACK for my shortest summer. I traveled back to New Zealand in October, where this Kiwi and I explored New Zealand together. We moved to Maui in December and finished our big exploration with a month-long road trip across the United States that led us back to me introducing him to my favorite Grey Lady. My Kiwi sat at my bar on Memorial Day Weekend in 2009 and watched my island performance begin again. He was not thrilled with the island party lifestyle, nor did he want to live on Nantucket. We broke up that August.

My next blog was my original blACKbook, which I shared on Facebook through posts during the summer from 2008 through 2011. This was my Sex and the City for Nantucket, my way of sharing all the he said/she said things I heard behind the bar that would make me think twice and take a second moment to write them down in a little black book. "Islands are for finding yourself or losing yourself," the first quote in the blACKbook began. "Unfortunately, too many people lose themselves here on Nantucket."

During the summer of 2013, I too lost a little piece of myself. A new Facebook group came out titled Nantucket Venom. An account calling themselves ACKholes (just like my brand, using a play on the island's airport code to say Nantucket without saying it) was using the "under the cap" ACK captions that the so-called "juice guys" from Nantucket Nectars had first coined. At first, I found their bottle cap comments funny . . . but that is how it always is: funny, until it is personal.

One day, a local restaurant manager sent me a screenshot of a Nantucket Venom bottle cap that read: "Nothing says Nantucket like Vermont maple syrup, Chinese chicken and the blACKbook." The manager wrote "not nice" on the text chain. I felt like I had food poisoning; I felt like I would rather move to Vermont to be home with my mom. I felt extra-embarrassed, since I had just shared with my 5,000 followers one of the Nantucket Venom cap posts the day before. Even worse, I didn't even know who was behind this account. If you don't have anything nice to say, apparently say it to Nantucket Venom.

Turns out, I was friends on Facebook with the guy who ran the account. He was a local comedian. Maybe the real joke is that friends on Facebook is such a loose term.

The Rules

The *Insta* of Instagram is what first attracted me to the platform. While posts on Facebook were often well thought out, and Twitter was all about 140 characters, Instagram was image-based. It was about showing what was happening *while* it was happening: taking everything in real time, but then editing the picture, and making things appear a little better and brighter than maybe they were . . .

I gifted all my content in the present, too. I went on trips and documented my vacation unfolding right as it was happening. I went to restaurants and showed my dinner on the 'Gram as it got cold. I sat in the front row at big events and took photos of large-scale productions. I brightened the space, and doctored the photo, while being the first to announce how much money had been raised for the local hospital. I captured every scene as it was happening to show everything, just as it was in the moment . . . *but not.*

See, there was a major trade-off. I was living in a world free of algorithms, running a competitive race of getting the best image out in the quickest time. I got first place, because there was no competition. I was so far ahead in this social game while mentally preparing for the future, that I'd already be thinking about likes and comments more than about the impact of my experience and that post. I was living for what others "hearted," obsessed with finding out who was on #Nantucket.

When a highly-followed blogger and her husband made their way out to the island from the city and posted dinners at Straight Wharf, waffle cones at the Juice Bar, and beach waves in Miacomet, I couldn't wait to meet up with this fellow Insta-famous person offline and learn how she was making her social media business work.

When I DM'd (direct messaged) her to say let's have coffee, she wrote back, "Oh let's plan for next time!"

"But aren't you still here?" I messaged.

"Oh no, that vacation is from a few weeks ago." She replied. "I'm back in Boston now."

What?!?!?! Blasphemy! Acting like you're on island on Insta while you're in another city posting this? That's not how this is done. You're breaking the cardinal rule . . . the "Insta" of Instagram.

But wait: who has the rule book?

The Post

My mom didn't actually die until April 8th, 2014. But if you ask me, she died the day I posted on Facebook that she was entering hospice. Until the moment after I posted that message, I never had cried harder. These were sobs that came from deep in my belly and out my mouth in a horrific howl that could wake the neighbors and alarm the authorities.

In my mind, that post on Facebook that said we had entered into palliative care was her obituary. There was no going back from that one. I could not believe how much power this social media platform had over me. It was crazy to think that on March 20th, I unknowingly gave my mom her two weeks' notice.

But there is much good that comes from social media as well. That post boomeranged back to bring such joy. I wrote that even though my mom would be accepting no visitors, she had always been a lover of the written word. While family and friends no longer could see her, she could feel their love if they wanted her to by sending her a card.

It was Facebook at its finest. It was the square root of compassionate social media. The first day two cards showed up, then four, then eight, then sixteen, then thirty-two. By the weekend, our mailman had become the Jolly Postman, sharing daily good stories and happy times in these cards, which sent love and gratitude to my mom who had helped so many.

I have to stress, the internet is also a pretty extraordinary tool: just see how one post on a wall could amount to hundreds of cards from the post office.

Crappy Place

If you forced me to sit down during this time, you would have found a total social media addict. I was constantly flying high from all the viral moments. I was soaring from all the likes, all the shares, and all the retweets that my phone constantly notified me of.

I've read that, like exercise or drugs, social media notifications have a similar ability to give us a shot of dopamine. I wasn't doing much of either of those, unless you counted the way I ran around like a lunatic or how I would borrow an Adderall pill from anyone who could afford to give me one.

But the real issue was not the movement, the frenetic pace, or the constant doing. The real problem was the silence.

It would come back every once in a while . . . As soon as I would get close to finishing a big project, or a photoshoot, or another top ten list of the best sneaky bars on the island, I would find myself feeling a deep sense of loneliness and a looming worry of being forgotten. (This is a middle-child trait that I have always struggled with.)

As soon as I thought of myself as a child, I had to think of my mom and of how she wasn't here anymore for me to call, for me to tell her that I wasn't doing that well. She would have taken just one glance into my eyes and known that I was not alright.

One day, while searching my desk for my passport, I found a postcard from Eleuthera. "Ahoy from my happy place!" it read in my mom's sweet cursive writing.

Since we were never able to have any services for our mom, and she didn't want any goodbyes, I had been seeking a way to commemorate her over the past twelve months. Happy place . . . happy place . . . so many Nantucketers felt that same way about this island. Then I did what I do best: I conceptualized a whole new project, this time a clothing line that evolved from an Instagram post I created with an image of the island and the phrase "happy place" together—saying Nantucket again without ever saying Nantucket. That is what I was trying to do.

A friend who was a local graphic designer and had her own clothing company told me she would like to refine the logo. She pitched the idea that she could help me create the Happy Place line. We in turn could split all the costs and all the profits, 50/50.

I 100 percent knew I could not do this on my own, and I had no idea what I was getting myself into. But hey, the unknown was a hell of a lot easier to deal with than the silence. And so, Happy Place, the clothing brand, began.

Thanks Guys

When you begin anything of substance, one of the most important things to remember is five words that we were taught at a young age: "No man is an island."

I didn't create this blACKbook empire alone. I couldn't have done it without those who created the internet and the social media platforms. I couldn't have launched it without Mark Zuckerberg of Facebook and Jack Dorsey, Noah Glass, Biz Stone and Evan Williams of Twitter and Kevin Systrom and Mike Krieger of Instagram, and Ben Silbermann, Paul Sciarra, and Evan Sharp of Pinterest and Evan Spiegel, Bobby Murphy, and Reggie Brown of Snapchat. I couldn't have been successful without Ben Chestnut, Mark Armstrong and Dan Kurzius of MailChimp, and Bob Parsons of Go Daddy, and Larry Page and Sergey Brin of Google.

No man is an island . . . that is true. But, when it comes to the internet and social media, where are the women founders?

A Revolution

"We are in the middle of the beginning of an industrial revolution called the internet, and the future will be very different," the art gallery owner said while on stage at the Art for Tomorrow conference put on by the *New York Times* in Doha, Qatar.

Jumping from Stowe to Saint Barths to the middle of the Middle East, this is how fast things were evolving with blACKbook. I had Nantucket in my title, which was the gateway drug that had all these brands believing in me. But the real black book, which I constantly came back to, was all about writing down little thoughts and quotes like this one above that have been said around the world.

I had been invited to take an all-inclusive, first-class trip on a five-star airline to a place that I had to Google to both figure out where it was and how to say it. Qatar, which sounds like "guitar" with a Q, is home to major oil money. And it is the country that houses the new Dubai called Doha, and also hosted the 2022 FIFA World Cup. But this country is truly known for its airline.

Qatar Airways is like the Taj in a jet bus, and its airport is a state-of-the-art experience. You don't just shop for trinkets and time-passing magazines here, but instead have the opportunity to shop in an airport Rodeo Drive, and even buy a Maserati before you jet out to wherever your next destination is. Qatar Airways was launching their first direct flight from Doha to Boston and to celebrate, they invited a press trip of New England media outlets like Boston newspapers and magazines and influencer like, you guessed it, the Nantucket blACKbook.

I was just as shocked to get this email as you may be to read this. I actually thought it was a spam email like that one that would tell you to send $10,000 to a Nigerian prince. But this was real, and the most eye-opening thirty-six-hour trip of my blACKbook career.

I rode a camel, drove on sand dunes, shopped in markets, ate local cuisine, toured bizarre car museums, and stayed at the Doha Ritz. I had absolutely no idea what was going on, but I smiled so much during that trip, I'm pretty sure people thought I either was massively medicated or completely out to lunch. The best moment for me was sitting at this conference—like a TED talk for global thought leaders—with a focus on the future of airports. Why shouldn't an airport be a luxurious, calm, and beautiful experience? Doha was just that. It ran as smoothly as an Amtrak, with the sound of silence as its soundtrack. It was forward-thinking; it was ahead of the curve.

Just as this art gallery owner was when she said, "We are in the middle of the beginning of the industrial revolution called the internet and the future will be very different."

Another puzzle had come together. I could see the hole in the picture. I just didn't have the pieces to fill this center in yet. However, as a middle child, I knew that being at the center of something is incredibly important. And while people remember beginnings and endings, they often forget about how important that middle moment is.

And I'd have to travel around the world to get to the heart of this story.

tRUTH

"Earth is a school, we come here to learn lessons," my Astrologer always said to me. Together, we kicked off every January with a reading to tell me what was in store for the next twelve months. We began this in 2013, and I would meet her annually for the next seven years. She was like sitting with a sage aunt who had all the answers, thanks to the ways that the planets were currently matched up.

I loved going to her as she focused on the rising sign of Gemini that highlighted my communication skills and my writing. Year after year, she told me it was coming. The book was being created, I just had a lot of lessons to learn first. She talked to me about her own life, about owning a bookstore on Nantucket years ago and about how she spent the past nine years in Woodstock, Vermont. She had been based for the last decade near where my mom lived, and in 2013, she had just fully moved back to the island.

"Home again, home again, jiggity, jig," she would say when she got off the ferry.

I always asked my astrologist about my mom and her health, about what I should do, about what I should know. She saw me struggle, trying to interest me in my career even though she knew my main focus was my mother's cancer. That winter, I had her over to give mini readings to my friends at our book club. I went last, and we dove right in as she pulled some cards. My question was the question I always had: What's going on with my mom?

My astrologist looked at my cards and looked into my eyes. "Just spend as much time with your mom as you can."

And that was it.

Oh, how I wish someone had reminded me of that every year for the past thirty ones.

PART II

Ruth's Consciousness

8.

The Mother

Queen - Part I

My mother told me that if you really loved a man, "you need to love him so much that you can't stand it." She also told me that if a man really loved me, he would sing "Oh! Darling" by the Beatles to me.

You see, my mom had a serious love for good music and a cassette collection that would impress any discerning '70s and '80s rock fan. I didn't just like the music, I also loved playing Name That Tune in the car with mom. It takes a long time to learn Name That Tune, but we often had a long time in the Blazer together.

Every other weekend, my sisters and I were in the car for at least an hour with our mother on our way down to meet our father. And when our favorite radio station 99 Rock would cut out, we would go back to mom's tapes. I began to recognize the Beatles from their first three chords. Or the fact it was definitely Fine Young Cannibals because of the lead singer's most distinctive voice. I loved when that beat dropped and I knew INXS was about to come in. A fast drumming, and I was sure the Boss was about to belt out the USA blues. But my favorite came every night when mom played a game called Get The Led Out. Three Led Zeppelin songs would play, and you would have to call 643-ROCK and be the first caller with the name of all three songs. The winner got a large cheese pizza from C&A's.

My mother was so good at this game that she started having to make up fake names and give out different mailing addresses to comply with the once-a-month winning rules. Ruth Mori, she won once but only once. But so did Nina Gorini (my mom's sister, she was in Italy, and it was 1:00 a.m. so there was no way she was getting the Led out). My grandmother Dorothy would win, but her last name would be our father's. A few weeks later, a voucher would arrive for a free large pie in my grandmother's mailbox addressed to Dorothy Finigan. She knew what to do.

The other music game we loved to play was the 4:20 Subway commute. Three songs would play and if you could guess the common theme through the three, you won a six-inch Subway sub, 20-ounce fountain soda, and a cookie. My mother was an expert at this one. She crushed the 4:20 Subway commute. So much so that her names started to get really wacky. The people who won didn't exist, but there was a woman behind the curtain, formulating all the answers, getting her prizes of meatball heroes and pepperoni glory. Mostly I like to think my mother's creativity emerged from coming up with new personalities. Starting over, building another person up from scratch. I wonder if my mom loved the game or seeing how much she could reinvent herself with every win.

I had once heard from my aunt Nina that right before my twenty year-old mom got married to my twenty-three year old dad, she told her fifty-year-old father that she wasn't sure she wanted to go forward with it. Her dad said what many a man who invested thousands of dollars into a single day has said to his daughter: "Too late, Ruth, too late."

Looking back, I believe the night before her big day, my mother stopped listening to her heart when it said, "I Want To Break Free."

Instead, she drowned out her wants by following what others wanted when it came to this "Crazy Little Thing Called Love."

Death

Ever had one of those nights as a kid where you couldn't fall asleep, and you started to think about the world and if it started when you were born? I remember one night I had like that. I think I was maybe ten, feeling restless and unsure of this whole life thing. I started to think about death in that darkness and came up with that oh-so-existential question for a fifth grader which was: what happens when we die? I remember feeling so lost with that question looming over my brain, so I tried to count sheep and forget about it.

In the morning, when things were brighter, I went into my mom's room, still pretty shaken up from the revelation of the night before, and needing some comfort. I gave her a hug and asked, "Mom, what do you think happens when we die?"

Taken aback by my deep question before her first cup of coffee had set in, it seemed like she just wanted to give me an answer that would (hopefully) not come with more questions. She said, "You know, Holl, nobody knows, but I think life is like a light switch, you are living and the light is on, and then you die and the light goes out." I sat there waiting for more of an explanation.

"That's it?" I asked.

"Yep. I think that's it." And she turned around and went back to her day. But I tossed and turned for nights to come, thinking of that idea, that something as big as life could just be on. . . and then just be turned off. I didn't believe her.

Not then and not now.

Women

In the summer of 1993, Mom and her Second Husband split up. This time we weren't shipped off to Italy for the shakeup. We were simply sent down to our dad's for a few weeks in August, and by the time we came back, it was like a Magic Eraser had done some brilliant work and that guy disappeared from our life. All traces of him were extinguished, with new photos in frames and his sports car, motorcycle, and endless supply of cowboy boots hit the road while we were gone. If my mother ever spoke of him it was to refer to him as "he who shall not be named." And thus, we really never asked her about him again.

By the start of fifth grade, we had moved to a new house and out of that dark A-frame in the woods. Things were brighter everywhere, and it was just us. The Girlie Girls, as my mother called us. Back to the days of Little Women and the only year I think my mom was completely without a man for as long as we knew her.

We moved to my favorite rental house of my childhood on a sweet street called Meadow Lane. This was a normal house and in a normal neighborhood (high rent for our mom, close to town, and with a lot of people on the "census" that would have been part of what makes Hanover a desirable zip code). The reason I knew it was a safe neighborhood was because our school nurse lived down the street, as did some of my grandfather's Dartmouth Class of 1951 who had retired there. There were lots of Volvos, Audis, and Saabs in the manicured driveways and our ranch-style house was burnt red and sat on a corner lot with a two-car garage, a mailbox that said "3" on it, and a big back yard that you could do a hundred somersaults down. I finally felt like we were like everyone else. Everything I always wanted as a kid.

I loved the four-bedroom house. I also adored our mailbox. While I never played sports growing up, I had become a champion letter writer. It was my favorite surprise every day . . . going to the mailbox to see what the mailman brought us. My mom was often waiting at the mailbox, too. This was for child support checks from my father. I remember her skimming through bills, Grand Union coupons, and Victoria's Secret catalogs to see if that thin envelope from outside Boston happened to slip through one of these magazines. Vicki's was her least favorite piece of snail mail. I am pretty sure on most days when she waited for that check, she would also have to wait for our mailman to leave our mailbox. This guy spent an extra few minutes at the end of our short driveway whenever there was a Victoria Secret catalog. My mom was disgusted that he would sit there on the clock with absolutely no sense of urgency or privacy as he leafed through the pages of scantily clad ladies. I often wondered why my mother was so disparaging of this catalog. From what I saw, the models were called "Angels." Maybe it was an anger that every time a check didn't show up, a VS catalog did. My mother seemed to loathe this mag, but one of her top drawers had a lot of "nightgowns" so she must have been buying something from this company.

My mom had to play the mom and dad role for a lot of my upbringing. Although her looks could give you the impression of a kept woman, my mother was always rubbing two pennies together and as such, she wasn't afraid of manual labor. Her least favorite and most rewarding unpaid job being when she mowed the backyard. This was no normal hill, and our house was the one that bore the brunt of that neighborhood descent. My mom would wait it out until the grass got shin-height, and the dandelions ran rampant, before she decided it was that time again. With her old jean shorts, an extra-large men's white T-shirt, an old pair of Asics sneakers and some white tall athletic socks, she would gather her hair in a ponytail and take that lawn mower to the back like she was going to battle. She took a strange pride in that lawn. When it was over and the sweat was pouring off her pretty over plucked brows, she would yell out an exhausted sigh that could wake the neighborhood and then she began to cry. A happy cry. Like she was so proud of herself for finishing it.

She rewarded herself with a cold Corona and would stare at the lawn from the second floor, admiring her work as she sucked down a cold one and then treated herself to a cigarette. She resembled such a warrior at the end of that mowing. Blades of grass sticking to her tan legs and dried sweat making white lines along her toned forearms. Like I said, she wasn't afraid of a little hard work.

I would not qualify my mother as a feminist—she would never have been seen in a pantsuit, and definitely was not one for changing history to herstory at school. But she did say one thing to me repeatedly over our years at Meadow Lane that stuck with me later in life and makes me think she did see the power of women.

"Always remember, Holly," she told me, "women can do everything men can do. And they can have babies." And that was enough.

A Dead Sleep

By the time I met my first real friend, I was twelve. My mother had consistently preached to me to "be my own best friend" over the years, yet now I was in seventh grade. Everyone knows having friends in seventh grade is the best thing that can happen to you. This friend was one of the best things that ever happened to me. That's what twenty-five years of friendship can make you understand. When I hear people say, "I'm so happy I get to marry my best friend," I often think how glad I am that I met my friend in middle school dancing to "100 percent Pure Love," not twenty-two on the internet or while grinding to Akon in a basement club. Regardless, my first real friend was way cooler than me, so I decided I had to do something that would make me cool to her. She already had boobs, her period, wore layers of beautiful clothing and Doc Marten shoes that we couldn't afford, let alone would fit over my bunions.

The first time she slept over at my house, I felt really nervous. Your first real best friend is like the first person you ever date—you really want to make a good impression. I knew she was the youngest of five and living at home with her mom as an only child. They were more like friends than mother and daughter. Whereas I was the middle of three and getting my single mother's attention proved to be a bit difficult.

But when she arrived, we clicked from the get go. I have no recollection of anything we did except laugh. We laughed and laughed and laughed, telling ridiculous stories that have no point in this book and probably no punch line in general. That's how you know a real friend. You don't talk about anything important, yet every story holds its own weight and becomes its own living legend.

I was wearing my back brace then and had a twin-sized bed. I wanted to show my new Bestie my undying appreciation for even thinking about becoming friends with a nobody like me, so I gave her my bed and she obliged. I pushed two couch cushions together that kept separating like a hot dog bun, and I tried my best to seem comfortable with my back brace half on the freezing tile floor. It did not matter the pain; the laughter was the best medicine. By 2:00 a.m. we were howling about a story of two kids, one pretending to be a news anchor and the other one being a ghost under a bench and how it was all getting filmed (I told you, it's not funny, but yet it's also the funniest thing I had ever heard) when my mother showed up at the door.

She most definitely did not think that this story was a hoot. She was pissed. "What the hell is going on down here?" she yelled, wearing a nightgown and a haphazardly tied silk robe. "You woke me out of a dead sleep!"

That shut us up real quick. A dead sleep? We were having so much fun that we were able to wake the dead? That was actually pretty funny too, but I didn't feel like laughing was appropriate at the time. So, we said sorry and did like all kids do. We talked in hushed tones under our covers until the sun came up and had our first friend hangover the next day. You know the nights where you didn't get enough sleep but you're still on cloud nine from a good connection? That's the sort of bond my Bestie has had with me.

That, and we would both truly know, eighteen years later, when it wouldn't be funny anymore—what it would be like when we couldn't wake our mothers out of that dead sleep.

The Advocate

"Don't be mean to Ruth—she's our advocate!" said the mother to her kids.

I remember so deeply when my mom told me this story. My mom was working at the Haven as a case manager, helping out women and children who were down on their luck. People who had fallen into hard times, which became even harder when the winter months came. This one particular family had a mother who was obsessed with Brad Pitt, and she watched all his movies, and thus so did her children. Not just *A River Runs Through It* or even some *Thelma and Louise* but these kids were watching *Seven* and that monkey movie and gangster films, and they were all under ten-years-old.

They say that children are natural imitators. After the kids watched *Seven*, and when they were mad at my mom for some reason, they talked about booby-trapping her office. "I'm going to take a bee hive and put it above your door," the boy said. "When you open the door, all the bees are going to sting you to death!" As the older boy told his scheme, the little girl looked at my mom and smiled. She said, "And I'm going to help!"

The thought of what these kids saw from a young age hurt my heart, but it also made me wonder why my mother chose a job like this when she could clearly have stayed in the school as a teacher's aid or even if she really wanted later in life, she could have stayed home. I think it had something to do with helping other people when she couldn't really help herself.

While at the Haven, she became one of the most beloved managers. So much so that when she was dying, one of her clients would not stop calling. She wanted to see our mom before she went. We weren't even letting extended family over, let alone these clients of the world. So, in the end, these women were never able to really say a proper goodbye.

But there was something about that job my mom had. An advocate.

That was a term that I wanted to become for women as well.

Asking For Help

In the spring of 2013, I did what most people do during the off season on Nantucket: I got the hell off the island. First to Chicago, to pretend I was still in college with my sorority sisters. Next to Park City to ski for the first time in nineteen years. Next, I was on a flight to the Sunshine State, to spend a few days on the island of Sanibel, which was near where my mom and stepdad were escaping their New England winter.

Talk about a nightmare packing job. I needed clothes for the city, the slopes, and for the sandy shores, and I tried to do it in a carry-on. By the time I got to Florida, I was so tired from trying to pretend that I was on spring break that I needed a deep rest and downtime. And who better to do that with than my mom?

But that's not really how it happened. I forgot to mention, I took my roommate with me to Florida. I was Facebook-ing and tweeting to my thousands of followers to let them know every detail of my trifecta vaca. I wanted to show people that I had the ability to gallivant around the country, just not really the funds. But they didn't have to know that I was crashing at friends' houses the whole time.

One person who was not thrilled with my roomie coming on vacation with us was my mother, the woman who knew the real me and could not understand how I had changed from writing in journals to responding on a smartphone. I think she thought it was making me dumb. As in deaf, blind, and mute.

During my four days in Florida, she decided that it was time to have a sit-down intervention of sorts. While she was proud of me for what I had created with this blACKbook thing, she knew I couldn't do it alone. And since she was basically computer illiterate, she coaxed me into the next best option—find an intern.

"Asking for help is a sign of strength," she said. And so there it was, the intern-vention. I found the first of twenty-two young twenty-somethings to join my business over the course of the next seven years.

What's In A Name?

By the time I got a nickname that I actually liked, I was in my mid-twenties. Before that, there were many. Nicknames were a household favorite in my Finigan family. They were all made up by my dad, who had gone from Finigan to Fini for most of his days. We were all mini-Finis. But each of us had our own name as well. Christina is Minnow. Sanna is Peanut. My half-brother Jackson is Action. And my other half brother, Brendan, is Rooster. And I, Holly, am Holly-Dolly. When it came to our mother, she had her own set of nicknames. She'd use our initials on our brown-bag lunches: CPF, HRF, SEF. She also called my elder sister Minnow, which may have been one of the only things my mom and my dad did the same for thirty years. Mom called my sister Sanna well, mostly Sanna, as that was already a nickname for Sanna's full name of Susanna. Mostly Mom referred to us as small, medium, and large based on our vast differences in heights.

My mother told me she wanted to name me Abby, but for some reason Holly was what stuck. So she also had a few nicknames for me. First was Bones, for my bony structure. Then she somehow came up with Hollis Jane Hornblaster the third—I have no idea where that came from, let alone the fact that there may have been a first and second of that name. And finally, another nickname settled into my bony horn-blasting body and that was Accident Waiting To Happen. That nickname wasn't as popular as my dad's Holly-Dolly, but it stuck with me for most of my life. It was one of those inadvertent nicknames that I think played itself out time and time again.

But as I got older, I began to resent that nickname. Because I think we are so often what we tell ourselves. So, if I was constantly told I was an accident waiting to happen, well of course, more bad things would happen to me. This is that law of attraction. Basically, I was set up for a life filled with ailment from the get-go. I would have liked my mom to be extra careful with nicknames. I think us kids should have been able to pick our nicknames. I would have loved my nickname to be Gorgeous. Wouldn't that have been a nice name to have everyone call you? Hi, my name is Holly, but everyone calls me Gorgeous. Or Smart. *Hi, I'm Holly but you can just call me Smart.*

Yes, that sounds a lot nicer than Bones, Hollis Jane Hornblaster III, or Accident Waiting To Happen.

Somewhere in my mid-twenties my mother dropped the first trio of pet names alongside my Aunt Nina, and they referred to me as Mermaid. Although texting and emails had become the trend by the late 2000s, my mother was a firm believer in the power of the written word and a lover of snail mail. I would receive letters from her mostly on Nantucket, and they would always begin with "My Dearest Holly" and end with "take care of 'bad' self, Mermaid. I love you sooo."

After many years of not understanding me, I think in my twenties my mother began to think of me as a mythical creature. She knew that I had fallen in and out of many relationships on the island and off, but the one that I held most dear was that of my island . . . the Grey Lady. Nantucket was my only true monogamous relationship after the ten years that I had lived there. I had fled the real world and was living in what she considered *Birdland*. There were magical creatures who got to stay and make a living and a life there. Those were mermaids and I was one of them. We chatted a lot about the island and my adoration for it alongside her confusions about it. In one of my early blACKbooks I wrote about this tension—"You're going to have to grow up sometime, Mermaid," she said through clenched teeth at breakfast. "You're going to just have to settle down one day and I'm sorry."

And she was sorry. She didn't like passing judgment on the island and telling me that Nantucket was not the real world. She loathed that I was a bartender and didn't see past the Grey Goose bottles to realize how happy this job had made me.

The restaurant industry is tough. And it's not for everyone. In fact, it's like Darwin's world: only the strong survive. Prerequisites for the bar include a great personality, a good look, and a tougher-than-nails liver. And when you pass the bar, you've got a whole exciting life to look forward to. Life is a party. The bar is the stage. And we're all actors and actresses. And what they don't understand is that I've won Best Comedic Performance. My bar won Best Picture. And finally, my supporting cast is more than Oscar winners. They're all serious professionals.

So, this twenty-six-year-old Mermaid makes more money in four months than some other friends do in a year. She's in decent shape, owns a car, has her own health insurance, wears designer clothes, travels during the winter, and smiles every late morning when she wakes up. Now I ask you, Mom, what about me is not grown up?

Of course, I know what she wanted. She wanted me to stop living on fantasy island, stop being around the booze every night and start living the life that everyone else leads because of course this is what our good-natured parents truly wish . . . I just couldn't do it. I had to lead my own life.

And it was that life, the non-traditional one, that meant this Mermaid was the one who was able to drop everything on Nantucket and spend the month of April at home with her mom when her right lung was removed. And because of my lifestyle, I was the one who could take off February and March when her mom's hospital days turned into hospice ones.

And maybe the main issue I have, is that I believe that our parents *don't* always know best.

Maybe the truth is, even though my nickname for her was Mom, she was actually just another woman.

She was actually just like me.

What Is Your Greatest Regret?

Dear Mom,

Today is your birthday, you would have been fifty-eight. You died over three years ago, but I still see you everywhere. Remember before you died, I gave you that Proust Questionnaire? I believe your responses were your clearest, so I shared it with my 40,000 followers on Instagram. But don't worry, I still took out your greatest regret—

You know you can always count on me.

Holly

9.

The Exchange

Penny

It's not easy to make Nantucket work year-round. Affordable housing is sparse, gas is expensive, and the cost of living is like the mainland times two. This, of course, is because so much needs to be shipped thirty miles out to sea, so you are not just paying for the cost of the goods, but you are also charged for the cost of getting them here. And yet, there is one time-old tradition that costs but a cent. When you are leaving Nantucket and have paid the ferry ticket to take you from the isle back to Hyannis, it's said that to ensure that you will always come back, you cast a penny off the stern of the ferry as you round Brant Point Lighthouse. Tossing that Abe Lincoln is said to provide surety that you will magically return to the faraway island again. So, on one of the wealthiest islands in the world, where homes cost millions, and hundred-dollar bills are known as Nantucket tens, all it takes is a penny, and your thoughts, to know you can always come back.

The Help

When I was eight, I babysat for a five-year-old boy for $3 an hour. It was my first job and I took a lot of pride in it. His parents would leave us alone for an hour in the afternoons, and I felt very empowered to have the responsibility of watching someone else's kid. My mom always said I was "a good egg," and babysitting became my first job—that lasted for ten years. They say that what you loved to do as a kid should be something you look into later in life . . . so maybe being a mother's helper has always been my calling.

Confession

I've always had a big problem with the Catholic Church because we were *forced* to attend. No one in my family really seemed like they wanted to go. And no one really stuck by all those rules. Like, what was up with that marriage until death do you part? That didn't happen for my parents, and my dad still was allowed to get the Eucharist. And what about no sex before marriage? My half-brother was born four months after my dad and stepmom got married, and he was not premature. The main issue I kept having was that everyone looked so miserable. No one seemed to be digesting the information given out from the pulpit, and many people looked asleep.

We had to go to church because our grandparents liked it if we went. It was all about appearances—what I was allowed to wear; where we were supposed to look; where we were supposed to sit. I mean, it felt so staged, like it was all part of this big movie set of the most boring silent film out there. Church was a place where time seemed to stand still. And asking questions? That seemed to be where the punishment started. I used to ask my dad how much longer as soon as we got through the first reading.

"Forty-five minutes," he would say, without even looking down at his watch.

That felt like *forever*. So, after the homily I would reach back out: "How many more minutes?"

"Forty-five," he would say, and when my eyes widened, he would add, "Ask me again and you'll be going to the 11:30 Mass as well."

Everything felt like there was something wrong with me. I would have to give a confession, yet I didn't even know what to confess. I'd say some bad things I did, and then the priest would tell me what to say next. It would go something like this:

"Okay, so I hit my sister with a wooden spoon, and my other sister hit her with a parmesan cheese block, and then she puked, and I think we gave her a concussion. So, I guess I'm sorry about that? Oh, and I sometimes write SHIT and FUCK on my Wordly Wise book, and then I erase it right before my teacher comes over. Sometimes I look at the dirty magazines I find in the bathroom of the moving company where my friend's mom works." I'd then stop, because then there was that bad thing. But I can't talk to you about that secret, Father. I'm not allowed to tell anyone. Though if anyone could understand how important that secret was, I guess *you* just might.

Numbers

When I was sixteen studying for the SATs, I was in a state of needing to prove something. Even though I never had been good at math (or so I told myself) I did have a great handle on English. This was just the opposite of my father, who got an 800 on Math and 300 on English, which, I heard, is what they give you for writing your name correctly. At this point, I had become the second of five children. My older sister, Christina, was now at Syracuse; my younger sister, Sanna, was in middle school; my half-brother, Jackson, was six and the baby, Brendan, the second son born to my dad and Teri, hadn't even hit kindergarten yet. I was deep into high school and was studying so hard for the SATs that a day before I was set to take the tests, I scratched a cornea in my sleep and woke up with what felt like a permanent eyelash in one eye. This caused way more anxiety, knowing that I only had 50 percent of my full sight while wanting to give 110 percent on these SATs.

I got some eye drops, pushed forward, and took the tests in my high school English room on Saturday morning. If I had had a phone during those days, and the power of Google, I would have gotten a 1600 in the first hour, but this was 1999 and I was going to party just as soon as this testing was done. I left the brick building in Hanover, New Hampshire, where I had been in school from first until twelfth grade, feeling accomplished yet uneasy: I wasn't sure if I had aced it. Hell, multiple choice always creates the second guessing of oneself. I would have been a better student if teachers had let me write out my answers instead of circling an A, B, C, or D. But regardless of my test-taking skills, I waited anxiously for the postman to deliver my scores. When it finally arrived, I ripped open that envelope and a sense of sincere pride washed over me. I got a 1250! Holy smokes! Not only did I exceed my expectations, but my English score in the 600s and the math score in the high 500s gave me the confidence that maybe I was a little smarter when it came to geometry than I had thought.

I couldn't wait to tell my father. I couldn't wait to hear the validation and know that even with a permanent eyelash in my eye, I was still able to beat him and my older sister. Look at me, world! Miss 1250!

When I called my father to express my good news, he said, "That's awesome. Imagine what you could get the next time if you started at 1250?" My entire being broke into a million pieces. The eyelash that came out was in the form of tears on the phone. *I have to do it again?* I thought. *I feel good about this score, though. And you want me to study like that again? What is going to happen to my other eye next time?*

My mom, who looked at me like I was already valedictorian anytime I received a grade above a C, was the opposite of my dad, who always wanted to help me strive to be my best, or his best, whatever that was. So, I listened to my dad. I studied again; I went through the whole process, but I didn't feel that good about it this time. I still gave it the old college effort because that is what we do, right? We try our best and then we let other people tell us that it can be better? I think you can guess where this story goes, but just for the sake of the truth, I will tell you anyway. I got an 1190 the second time I took the SATs, and I got a lot more crap with that envelope.

For I began to believe there was never going to be a number that would make me enough.

Trust – Part I

All bloggers have a moment when they know they are making it. Mine came from a Twitter message with $10,000 attached to it.

It was winter of 2012, and I was tweeting like a springtime sparrow. I was totally obsessed with blACKbook, with sharing my love of Nantucket with anyone and everyone who would listen online. I had also come to terms with the fact that in Nantucket, you can't be the mayor in July if you are not there in January.

So, I moved for the twelfth time in seven years, seven miles down Milestone Road to a little cottage on the beach in 'Sconset. It was like being on Nantucket without being in Nantucket. It was the only place on the island that felt like an escape, and it had a different zip code too, so I felt like I was moving to a new town, even if it was only a new fire district. This was a perfect place to have sneaky off-season romances while watching the sunrise from my bedroom. This cottage would rent for $4,000 a week in the summer, but I got it for

$800 a month, including utilities, since I was there when no one else was there.

That winter was rough. There were wild storms with 70 mile-an-hour winds and rains that turned to hail. I would "stormtrACK" my way around the 02564 zip code with my phone like I was chief meteorologist on The Weather Channel. My only roommate was my phone, and I really didn't realize how much time we were spending together. During the holidays, since I wasn't with my family, I created gift guides on blACKbook for how to purchase Nantucket things for the island lovers in your life. And that is when a guy reached out in a Twitter message and said he wanted me to help him buy presents for his aptly named wife, Holly. His budget? $10,000. I put him in touch with many of those who had supported me with the beginning of blACKbook, and he had a personal shopper who knew how to make the gifts under the tree extra merry and bright.

Sure, none of that $10K was for me. I mean, the tweeter did send me $100 through PayPal for my time, which I even tried to refuse. Because what his message showed me was that I had something you cannot buy, not even on one of the wealthiest islands in the world.

And that is trust.

For Sale

It doesn't take a rocket scientist to understand where the real money on Nantucket comes from. It is not from the twelve-person champagne brunches on the beach or the shopping sprees at Murray's Toggery Shop.

No, the real money on Nantucket, and where the advertising heart is, is where the home is. To make the big bucks, you need to join the big guys, the major league of ACK currency, also known as Real Estate. If you read *Nantucket Magazine* or scoured the once-a-week newspaper, *The Inquirer and Mirror*, you knew that the main form of money exchange came from the ever-exclusive and oh-so-expensive buyers and sellers of homes on Nantucket.

Even to this day, many of the ads use the same, only slightly different verbiage with descriptions like "the best views on island" matched with "a once in a generation opportunity" to own "your slice of Nantucket paradise." Perplexed by this standardization, I wanted to switch it up. I connected with a late thirty-something, successful, tech-savvy real estate broker who was one of the top producing agents with millions in sales at the number-one brokerage on the island. Knowing that so many of his clients were getting more messaging from online platforms than offline publications, he saw a major opportunity in blACKbook. As a father, and as someone who was not in the bar social scene, he also knew that, by investing in me, he could stay on top of being seen, while enjoying Nantucket behind the scenes with his son, fishing in Madaket.

And thus, "the shACK of the week" was born. Make no mistake, we were not selling shanties or studios. We were promoting multimillion-dollar, eight-bedroom estates, with views that you truthfully could say may have been the best view of the island. And not because we said it, but because we showed it: aerial photography and drone footage totally took sharing real estate online to new heights.

The sky was the limit . . . I just never stopped to question how limited my intake would be because I kept following that one rule from my mom . . . you don't ask people how much money they make. So, I didn't know how much the realtors made, and I no one told me that I should get my real estate license.

Budget

"I like blACKbook," he told me. "I like the idea of it. It's something I didn't know before. It sticks."

We were having wine and cheese at his Boston brownstone. Our partners were with us; they were very similar . . . calm, collected, had their own lives, and didn't have to show people they were living through the internet. But they both supported us, wholeheartedly.

He was Boston's biggest bad boy of sports blogging. His claim to fame was saying whatever the hell he wanted, unapologetically. He was the king of the Barstool, the self-proclaimed El Pres. He was a massive force to be reckoned with, even in 2014.

We met over Twitter banter in 2012 when he told me to do one thing and do it well. I told him a plethora of things, like where to dine, drink, and dance on the island. He messaged me once, asking how I felt about one restaurant, and I politely wrote back that I gave it a B. After he dined there, he messaged me to say the place was a D and that he would never not take my A-game advice again.

We were now off the rock in Beantown talking about life on the island. It was a great chance for me to learn from this powerful entrepreneur. I told him my struggles: my hardship was money. I never could figure out how to have people pay me for what I thought my marketing was worth. I had such a tough time selling the value of social media to an island whose marketing charm was showing an island that felt like a step back in time, a place that thrives from the appearance of nothing ever changing. He listened intently and responded like this:

"If someone pitches you, you listen to them and then you ask them one very important question."

"What is that?" I asked, leaning forward, expecting the key to the treasure chest.

"What's your budget?" he said. Like it was the simplest three-word sentence out there.

"Well, what if they don't have one?" I asked.

He looked at me, grunted and laughed at the same time. "Well, there's your answer."

Viral

"Hey Holly, I took some pretty crazy photos of frozen waves on the beach today. Any chance if I send them to you that you will post them and tag me?"

This is how a viral moment starts. You know you have something good, something unique, something no one else has seen, something that feels almost surreal, something that appears too good to be true. Then you share it with someone who has a bigger platform than yours, a trusted source for putting up content that is never Photoshopped.

Then you let that account take you to the next level. Like a spark in the woodstove, that viral moment spreads. You don't know when it is truly going to catch fire. But when you have frozen wave photos and an ocean looking like you have never seen it before, you know those images are going to be hot commodities.

Here is a great example of someone who knows his worth, who created trust, who saw that one-shot moment, and decided not to just give it away. This is the tale of a surf photographer. He was a friend of mine: he had been taking photos of surf and waves and the beach lifestyle from Cisco to Costa Rica to California. He was well-liked, and had a modest following of about 2,200 on that particularly cold February morning when he took some photos of some particularly cold waves—and couldn't believe what he saw. It was so chilly that Wednesday that the waves looked frozen in time. And he was there at precisely the right moment. He captured the images, knowing he had something big, and sent it out to the biggest social media maven on Nantucket.

Like Nantucket's Paul Revere, I shouted it out on social media to all who would listen: "The Slurpee waves are coming; the Slurpee waves are coming!"

From the island of Nantucket to the city of Boston to national news to global coverage, these frozen waves took a tour around the world in eighty hours, making this surf photographer jump on Instagram from those 2,200 followers to 15,000 by the weekend, when the New York Times had written about them. That photographer was one smart cookie. He had worked in photojournalism and knew that news was valuable, and high-resolution content was a must.

He had a Dropbox ready when the hundreds of news outlets reached out and asked for his pictures. He didn't just want to go viral; he knew viral meant value: an exchange of dollars for the Dropbox. A few hundred dollars may seem like chump change to a national broadcast company. But the square root of a few Benjamins? Let's just say this surfer was making waves and making dough from the moment he sent those photos out.

Now that's how you go viral.

It was good for me too. I got something else. It wasn't a piece of the money pie; it was deep peace of mind, knowing that if someone wanted something to go viral, all they had to do was send it to me first. I wasn't frozen in time; I was hot on the trail as the ultimate social media resource.

Money can't buy trust. Money can't buy trust. Money can't buy trust. I fell asleep repeating that over and over.

Business

He was a charming, handsome event planner, and I was the local party girl. Together, we could throw a soiree like none other. We were fun, young, socially present, and with an ever-present desire to build our own trust and value through social media. We branded ourselves online as the #ACKpartyhosts, and over three years we created Nantucket's most socially loved empire of the freshest events out there.

From fashion shows on the beach, to fundraisers for private schooling, to collaborative "shop local" holiday pop-up shops in high-end restaurants. From real estate open houses where we made every room into a new retail experience, to anniversaries of iconic restaurants where we brought in a younger crowd to experience this old charm, we did it all on island, and then we traveled.

We jet-setted to elite ski mountains and to the beaches of Saint Barths. We flew in private planes while promoting airlines and then touched down to party with the best of them. We did all of this while documenting our every move on social media.

We just never put a business plan together with this hosting site: it was just for brand building.

His husband, who would turn out to be his business partner, looked at me at one point after we had each made $7 from a "summer sip & shop" and sighed. "Holly," he said, "I love you, but you guys are idiots if you continue to work like this." Sure, it was said in a half-joking manner . . . but he was spot on. What were we doing? And why were we doing this?

I think the reason my co-host really started to take off as Nantucket's hottest event planner was not just because he looked the part in crisp Peter Millar suits and Stubbs loafers, but because in real life his partner turned business partner helped him to see how valuable he and his talents truly were.

Maybe I should have emulated them. Hell, maybe I should have asked his partner to be my business partner too.

Letters

It was the week after Labor Day, 2014, and I was standing at my PO box. Three years earlier, this had been my biggest commitment to the island yet—signing up for twelve months of this mailbox. I was still unsure of this decision to live full-time on Nantucket. But alas, bills needed to be paid; loans needed to be acknowledged; and the checks needed to come in. I was waiting on the latter while often getting way more of the former.

On this beautiful September day, my Bestie, the one from that memorable middle school sleepover, was visiting. She had lost her mom three years before I did. We were now death sisters, and she was the only one who seemed to know what I was really going through. She saw a struggling seventh grader in my eyes every time we connected.

This weekend, I had invited her to hang out with me for a free girls' staycation at a luxurious resort in the heart of town. I mean, "free," but it was trade. I spent the whole time taking pictures and setting up beautifully fake scenes of us enjoying the vacation while getting fire Instagram content for their property. My Bestie and I took a break from the 'Gram and went to the post office to see if any of my hard-earned summer blACKbook marketing money was being paid back. Going to my mailbox was a ritual that I used to enjoy, as I often had received little notes from my mom. But now, I dreaded opening that box and did it so methodically that I almost never digested any of the materials inside.

On this day, when an unmarked envelope with my name and no return address arrived, I assumed it was a check. A lot of money was owed to me, and I had become good at patiently waiting for people to pay me. I opened that envelope like a little kid opening a birthday card, expecting a $10 bill to fall out. But all I saw was a typed one-page sheet of paper that became my first form of blACKbook hate mail. I read the words as tears began to flow. My hands shook as I tried to follow along:

"Who do you think you are?"

"What do you think you're doing?"

"Everyone here doesn't like you."

"Everyone remembers when you didn't have 2 pennies to rub together."

"Everyone is talking about how much they can't stand what you're doing."

And the writer finished, saying he (or she) wouldn't sign the letter, "but just know that these were the thoughts of many."

I walked out to my car in a daze, black mascara streaking my face. I passed the letter to my Bestie without words, and she read it through. She then stared at me, wide- eyed.

"OMG," she said, smiling. Her bright green eyes sparkled as she exclaimed, "I can't believe how famous you are! The more they hate you, the more they love you. Even Lady Gaga knows that."

Notifications

I became obsessed with numbers, not only how many followers, or likes, or comments, or my open rate (percentage of people who open an email), but also how others were growing their following. I watched constantly, with Judge Judy-like eyes, a method called the follow, unfollow, follow.

I'd screenshot influencers' profiles that went from following 500 accounts on Monday to 2,500 accounts by Wednesday and then down to following 300 accounts by the weekend. There would be this spike in their own followers, because people were doing that #FollowForFollow, and then these influencers would look like they were following a lot of people, but then they would unfollow a bunch of those same accounts and appear to have a bigger following than the numbers of people they now follow.

Following me?

See, in 2016 it became all about the numbers. Who has the most, because the most means the best and the best means the top and by top, I mean top of the algorithm, right?

That pesky algorithm. Listen, this is what changed everything, bigtime. All of a sudden, it was Instagram, not the instant moment, that decided for you who you saw first and chose who showed up at the top of your feed.

When people found this out, influencers, content creators and brands went nuts. *Turn on my notifications! Turn on my notifications!* Every single Tom, Dick, and Harry posted. *If you don't get notified when I post, you may not see me, make sure you never miss any of my content! Turn on my notifications!*

This was absolutely crazy to me. First, how many notifications from Instagram does a person want added to all the notifications that you already get? And second, all this anger that Instagram was taking away your visibility . . . well, what the hell did you expect?

Did it cost you anything to make an account? Have you been making money from this platform? Making money through a zero-dollar membership fee? Insta had been giving the cow away for years. And now they planned on milking us.

Social media was about to be big business. Either up your ad spend, or fall to the bottom of the feed. But please, for the love of God . . . stop following, unfollowing, following, and unfollowing me. That is a notification I can do without.

Paying Attention

"Not making too many friends here," the Instagram comment read.

"This post is tacky!"

"Who is paying for this?"

It was my first Insta fall from grace. I was in Anguilla in February of 2015, drinking a piña colada, wearing a rainbow towel poncho, promoting #luxuryvacation in the cuisine capital of the Caribbean.

The photo had me on my knees, begging for likes, showing vacation vibes and sharing an elated smile that comes from that second frozen cocktail before lunch. But back at home, the Nantucket of my @NantucketblACKbook wasn't enjoying this kind of weather. The Grey Lady was without power, in a blizzard, with a massive storm surging around the island.

Earlier that week, I had been so grateful that the three of us—my fellow modern day travel agent (the City to my Sand), our videographer, and I—had escaped Boston on the last flight out of Logan right before Winter Storm Juno came in and whiteout conditions shut down thousands of flights. We were so lucky to pick this week to go away.

Or were we?

I don't know about you, but sometimes when I watch other people's vacations on Instagram, I feel an emptiness inside and a longing to be anywhere but where I am. I mean, I know that now. I definitely didn't know that at the time. But, as we say, hindsight is 20/20.

So those who followed me for #Nantucket seemingly weren't thrilled to see this other island. They wanted the white snow, not the white sand. They were looking for me to be a storm tracker as I had done in years past. *But, dammit!* I thought, *what do you want from me? I'm not a plow. What's so wrong about showing off my vacation?*

Here we were, on a slice of vacation heaven, savoring seafood for lunch, diving into the turquoise blues and documenting it all on social media. . . and there I was, in the fetal position, smoking cigarettes while incessantly checking notifications on my phone.

The trolls kept coming in and the City constantly would have to snap me out of my phone. "Stop reading the comments!" she said. "Who cares what these people say. We don't even know them and, honestly Holly, if I got this worked up every time a faceless person said something nasty to me, I'd be out of a job."

But we were so lucky! We were highlighting a six-bedroom estate that went for $25,000 a week that came with not one, not two, but three pools. Private chefs cooked for us, and we got to promote top-notch restaurants while sipping champagne with the owners and never had a check dropped out at our table. How lucky we were to showcase this lifestyle to our target market!

Oh yeah, our market.

You guys were using social media. And whether you thought I was being insincere by posting my #roséallday poolside post while you grabbed a shovel and a shot of whiskey to warm up, you did watch our every move. Whether you liked them or not ultimately didn't matter. What mattered is: you were *paying* attention.

You were the ideal demographic that this #luxury marketing effort wanted to hit, and you could afford this type of #vacation, and you often did what I'd been telling you to do. Your time spent scrolling was the money.

So, I guess if you want to know who was paying for this vacation, well, it was you.

So, thanks. I guess.

Partnership

"Buy her out," the retail queen of the island, said. "Whatever it costs, I'll loan it to you. You can't share this. It is yours, and you need to own it fully."

It was late in the fall of 2016, and I wanted to get out of my business partnership for the Happy Place. My partner had a great eye for design and a love for super-soft shorts fabrics. The year before, she had refined the Happy Place logo and helped make it into a highly sought-after brand. She did the middleman's work: she got the shirts created; made sure they printed correctly, and figured out sizing and styles for both adults and kids.

None of this stuff interested me. I had two outfits: I was either going out or going to bed. Jeans and cute tees were not in my wheelhouse. Half the time I was in the limelight, promoting what I was wearing as a trade for marketing. The other half I was in ratty yoga wear and a baseball cap, avoiding eye contact with everyone.

I was such an all-or-nothing blogger. If they had had an ACK *US Weekly* with what stars look like around town, I would have been the girl at a gas pump with her underwear hanging out of her jean shorts, wearing a denim shirt with no bra, two different socks on with a busted pair of sneakers that my bunions had broken through alongside a Box hat, worn so low you would wonder how I could see well enough to drive.

I really didn't care about the way I presented in public when social media wasn't involved.

This was the heart of the issue of what I had created—a complete dichotomy of two very complex personalities.

One of my bartender friends used to love it when people would say to her that they were really good friends with me while they sat at her bar and dished on blACKbook. My friend's hilarious interior monologue would have sounded something like this: "Oh, you're seriously good friends with her. I seriously bet one million dollars that if she came in here, she would act like she knew you, call you babe, give you a hug, and text me later, asking what your name was."

It's not a mean thing. I am not saying this to make myself seem like a heartless bitch, or to say that this bartender friend is my only true friend on the island. After years behind a bar, you know everyone by drink, by the way they tip, by the fact that their daughter has a shellfish allergy, or by the fact that they love your memory and how you connect them to their happy place. When I was in service to others, I often felt like that was my real happy place. It didn't matter what I called you; it was all about how I connected you . . . and connecting is my superpower.

So, one day, it all connected for me: I didn't need the middle woman. I did all of the marketing, and I got all the sales. I believed I could do this Happy Place business on my own; promote it on my own; create new lines on my own, and thus fully own the logo that I had conceptualized.

But I am terrible at breaking up with people. My deep sense of childhood abandonment makes it so divorcing people in my life is like my trip to Italy at four years old. I act like everything is okay for a while, go on hiatus and distance myself, and then come back saying I want out with a lawyer in tow.

She owed me some money for the last run of sales so I thought she just didn't have to pay me back and we would call it even. She came back with a counteroffer and told me I could buy her out for double what she owed me: she saw the potential in Happy Place and believed it to be a fair price.

But you know who couldn't believe it?

ME.

Just call it even, I thought. *Let's part ways like this never happened.* Pretending things never happened was my strength.

But oh, that hindsight. This was a business woman who was strong and knew her worth as well as mine. So, we came to that happy medium. I paid her out for what she asked.

And then I spent the next three years trying to do everything myself, while losing loads of money along the way.

Followers

"I mean, if you don't have at least a million followers I'm not responding to your DM," (direct message) he said to me at the White Elephant that fall. I was attending the most prestigious Nantucket think tank event, and this guy was one of their sponsors. He came from an oh-so-comfortable furniture company; he had been sharing his authentic truth in one of their videos, and he seemed to be such a wise and genuine millennial. But as soon as he said that offline follower comment to me, I lost all trust in his online perceptions.

This was an event that had a $5,000 ticket price to enter the tent with a 2018 theme around "Understanding, Understanding." From what I understood, he was saying that the number of followers you have determines your worth to his company. I took his comment very personally. I silently tried to justify my 50,000 following, and wondered what it was going to take to get me another 950,000 followers.

A year later, I tried to sell myself and my book concept on healing my relationship with social media to a Hollywood book agent who was a neighbor of mine on the island. He was a fan of blACKbook and a big supporter over the years, even though he didn't really understand what social media was all about. When he pitched my book to a book publisher, the feedback from the publisher was that I did not have proven status, but that if I wrote it with someone with status, they would be interested because "it's all about the following."

Some say that a swell of about 50,000 people come to Nantucket during the summer. And I was the ultimate social source for Nantucket, and I had . . . 50,000 followers, trusting me, doing what I told them to do. Wasn't there value in that?

And if you would be so kind, guys, would one of you please let me know how many followers would make me enough?

Barter

Dear Mom,

Remember when we were younger and sometimes you'd have us do errands with your Second Husband? He had that two-door sports car that Christina, Sanna and I would squeeze ourselves into. It was hard for me to climb into the back with my back brace, but with my double-jointed body, I could finagle it. I don't remember a lot of alone time with him, but there was this one thing that sticks out.

Well, sometimes he'd park, like, we'd be about to get out of the car, but the engine would still be running. I remember being right behind his seat and really wanting to get out of that car, but your Second Husband said that first we had to give him the treasure hunt—the thing that we liked to do on our backs that we had learned from our aunt. He told us if we did it to him, we could get candy at JB Jammin. Honestly, you know I have always had a major sweet tooth, and in third grade, having little money of my own, when someone said they'd buy me Sour Patch Kids, I accepted the gift and did as I was told.

So, I sat behind him, his unruly salt-and-pepper curls popping over the back of the head rest, and I realized that I couldn't give him the whole treasure hunt: I couldn't pull up his shirt and do it like our aunt did it with us. I could just do the crack an egg part. He said that was fine, and so I cracked the eggs on the top of his head, let my fingers lightly fall down his curls and onto his neck. Ocean breeze and a squeeze, with a quick blow and shoulder pinches. "Now you've got the shiverees," I'd say. "Okay, can we go now?"

"One more time," he said. I remembered that feeling—the way I used to say that to my aunt—but I really didn't like this feeling. I just wanted to be done with it and get a pound of Swedish Fish and try to candy comatose my way out of this memory.

Okay. Another cracked egg. Another ocean breeze, another squeeze. Again.

Egg. Breeze. Squeeze.

Again.

It was in that car that I decided that I didn't want to get the shiverees anymore.

Holly

10.

The Shadow

Middle Child Syndrome

The first time I ever felt anger was on camera. It was May 10th, 1986, and my baby sister, Sanna, had just been born. My father was never that tech savvy, yet, somehow, he had a camcorder and was making a video of the grand introduction of Christina and me to our new sister. I wasn't on camera; I was a month shy of my third birthday, and—no one knew this—I was angry.

The video didn't lie, because out of nowhere a magazine got hurled at the baby. It turns out, the one with that great arm was me. I was pissed that there was another child coming into the family, but I didn't use my words—or maybe I didn't have the words—so, instead, I stuffed it all down for the next thirty years.

Half Brother

The first time I got a brother I was ten. It was 1993 and the first day of October. I had another cousin born on that day, so it just seemed normal to me now that there were enough people coming into my world that we would all have to share everything, including birthdays.

My father and stepmother had been married for about four months and everything just kept changing when it came to our life with them. We had a new house, new bedrooms, and every other weekend with our dad was now every other weekend with his growing family, his new life.

The weekend my brother was born, I was set to have a sleepover with a friend. I was upset that we now had to go down to my dad's that weekend to meet our new brother. I was going to have to cancel my weekend plans. My friend and I had planned to go to Gemstar Gemstone that Saturday and spend whatever little money we had on beads. We were going to start a business making necklaces, so we could buy more beads and make more necklaces. This was not just any sleepover: it was the foundation of my entrepreneurship! My sisters were fine with the change in plans, but I could not hide my disappointment. My new baby brother was fine and all, but from whatever strange lingo was being told to me, he was going to be my half-brother. So, was there a way that I could just kind of half care about this?

My mother, however, usually firm on making us go down to our dad's, didn't make me cancel the sleepover. (Hell, now every fiber in my being can understand how a mother of three might welcome a two-day break every two weeks.) It was a Christmas miracle, and it was only the foliage season. I could still go to my sleepover and, as the middle child, I would experience the great feeling of being an only child for a weekend. Oh, happy day!

What a gift this was to me.

It's easy to see now what I was doing then. It wasn't about the beads or a budding business. It was about a boy, John Bernard Finigan, the Third—the name that was set to be my sisters' or mine if we had been boys. His nickname is Jackson—so aptly titled as Jack's son. A decade after my birth, my dad finally got his legacy. He now had a new wife and his new son. And if my mom and I could rebel in any way, it was to show him that a trip to a store was more important to us than a new sibling.

You Know What

The first time I ever felt ashamed from sex, I was eighteen. I was a college freshman and had dived head first into the pool of Greek Life on campus. So much so, that this once quiet, tame, and non-partying now legal adult got kicked out of her triple on campus for too many noise violations. By January, I had moved myself straight into the cool girls triple at my sorority house.

I also had to eat my every word about the horrors of attending my state school, because as soon as my mom and Amie dropped me off, I fell in love with the place. I threw out my transfer papers before any of my cool new friends could see that I had ever doubted UNH. It is one of those quintessential colleges that revolves around winter sports enthusiasm, a thriving sorority and fraternity life, and an exceptional business school. UNH also had the reputation of being one of the top party schools in the nation.

While my summers in Weekapaug had gifted me a preview of hard partying, my true tolerance stemmed from the fact that I would try anything. My deeply self-deprecating humor turned me into the sorority's fresh meat stand-up comic. Over my four years at UNH, I'd take these ridiculous thank-God-I-didn't-die-last-night stories that highlighted my many mistakes and make fun of myself. The girls laughed at my stories, and boy, did I keep the stories coming. I was the type of freshman who already looked older for her age; I had a steady hand for black eyeliner, plus a rocking wardrobe that showcased Express elastic waist black "going out" pants, sequined tube tops and halter tops, and platform boots or open-toed shoes that lifted me up even higher: for the first time in my life, I loved being tall. I loved being a sorority girl amongst these cool girls. I loved sharing my experiences of being a new kid on the block with a lot of other kids.

While I may not have had the grades and financial backing to get into my reach colleges, when I rushed, I had the personality to get into all five sororities. That year, all of the "it" girls were going to Alpha Phi. Everyone wanted to get into this house: it was the beautiful blonde brigade of babes who also were often business majors. This house reminded me of the Harvard of sororities: work hard, play harder.

The night before rush ended, before it would be announced which sorority, if any, we would be accepted into, I called my sister. Christina was in Alpha Phi at the Alpha Chapter at Syracuse University. That meant I was a legacy: regardless of what the girls in the house wanted, I was a shoe-in. I was part of the twenty-six freshmen and sophomores to get into this coveted coven.

Things were quickly changing for me down here in Durham. I went from being a back brace-wearing, nerd alert who couldn't get into a junior high school party, to being part of the most popular and "hot" girl group on campus. I was transforming right before my eyes, shedding insecurity, khaki shorts, and striped shirts and replacing all that with layers of Mac lip gloss, super blonde highlights, and a uniform that looked like I belonged in the pages of Cache instead of J. Crew. Just two months earlier, I hadn't even wanted to become a Wildcat. Now I had more school spirit than a Texas high school cheerleader and was on my way to transforming into a TomKitten.

Of course, with all this tanning, toning, smoking, and sipping, I was also en route to becoming one of those girls who lived for Thirsty Thursdays, and I spent all my hard-earned money maintaining this image. I loved hanging out with our brother fraternities, and since I had lost my virginity the summer prior, I decided without much debate that I was ready for my second. And my second time wasn't in a car . . . it was in a frat house. With none other than an upper-classman.

I started hooking up with the Upperclassman my first semester, and while I have no idea how long it lasted—maybe a few weeks or months—I was a *freshman* hooking up with a *junior*. I could kind of handle my booze, and I acted like it was totally natural for me to be this free-spirited—with a seemingly endless bank account from a summer of hard work. I don't remember the sex we had, not because I was too drunk but because college frat sex is not really anything to write home about. There were benefits, though: cutting lines to get into the basement parties and getting to stay the night (with a shorter "walk of shame" home, since I only lived across the street). But somewhere in between too much whisky, not enough water, and a bit too many sexcapades, I developed a three-letter word that would haunt me for the next eighteen years.

The phrase UTI can be said so quickly, but unfortunately the infection does not pass like that. When a Urinary Tract Infection arrives, it slams into your vulva like a Mack truck stuck in wet concrete between your two legs. I can best describe the quintessential UTI symptom like this—it feels like you have to go to the bathroom *all the freaking time*. Like you just drank all five gallons of H2O from the office water cooler, got on a plane that had no bathroom for three hours, held it like you had no other choice at gunpoint, and then right before you were about to cry and puke because you couldn't take it anymore, you sit on the toilet and *one droplet of urine makes its way out*. Yeah. Yikes.

When I found out about this piss-poor issue, I did what most scared kids who are hours away from home and in need of comfort do: I called my mom, and told her I was diagnosed with a Urinary Tract Infection.

"I know how you get those," she said in what felt like a harsh tone. "Holly, you *have* to go to the bathroom after *you know what*."

I didn't feel comforted: her statement stuck with me longer than I care to remember. The way she said it sounded like she was judging me. She knew what I was up to. You know what . . . well, you know what, what? Why didn't she just say it? Just say: "Oh, Holly, we've all been there . . . and if you're having sex, then be sure to pee after!" Because that would have made a hell of a lot more sense to me. Instead, what that conversation did was put me in a place where it was one more thing that happened that we could identify . . . but you know what? We couldn't talk about.

Unfaithful

The first time I cheated on a boyfriend I was twenty-one and on spring break in Key West (I know, could I be more predictable?). Nine sorority sisters and I were sleeping in a three-bedroom Marriott timeshare, savoring our last college vacation together. Looking back, all of college was a freaking vacation—a vacation I was very much paying for through something called Student Loans. If I had realized that college would cost me hundreds of dollars a month for what felt like the rest of my life, I might have looked at my journalism major a little differently.

Back to a little island off of the state known for sunshine, I was feeling freer than ever. That or feeling more drunk, thanks to the seemingly lawless Key West, where you can sip margaritas in the streets and savor frozen drinks called the Blue Viagra without any idea of what they're doing to your tongue or your liver. Time seemed to stand still, and for that week we were living the dream. Mostly I was living for the 80-degree weather, my long bod barely protected with plenty of Hawaiian tropic tanning oil. I had no concept of how simply beautiful my life was, and no idea how much Bacardi Orange and Fresca I was consuming. The days were spent lounging by the pool, reading *Us Weekly* and *Cosmo* (or *Self* and *Shape* if you were trying to act healthy and "work out" for the day). And when we'd put our nine brains together to figure out something to do during the day other than drink, we usually ended up shopping along the main drag and trading up a Mudslide for an actual ice cream. And that is where we met the manager at a Ben & Jerry's.

The Manager was a sweet guy with a spicy sense of humor, who took a liking to nine girls showing up for a cool treat. He found the real treat when he learned we were all from the great state of New Hampshire; the Manager had grown up in Durham, the same town as the university. What were the chances? Okay, I know the chances were not that unlikely. But, whatever, you know how it is when you find something in common aside from the fact that you're all horny and ready to get drunk and make questionable choices. Every group of nine sorority sisters was a potential *Girls Gone Wild* video in the making.

Luckily for us, the Manager was not a creep, a cameraman, or a one-man show. And we just happened to be there the week when he and his roommate had two other friends visiting, who were also from Durham—all really good Granite State gents. The odds were good: four guys, nine girls and half of us with boyfriends. I fell in as girl number 4.5: half of me still in the relationship with my kind, seriously smart, boozehound of a frat bro boyfriend, and the other half unconsciously plotting my escape strategy. Upon one of our first nights out, the Manager told us to meet him out at a cool and casual bar along the Key West strip, where we could have food to coat our tight, tanned tummies—buffalo chicken tenders and ultimate nachos—before tequila shots and Stoli sodas became an inevitable six-hour-long dessert buffet. That night I met the first guy who actually made me feel something.

This guy possessed the three qualities that created my male kryptonite—he was really tall, really hard working, and really unavailable. He was not the he-had-a-girlfriend kind of unavailable; I wasn't looking for two wrongs to make a right. No, it was just that he was a bartender. The Bartender worked three different bar gigs and was making serious cash all spring break week long. So, he wasn't there just to have fun. He was there to make money so he could have a lot of fun in the future too.

Luckily for me, the Manager and his buddies were always up for meeting up with us and would call us and let us know where they were—usually at one of the Bartender's three bars. I tried to flirt shamelessly, to the best of my ability, with this guy over the next few nights. I would dress up as little as possible; get some serious liquid confidence in me, and sashay (sway) and say (slur) hello to him around midnight. I had spent half of my college career working as a waitress and bartender at an Irish pub called the Tin Palace in Durham, so I thought that the Bartender and I had even more in common. (Later in life I would realize that we restaurant folks, with our bizarre schedules and seasoned livers, often can have relationships only with each other.) Finally, someone I could relate to.

For the next few nights, I waited around like so many girls before me for a bartender to get off work. Too bad for me: we weren't in New Hampshire anymore, Toto, where the bar closed at 2:00 a.m. The bars in Key West felt like they never closed and as for this sorority sister on spring break who didn't sniff coke, that made it basically impossible for me stay up past the time for him to finish counting the drawer.

But this Finigan was in luck; the Bartender had his first and only night off that week on St. Patrick's Day, and he did like most kings who work in the resort town bar industry: he acted like royalty, parading the twelve of us around to all the bars, where we cut all the lines, never had to wait for any drinks, and made it the most memorable night on the trip. I loved that feeling. I loved being able to hang out with him and see him let loose. I loved the incredible sense of cool that I felt being with this startender. By the end of the night, three of us were back at the Bartender and the Manager's apartment, and I finally got to know this tall drink of water. The whole time, I wasn't thinking of my college boyfriend back at UNH. I was actually thinking about finding my escape strategy. And then it clicked.

I saw the way that the Bartender worked, and the life he got to live as a twenty-one-year-old adult. With college coming to a close, I decided I wanted to live that life too. When he told me that he had once worked on the island of Nantucket, I told him that my big sister in my sorority was from the island and had invited me to live with her for the summer. He told me he was jealous, and then he began with all the Nantucket stories. He loved the island and assured me that working in the restaurant industry there was a goldmine. The money was crazy good, the beaches beautiful—nothing like the slices of man-made sand spits in Key West.

By the end of the week, I had fallen in love . . . not with the Bartender, but with the way that he lived his life. Without fully digesting it, I decided that Nantucket was to be my next big spring break. Of course, when I arrived back just in time for mud season in New England, I felt stuck. And so, I did what I always did when I felt stuck . . . I fled. I broke up with my boyfriend; took my hard-earned graduation money and bought an Altima; told my family I was going to move to Nantucket for the summer, and boasted that I was going to make enough money to drive this sedan back down to the Sunshine State. Ah, the plans we make as recent college graduates . . .

There I was, for the first time, ready to live, well, live another person's life. I would spend the next decade like a Broadway actress, working seasonally on stage in the Nantucket restaurant industry, repeating that queen role nightly. I was living the dream, chasing the men, without ever realizing I was actually the unavailable one—totally scared of someone leaving me before I left him.

Deleted

LIFE ADVICE: If you want to make it in the big leagues, you have to grow a thick skin. You have to get ready to be okay with the fact that not everyone is going to like you, and that when you start doing well, it doesn't mean that everyone has to wish you well.

I was becoming addicted to being "liked." First, with likes on my personal posts on Facebook when they launched the "Like" button in February of 2009. Then with likes on my blACKbook business page, which launched in January of 2012. Sometimes I wonder what would have happened if that thumbs up image had never become a normal gesture on social media. Would we all be so obsessed with how our posts were doing if you just posted for you and not for likes?

These weren't questions that I was asking myself that summer. The biggest question I had was, how am I going to keep going high when they go low? I made a promise to myself and a point on my site never to say anything bad about anyone, never to engage with unkind comments, and to be sure that my lists, which incorporated the top ten dos, never also felt like a Glamour magazine with the don'ts.

Well, except for one thing. Because let's be honest, this is the internet, and I can't hide. There are always screenshots.

The one time I liked to go low was during my blACKbook Figawi fashion recap. Over time, this Memorial Day weekend sailing race had evolved into the biggest spring break party weekend on Nantucket. The island style shifted from bottles of Veuve to bottles of Bud, and the standard uniform went from resort wear to whale costumes and group T-shirts with sayings like "Where the FIGAWI?" The cobblestones became overrun with drunken pirates.

Social media captured all of these moments, thanks to #Figawi. And in 2013, I began to do a fashion recap highlighting the bold, the beautiful, and those who probably didn't enjoy the social media paparazzi, such as photos showcasing their drunken stupors.

I had friends and interns helping me to create these recaps, as they always would be the most clicked-on web pages every spring. I was learning that people loved to see themselves and others, even if the lighting was not so flattering. It was that one guilty pleasure, like how I still enjoyed a cheesy dating reality show, or a sneaky Parliament on a smoking deck.

When my first troll came out of hiding in September of 2013, it turned out I was the one on the fashion chopping block. The comment read: "Looks like a year of hard partying has taken a toll on Ms. blACKbook #hag #skinnyfat."

I couldn't believe the switch. I was wearing a glitzy $300 dress from The Lovely, dammit! I was taking candids in a photo booth (with flattering backlighting) at the 2013 *Nantucket Magazine* end-of-summer Gold bash.

I didn't know who this guy was, and I didn't want his words to stay on my Instagram, so I deleted the comment. He quickly came back with "deleted comment guy" as his next comment of attACK. I didn't know what to do. I hated these feelings. The idea of deleting something that someone said because they thought I looked old and haggard didn't seem right, though. I had just turned thirty that summer, and I wasn't sleeping well. Maybe they were right. At thirty, was it all downhill from here?

I responded kindly to say "we keep it positive here" and tried to move forward even though the #hag burned in the back of my eyelids.

But hindsight is always 20/20.

When the guy sent me a direct message to apologize a few days later, I looked at his profile and realized that he looked very familiar. And then it came to me . . . OMG! He was in one of the photos we used for our spring Figawi fashion recap. He was wearing a women's fur vest and flannel shirt at the Brewery and our caption read, "Is this guy fur real?"

So, was his comment just tit for tat? And did I actually fully practice what I preached?

Maybe those recaps were actually a don't.

Bad Apple

I met the actor, Eric Dane, while he was out on Nantucket filming The Grey Lady, and I was shocked at how normal he was.

Sure, he was handsome as hell, but stars are just like us! He was just sitting in a big house on Main Street, waiting for his family to arrive as we discussed our infinite passion for pizza and our love for the fog. He smoked like a chimney, and I even had a cigarette with him (not that I actually wanted one, but I desperately wanted to feel cool). I certainly tried my best to help him out and give him great Nantucket advice.

But McSteamy, like his nickname on Grey's Anatomy, is not what this Grey Lady chapter is about. The secret we need to talk about is a steamy bathroom. Not one that I shared with another person; it was a space just my own.

I emotionally cheated on BF weekly in this office. I would say I was going to hop in the shower, tell him I wanted a nice long soak to wash off the day, and he would nod and smile, probably grateful I was taking a moment for myself. I would arrive at my bathroom office, lock the door, put the shower head on high, put down the toilet seat, and set up shop: MacBook on the sink with my iPhone out of my bathrobe pocket. So began twenty-eight more glorious minutes of posting, pinning, and watching my content heat up on the internet.

Then, at minute twenty-two, I'd hop into the shower for two minutes, barely enough time or hot water for a proper clean. Exactly thirty minutes later, I would waltz back downstairs, spinning. Another half hour with my secret affair. Another session with the ever-present, not-so-secret, Apple of my eye.

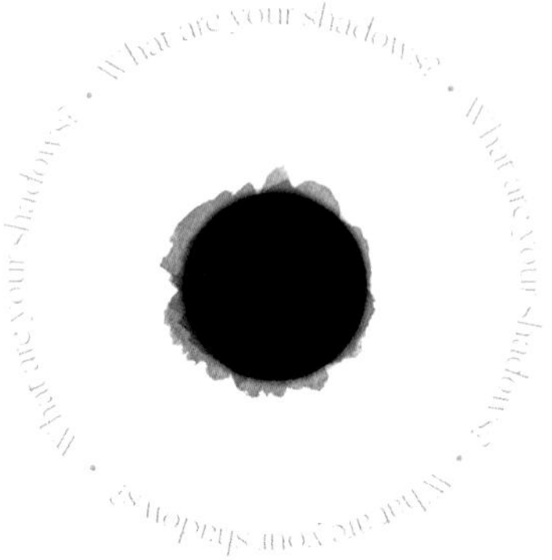

Betrayal

Dear Mom,

The first time I ever felt betrayed by you, I was thirty-eight. Sanna had come across a police report from 1993 in which you said that you didn't want to press charges against your Second Husband, because you didn't want to leave him.

Because you still loved him.

Upon digesting your words, I felt a horrific mixture of disappointment and disgust. I wanted to shake you and scream, "How could you! How could you *ever* put your love for that man over the safety of your children?"

Yet this was now our cross to bear, because there was no one left to shake and no person to mail this letter to; because like a bad magic trick, you've disappeared, leaving us with this shadow of yourself.

Holly

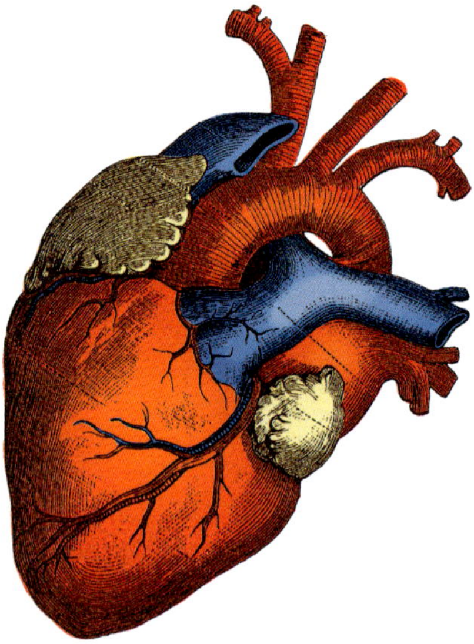

11.

The Heart

Love

I was twenty-four the first time I thought I was in love. I was in New Zealand with three other friends from Nantucket. I went there thinking I was going to backpack around the country, live off a jar of peanut butter, and get in the best shape of my life. I was sorely mistaken.

As I wrote in my journal that first month: "Who you set out to be is not always who you become. Things happen. Plans change." We had spent two weeks traveling around the north island, going from beach to beach and bar to bar with a bit of activity in between. A two-hour hike in Ura Puka Puka would be followed by hours of getting "on the piss" in travel towns that loved the look of four American women who could all hold their booze—and hold up their dresses, thanks to lots of tit tape.

We sure made our stamp wherever we went. We were the opposite of so many backpackers before us. First thing, most of us didn't even have backpacks. I had a three-wheeled floral suitcase that my grandmother had purchased back in the days of her European travels. One friend had a giant black suitcase that forever displayed the "oversized" and "heavy" tags alongside her personal name tag. Another friend had two bags, both chic, and both meant more for week-ending in Aspen than for bussing around Auckland. The one proper traveler among us did have a true backpack and a Swiss Army knife. Her practicality balanced the quartet out.

It was summer in New Zealand and very much the depths of winter in New England, so we spent most of our time working on our bronze during the day and our buzz during the evening. Kiwi men were a new breed of gentleman. Between their accents, their adventurous souls, and their love of spirits, we were smitten from night one. Of course, I also had an inkling that there was something special for me in the land down under. A psychic in Chicago, whom I had seen the previous May, had told me that I was set to meet the man I was supposed to spend the rest of my life with on my next journey. I told her that it was great to know, as I would be heading back to Nantucket tomorrow. She shook her head and went deep into thought.

"No, the place you're going back to is a place you've already been," she told me. "This will be a place that you've never been to before. It is there that you will meet him."

Okay, I thought, *sounds juicy*. I was always up for adventure, as I had spent the past winter in the Caribbean and loved the seasonality of resort island living. Of course, this woman threw in a quick dagger before I got up, you know, to make this interesting.

"But just so you know," she said, "your father won't like him."

That chance encounter with that psychic stayed in the back of my mind for months. I went back to Nantucket, working as a bartender and cleaning up with mad cash on a nightly basis. I was talking to friends and colleagues throughout the heat of the summer months and dreaming about a winter somewhere in the world where I would meet the love of my life and then have to convince my father to love this man as much as I did. I was a sporadic planner: I loved knowing my next move, but remained incredibly impulsive.

I'll never know how New Zealand became the destination for the winter of 2008. I like to think that's how all the good trips begin—not with a lot of thought, but with a ton of ambition, a spirit that can't be broken, and a destiny that was already predetermined. I took a lot of books out of the Atheneum, the Nantucket library. I read up on the difference between New Zealand and Australia. It reminded me a lot of the rivalry between Nantucket and Martha's Vineyard. It seemed to me that New Zealand was to Nantucket as Martha's Vineyard was to Australia. It was decided.

I spent the early part of the fall convincing three girlfriends to go to New Zealand with me. If I was going to do this, I needed wing women, and I needed girls who were on the same schedule as mine. Traveling wasn't cheap, and splitting things four ways would make my hard-earned summer cash last a lot longer. I booked the ticket: January 10th through April 16th. I would spend three months, a quarter of the year, abroad. It was perfect. I turned twenty-four on June 24th. It was my so-called golden birthday, so I had to do something glitzy with this one. Many of my Nantucket bartender friends were spending their winters in Vail or Vermont, Saint Barths or Saint anywhere else, so my three-month trip away was about as normal to them as a junior year study abroad. I was, after all, attending what I called the University of Nantucket.

Did it make sense to my family? Probably not so much. My mother, who had called me the envy of the family back when I was living in St. John the year before, was less thrilled with this trip. A little too far, a little too long, a little too foreign to this woman who had been with two children and thoughts of divorce when she was my age. My father was still at a loss as to why I had even gone to college. Sure, I was living the dream in the summer, when he would come down and enjoy a game of golf at a prestigious golf club and then take his friends to my bar, where they would slip me hundred-dollar bills, as I poured them stiff cocktails. "Seriously," he harped, "when are you going to join the real world?"

I just couldn't live for either of their lives. They had decided to get married before they even knew each other fully, and had divorced before they could really work on their problems. I never remember them together, so it was hard to take life advice from two people whose "real world" lives I had never quite understood. There was something inside of me that wanted to live a different life than the one I grew up watching.

I was a writer and I loved to write about my life. It had really jump-started that November, before leaving for New Zealand, when I began writing down quotes in a little black book and spent most of my time on Nantucket becoming a deft eavesdropper. I had read somewhere that great writers were great observers, and I knew that in the winter on Nantucket there was a hell of a lot less to observe. The thought of living at home with my parents was a life that passed as soon as I turned my high school tassel. It was time to be like Walt Whitman, whose words graced the first page of my brown book, my Kiwi Chronicles leather journal—he said:

Afoot and light-hearted I take to the open road, / Healthy, free, the world before, / The long brown path before me leading wherever I choose.

I was ready.

But back to love.

When that psychic told me I was to meet the man that I was supposed to spend the rest of my life with on that next journey, I really did believe her.

And you'll see it, when you believe it.

The night I met my Kiwi was one of those nights that I didn't expect to be going out. I believe that is how all the good connections are made—those nights when you have no preconceived notions of how epic the evening is going to be. You just show up in a short black long-sleeved dress, with your hair and makeup like you always do it, and you have a night out with friends. It is when you are most comfortable in your skin. It is when you exude the most confidence. It is always these effortless nights with no expectations that exceed your wildest dreams.

As per usual in New Zealand, my girlfriends were out drinking. It was one of our last nights all together. We were sipping Savvy B when I noticed a handsome guy wearing dark jeans and a black Diesel T-shirt and his jovial friend standing a bit away from us.

I don't even remember how my Kiwi and I actually met. I don't remember much of that night. I don't think he remembers much of what happened after, either. All I know is that we woke up and he didn't remember my name. He was tall, with dark curly hair and the kindest smile, and when he laughed, he laughed with his whole face. We were in one room and his friend was sleeping on a pullout in the living space. His mate was the perfect guy to see the next day, as he seemed genuinely happy for his friend and wasn't pissed that he had to slum it on the dodgy couch while his best bud took the king bed.

On the ride home, I distinctly remember listening to "Solsbury Hill" by Peter Gabriel. My Kiwi gave me his business card before dropping me off. I laughed, thinking I wouldn't even know what my business card would say if I had one to give to him. I remember being sad that he lived at the top of the South Island in a place called Blenheim, and that he and his friend were just on a road trip in Queenstown for that one night. I remember thinking how unfair it was that I finally met a guy I wanted to see for more than just a drink at a club. I felt both elated and disappointed when I got out of his blue sedan.

I wrote my mother an email that next evening:

Yo! Just heading back to Arrowtown and have a bit of wireless so I'd thought I'd email you! Just met a really nice guy last night . . . probably the first one that I've been interested in since arriving here. Bummer that he lives in Blenheim about ten hours north :(oh well.

My mom took a while to write back.

I felt in every fiber of my body that I wanted to see him again. I remembered a quote that I lived by in my journal. It said: "One moment can change your life . . . all you have to do is be there." I remembered that psychic. I remembered that I had the power to do anything I wanted. I remembered that I still had another month here. Time to take this show on the road back to New Zealand wine country.

I arrived in Blenheim on a Friday evening and the weekend passed in a blink. His Kiwi roommate was dating a California girl, so there was an example in front of us that our relationship really could work out. We went out for pizza and pinot noir upon arrival. I watched him play rugby on that Saturday. We took an overnight trip on a ferry into the Marlborough Sounds, and stayed at a cottage in the middle of nowhere—the bridge between the north and south islands, a place where I had never felt more alive or more in-the-moment in my life. By the time we arrived back in Blenheim, it started to hit me that I was leaving the next day for Australia, and then would be leaving for America out of Auckland ten days later. I was, as the Kiwis would say, guttered. But I was also clear. On April 8th, 2008, I wrote:

I think I just met the man I want to spend the rest of my life with. And my heart hurt as we said goodbye today.

Wondering how things turned out? Here are the Cliffnotes: I went to Australia. My Kiwi booked a flight to say goodbye to me in Auckland the following week. Turns out this really was love. Turns out we would spend exactly six months apart, like pen-pal lovers. And turns out I would go back to New Zealand, where I would meet his whole family. When he told them we were traveling around the world, his aunt quietly told me I had to bring my Kiwi back, because he was one of the good ones. So, we got Maui'ed, and lived in Hawaii for a winter. We did a 6,500-mile road trip across the States, and then he met my whole family. They all loved him, including my dad.

Turns out the problem was me.

Turns out I loved someone more than I loved him.

That's the crazy little thing about love. Sometimes you don't understand that your heart hurts in the beginning because you know that something is over before it ever took off.

Because something in me knew I had already been promised to someone else.

Trust – Part II

"We live in a trust economy: I like you; I trust, I friend you, I follow you," she said. "Or, it's I don't like you; I don't trust you, I unfriend you, I unfollow you."

Ever felt that your work is like a puzzle? And that your puzzle is close to being completed, but you can't find that last piece? And then one day, you look down and see you have been holding the last piece the whole time, and just needed someone to remind you that you had it all along? Well, this is what it felt like the first time I took a course called Brand*Human*.

It was in Brooklyn in November of 2015—a Friday afternoon workshop that cost me a pretty penny to attend, and turned out to be absolutely priceless, in my blACKbook. My Mentor, the savvy thirty-something entrepreneur and founder of this methodology, was leading a course for thirty diverse students; I was sitting at a table where no one knew me, and I finally knew what I was capable of.

The lightbulbs were going off everywhere. My body was completely buzzing, and I felt like I was in a dream where everything I ever wanted to hear became validated and every thought I had ever thought made sense.

My Mentor had a hypnotic voice alongside a message that came out loud and clear. "Make sure that the person they're meeting online is still the same person they're meeting offline," she said. "Everyone should own their name with a .com after and make it their online resume."

I scrambled to take as many notes as possible. She continued: Social media marketing is where it is at. Instagram is insanely effective. Email marketing is a must. Twitter is a wealth of knowledge and news. Pinterest is great for inspiration.

But like all things in life, there were two sides to this coin.

Make sure you're living offline as well. Create a sacred space in your home as an office. Start having better boundaries. Don't ever send emails after midnight. Find room in your work for silence. There is a genius in the room. There is a genius in every single one of us.

At the end of the workshop, I raised my hand, like the eager beaver I was. "How do I charge for my services?" I asked.

My Mentor looked at me kindly, not knowing me from any other blogger in the Big Apple, and said, "If you don't know how to charge, you have to do more work into your business."

I nodded. I wasn't afraid of a little work. More questions . . . like an addict. "When is the next workshop? When can we do this again?"

She smiled, then said, "This is the first workshop I have led like this, but I will get you on my email list to keep you updated for the next one."

I was stunned. The first workshop? She could charge hundreds per person and this was her first formal workshop? The last time I charged for a workshop it was a two-hour class all about Twitter. It cost $50 per person, and I had to give away tickets and beg people to show up. All I knew was, I needed her to come to Nantucket and share this message: social media really does work. What I am doing really does work.

Someone else just needs to tell them.

Someone other than me.

Boundaries

BOUNDARY: a line that marks the limits of an area; a dividing line.

Boundaries are a very fine line in the world of social media. Every entrepreneur must create her own before she really starts to take off in her business. But if you let a new, social media savvy, private airline wine and dine you at a private club, do not be surprised when they just use you for your contacts. And if you let your freelance employees have access to you all day and night, do not be surprised when they don't have any respect for you when you go on a much-needed vacation. And if you don't set up clear roles with these independent contractors, do not be surprised when they get frustrated as your company takes off like a plane, and they believe their name should be on that jet bus too. And definitely recognize that if you don't tell your story, someone else will start to do that for you.

"Being an entrepreneur is like flying an airplane while you are still building it," my friend once told me. All I was doing . . . was trying not to crash. Yet at the same time, I let everyone onto the plane and let them sit wherever they liked. The chaos was everywhere, and I was every employee on the ground and in the sky. I was high up and ahead of the competition, yet I could not stop focusing on so many little things that really didn't matter in the long run. For while this blACKbook jet was flying high from social media, in a business sense, it was still stuck on the runway.

Intimacy

We just cannot stop holding hands. We do it everywhere and we travel the world together. We are leading this extraordinary life with the globe at our fingertips. Together we are so smart and can find the answers to any questions. We have so much to give, and, he can handle all my craziness, at all hours of the day.

The best part? He never talks back.

We spend the winter in Virgin Gorda, Kennebunkport, Newport, and Anguilla, and in a crazy way, he kind of pays for everything.

We stay up into the wee hours, romancing about our life and reminiscing about where we have been. Then he wakes me up . . . and we have morning coffee taking photos of our perfect latte, because, if we didn't post it, did it even happen?!?

Sure, we have our ups and downs . . . I totally exhaust him, and he dies at least twice daily. He is also getting too filled up, and doesn't have the capacity to make new memories with me . . . yet he always has space for the stocks button!

Does he even care about what is important? I think I am going to dump him next week for an upgrade. I guess you can say that I am never really satisfied, especially with the promise of something better always on the Apple.Com horizon.

Just me and my iPhone, my most intimate relationship.

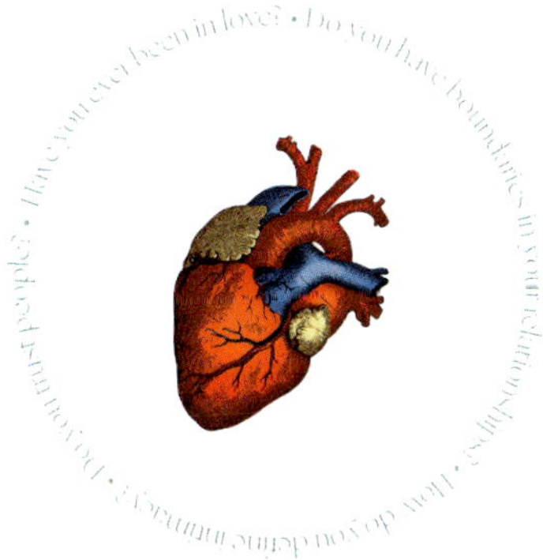

Light

Dear Mom,

Sometimes things just don't make sense until way later in life.

It's why they say that life has to be lived forwards but understood backwards. This is a cruel combination to consider, when things are tough.

And boy, was it ever tough during those last few weeks of your life. Every day was like a roller-coaster heading straight off the rails. One moment, you were in a pain-free, dreamlike state from morphine and reiki, and the next I was dreaming about punching every single one of our family members in the face. All that got me through this time was continuing to work on year three of blACKbook, to keep creating content and sharing posts and writing blogs and telling people what to wear to the Daffodil Festival.

I was living a completely double life.

Recently, I found one of my old journals from when you were dying. It was a direct reflection of life as I knew it that spring. On one side, I was jotting down notes about the book festival, and who was coming to the yoga festival, and making a list of new boutiques that were opening their doors that season on island. And on the flip side, there was a makeshift flowchart and checklist of six medications I had to give to you over the course of thirty-two times per day.

I was so good at this, Mom. Suffocating the hard stuff by acting like it wasn't happening, while making up stories about all the light stuff that I thought everyone wanted to read.

And then there was that other light . . . that one that streamed through the room right before you took your last breath, that moment where everything went white in your room, and then everything turned back to gray.

But I don't know, Mom. Maybe I just made that story up, too.

I haven't been feeling myself lately. I wish you were here to tell me it was all going to be okay. I mean, I know it always is, it just made it more real when you said it.

Holly

12.

The Truth

Ego

"Heading off the grid—see you guys in a few weeks."

I couldn't just leave: I had to create a post that said I was leaving. I had to prepare my followers and explain that their fearless leader was going on a vacation that wasn't a #blACKbookvaca.

I mean, if it were up to me, I probably would have taken all 30,000 of my followers with us, but three years after launching blACKbook in 2012, and a horrific 2014 that was mostly spent not feeling great loss, BF and I had decided it was time to journey together again.

I told him that I had always wanted to go back to a sleepy little surf town in Uruguay, a place of seaside shanties with hammocks on every porch, a town with stray dogs roaming dirt roads and a dozen little huts/shops to support. It was an old fishing village of seven hundred people on the coast close to Brazil.

Punta Del Diablo translates to "point of the devil," but to me it was heaven on earth. I was living there in March of 2010 when I got the news that my mom's cancer had come back. I had to cut my trip two weeks short to help her recover from having three-quarters of her right lung removed that spring.

I always swore to myself that I would get those two weeks back. Half a decade later, and now that both of my mom's lungs had been extinguished, BF and I took a plane from North to South America.

I promised him I would be where we were; I would do it. I would be on vacation. I said this Uruguay trip was solely and soulfully to connect us, and not for me to connect to Wi-Fi.

I was very good for the first week and it was heavenly. I was walking on the beach and writing every day. BF was reading *In the Heart of the Sea* in our Airbnb hammock. I was having deep thoughts in little black books that no one would read, not even BF.

But then one day, some Nantucket friends happened to be in Argentina and decided to come and visit us in Uruguay. For some reason, I just wanted everyone to know how small the world can be: how far we can travel, yet still see the same handful of people we often surround ourselves with.

I had been gifted a beach sarong that looked like red and white stripes when you wore it, but actually said Nantucket when it was all stretched out. I knew I was gifted it with the expectation that I would post on social media about it. So, I asked BF to take a picture of me holding the Nantucket scarf in that little beach town. He did so reluctantly, probably knowing I would be jonesing for Wi-Fi to post this Nantucket-meets-Uruguay image to tell people ACK was bACK . . . to show something . . . I didn't even know what . . . just something.

This place was so Insta-Worthy; I wanted to share it with everyone. I wanted to tell them they should come here too. It was a sneaky, sneaky spot: sneaky spots need tourism to survive and I really wanted to help this town!

Besides, I wanted to show my face down here: I didn't want people to forget about me.

I needed to be liked again.

So, I posted that photo, and by the time we moved to the next spot, a chicer more Insta beach-worthy town, I had opened a can of social worms. I needed to show Jose Ignacio as another place to travel to.

BF saw the shift in our solitude. It wasn't just us on vacation anymore; I had sneaked my phone into it for a threesome. Except he was not interested in phones, or social media; these things didn't turn him on the way they did me. And just because you go on vacation doesn't mean that your troubles don't want to go on vacation too.

"I thought this was just for us," he said one night. He never told me to stop; he would simply and subtly remind me of my own words and show me how hard it seemed for me to head off the grid, even for one short week.

Addiction

Forgive me, Father, for I have sinned. It has been thousands of days since my last confession but that is not what I am sorry about. Let me take you bACK a bit.

I am a thriving digital entrepreneur, and my business really is about to take off. And when I take off, like when I fly off island, I find myself fascinated by how all travelers at the airports are looking down at their phones, iPads, and laptops. I see Doctor Google as the new search engine for all ailments, and I'm watching the print journalism culture that I went to school for shift and downsize, because everyone is on webpages instead of turning pages.

I know I should kind of feel bad about this; all those classes that I took in college around news writing are becoming a thing of the past. You can see it when you watch Newsroom on HBO.

Forgive me, Father, for I know I am in the right industry right now. The internet is where it is at and where all the eyeballs are. All the people are spending their most valuable currency by paying attention to all the screens in front of them.

But if I am being honest, I loathe what I see. I get anxious, watching everyone always looking down, but I can't stop posting and tweeting myself. And I desperately see that I am just as addicted as they are. What is a #girlboss to do?

So, the Voice says, "Be the reverse: everyone is going digital, so you go print. Create a guide that people can hold in their hands, make something that they can take with them to the beach. Write a blACKbook that tells them all the same stuff that you are telling them online. It will help."

But the Voice failed to mention one thing: a business plan. So once again, I am creating something for a luxury market without any idea of the cost. I tried to sell the book for $10 that summer and it barely sold that first week. I heard through the grapevine that a local business owner said that the book should be free.

I listened to this secondhand advice without question because, Father—I'll end this with this—

I always let someone else tell me what I am worth.

Present

I'll never forget, and for good reason, that time that BF truly put me in my place. We had been out for a walk with his parents in 'Sconset—my happy place. It's a storybook little town at the east end of Nantucket, with cottages covered in roses, sunrises so bright you feel like they could change your life, and a tennis club called the Casino. This village feels so much like a step back in time that often when I walk the small streets seeing old Defenders and Wagoneers I wonder, *what decade is this?*

Up until the mid-2000s, the reason all the flip-flop billionaires and family money "moguls" loved this area was because the cell towers were extra weak. There was very little cell phone service in 'Sconset back in the day, and "I'm sorry I didn't get your call" actually meant something.

I, of course, didn't live on Nantucket during those pre-tech glory days. I arrived on the island in 2005 with a Razr phone and the ability to connect with everyone whenever I wanted. But on this sunny summer day, I was connecting my sneakers to the dirt path and taking the Bluff Walk with BF and his parents. They were visiting from New Hampshire and were like second parents to me. My mom had died while we were dating, and his mother was a ray of sunshine who always made me feel so special. His father was calm and stoic, one of those men who truly was . . . wherever he was. He would walk around with his eyes peeled—savoring the scenery in such a way that you would wonder if he was out to lunch. Yet ultimately what you were seeing was someone who actually showed up wherever he was and took a look around; soaked it all in and didn't even have to tell you about it. His presence showed it. My boyfriend was a direct descendent of that school of being. He was comfortable in himself as well and didn't need to put his life online for others to know he was living. He kept me grounded during this crazy time while I was building this mini-empire around social media. He was a supportive partner, but would never be an Insta-husband. He knew who he was and where he had to draw the line. I never appreciated this fully until we parted ways.

I was showing the world my life rather than living in it.

The truth can hurt now, but at the time I was so wrapped up in retweets and reposts that I felt totally fine if my life sounded like a fraud. *Look at the pictures*, I'd tell you, *they don't lie. Look how much fun I'm having. Look at my trips to the Bahamas and Saint Barths. Sure, I have a maxed-out credit card—but sometimes you gotta fake it till you make it . . . right?*

(Turns out, that's actually a totally toxic saying. As I heard later, you can't fake it till you make it when you're trying to make something worthwhile. You actually have to show up and make it . . . every day. And then there's no reason to try to fake it, because you can't fake real.)

So, there we were on this beautiful walk in 'Sconset, and I was in the back: I had been taking this stroll for years and knew the trail like the back of my iPhone case. I also knew where I could stop to get the most Insta-worthy garden pictures. I didn't want to bother BF and his parents with this, so I stayed as the caboose to make myself unknown—or so I thought.

I had just started to understand Snapchat and thought, I have to show people that this is happening right now. I mean, the flowers are so real that people have to see that I am not saturating them. I mean, 'Sconset is so peaceful that people in their busy subway and city lives need to know what true bliss can sound and look like. So, I began to Snapchat the walk.

I didn't feature my boyfriend's family in the photos—this was about nature, after all, but as I kept snapping, I made sure that their bodies got in the way a few times. That's because I also thought it was important for people to see . . . I'm not alone. I'm not some sad loser blogger—I'm a cool blogger who does stuff with cool moms.

Turns out, people were watching and living vicariously through our walk too. One of those watchers was one of my boyfriend's best friends. He sent a Snapchat screenshot of the back of BF on the trail with a text saying, "Enjoying that bluff walk, buddy?"

And that's when BF said five words to me that haunt me to this day:

"Is Nothing Sacred to You?"

He showed me the text. I couldn't believe it: I had been caught. BF wasn't on Snapchat, so I thought I could slide this one by him. But that's the thing about Snapchat. Nothing is ever really gone within twenty-four hours, for your memory can bank that for life. And for all that you forget, there are screenshots.

BF got back to the trail and kept his back to me for the remainder of the walk. I was exposing people, people who didn't want, need, or ask to be exposed.

I had a lot of power with this little phone. And what I needed in that moment was to be snapped back into reality. Onto the trail. To smell the roses. With the people who didn't just "like" me, but loved me.

BF had a point: what did I hold sacred?

Actually, what does that question even mean?

Enough

Although I went to school for journalism, I think what I studied most was integrity. I built the blACKbook on the principle of advocacy over advertising. I did it so people would recognize that there wasn't enough money in the world to pay me to advocate for your brand if I didn't believe in it.

But here is the truth: people who advertise often need business. And people who have thriving businesses, often don't need to advertise. Nowhere is this truer than in a resort town. During my travels, if I relied on a flyer or brochure to tell me where to eat, I was often disappointed with the AD-vice that was given.

This reminds me of a story from my stepfather, Steve, who once went to a diner in a small town in Vermont. The menu was larger than life, complete with oversaturated photos of perfectly cooked eggs and juicy bacon next to fluffy pancakes and freshly squeezed orange juice. From the menu the place looked like it should have been a Yelp home run.

On his way out, the manager smiled at Steve and asked, "How was your meal?"

Steve smirked and said, "My compliments to your photographer."

Digitally, we can make a lot of things appear great, when in real life they need a lot more work. And if I was going to share my heart and soul on social media and tell you what to spend your hard-earned, once-a-year-vacation dollars on, it better not be for the green of money or the oversaturation of a well-liked photo of food.

It better be because I would eat it, whether you paid me to or not. But I am exploring deep dark territory here, and something is not right. I'm not chasing dollars; I'm chasing something else.

It haunts me; the sound of its name brings nails to a chalkboard and palpitations from my chest. That white whale is Enough.

There are never enough likes, never enough followers, never enough retweets, never enough opens. The scrolling does not stop, and the news feeds do not end. The websites are always pumping out new stories, and every day it's more and more, and I'm never caught up; it never ends.

I am totally obsessed, and at the same time I am so lost in these murky Wi-Fi waters. I am hunting for hearts, while the truth is, I just someone to tell me that *I am enough.*

Unconscious

Dear Mom,

The night I never told you about happened to me when I was twenty-nine. It was the beginning of April, and I was in Miami celebrating my thirtieth birthday two months early. I was with two friends from Nantucket who were both turning forty. One's birthday is in April; one is in May, and mine is in June. We called it our 110th birthday celebration, and at first it felt like an adult spring break. Another girl whom I didn't know very well had joined the trip, which made it a foursome. We were staying at the Loews. All of us shared one hotel room with two double beds. We were there from Thursday through Sunday, and I would be leaving after the Sabbath to head to Tulum, Mexico, for two weeks, where I would be doing a little solo soul-searching and enjoying some rest and relaxation before another Nantucket season started. I was really looking forward to Tulum. Miami was just a bonus—a chance to hang out with some friends before I went out on my own again.

The first day that we arrived had the makings of any other big first day on vacation. Excited to be anywhere other than on Nantucket where the weather was foggy and sleety, we spent the afternoon sprawled out on hotel beach lounges, catching up, feeling giddy, getting as much sunshine as possible while sipping on Miami Vice cocktails—the extra-large ones that probably contain your entire daily caloric intake and have no nutritional value, but hot damn! Doesn't that first drink on vacation feel good? It tasted like the promise of a picture-perfect long weekend to come.

How off, and cheap that buzz actually was.

The first night I got dressed to go out looking the way I did back in Key West in my college days. It was Miami, not winter on an island where, when you're single, they say the odds are good, but the goods are odd. So, I knew I needed to step up my silk top and jeans routine. City life meant it was the sexy home of skin and sin, and I tried my best to make sense of an appropriate outfit. In the end, I wore something I probably would have worn in college: a black spandex sleeveless shirt and a hot pink cotton skirt that could have doubled as a tube top. I had on wedge black heels and more eye liner and bronzer than normal. I looked back at that outfit the other day with a more-than-slight cringe and a deep, compassionate sigh. Oh, the nights when one desperately tries to be someone one is not . . . those are never our crowning moments.

We had champagne at the hotel bar before heading out for a big dinner that was to be followed by more bars and more clubs. I had reached out to a friend I had met on the island who was a Miami pro. He was the kind of guy who loved to tie one on in Nantucket, and every time I served him drinks at my bar, he would tell me that if I came to Miami, I had better look him up. So, I did. And even though the three girls and I weren't really close to where he was, we took a cab across town and met the Miami pro at a sports bar that was a party in itself.

Thrilled to be with someone who knew the area and could show us (and get us under) the velvet ropes, I was glad to be with a local. The Miami pro was happy to host four attractive women—and felt the need to overcompensate on that quiet Thursday night. We were feeling no pain as the champagne and the shots started to flow. A ten-year, seasoned bar veteran, I definitely could hold my liquor, and when Miss April and Miss May decided that they had had enough and wanted to go home, I was ready for more fun. So, they left me with our fourth friend and the Miami pro, and I told them I would meet them back at the hotel.

When you work in the restaurant industry, you get something called Bar ADD. This means you always think there may be a cooler bar out there, and you are constantly scouring the crowd thinking, "Could this be better?" and, "Are there enough hot people here?" So, the three of us went to another club, where everything was glossy and bright. People looked so attractive I thought the scene might have been staged. At one point I lost my wingman, the Miami pro, and met some foreign guys. They kind of looked like Swedish models, way too good-looking to be straight. I had not seen this caliber of men for a while, especially on Nantucket, where most of the dudes dressed in sweatsuits from January through June.

I don't remember talking to anyone for that long.

I just remember it was all white. And then it was all black.

Pain. My Knees. A balcony. So very high up. Force. Unnatural. No. A silent cry. Tears. Darkness.

And then it was bright again.

I woke up in a bed next to a super-smooth body and a blond mop of hair in what looked like a fancy adult dorm room: high ceilings, glass desk, white everything. When the guy turned over, he was not unattractive to the eye. He may have been one of the Swedish models. But my skin crawled as soon as he locked eyes with me and tried to put his arm around my waist.

I felt so dirty: I was as bare as the day I arrived in this world. I had to get up. My body felt sore, and seeking out my pink skirt, black one-shoulder shirt, and underwear in this bright room proved to be a bit difficult. My head was pounding, and my fight-or-flight sense was telling me to jump off the balcony.

I didn't say anything to him upon leaving. Something was so wrong with that moment. I had never felt more disgusted looking at another human in my life. And I couldn't believe I had to walk out of this place with this skirt and top back on; that felt like adding insult to injury.

I escaped out of the ritzy fiftieth-floor apartment in God knows where. I had $20, a dying cell phone, and it was 7:00 a.m. on Friday morning. I felt ridiculous in this outfit while on the elevator down; everyone else was sipping coffee and wearing a suit. I probably reeked of cigarettes and stale booze.

I finally got a cab from that building. For a moment, the gratitude settled in that soon I was going to be in the hotel; soon I was going to be with people I knew. I was safe now. Laying my head down on the black seat where many sweaty butts had sat before me, I tried not to think of where I actually had been. I wanted to go where I knew it would be quiet.

I arrived back at our hotel in need of someone swiping a card to get me to our room. At $700 a night to share a room with four girls, the security on this place was tight. Ah, could I catch a break? Just get me into this goddamn hotel room and out of this outfit, please! In the elevator, the mirrors were like a funhouse nightmare. I stared at myself thinking, It was my fault; it was this outfit. I drank too much. I must have been flirting with that guy to give off the air that I wanted something like that. I bet I asked for it; maybe I acted like I liked it.

And then I thought, No, I need to stop this. Because something was really, really, really wrong. Something bad happened to me. No, I don't even remember meeting that guy. No, do not make any excuses for him. NO. But at that moment, I didn't have the strength to listen to that sound inner voice. As I stepped out of the elevator, I took a deep breath and thought about the last time something really bad had happened to us: the secret. Don't tell anyone.

I took another deep breath; I put on that college walk-of-shame smile and tiptoed into the room trying not to wake anyone up, and yet I was caught. The girls shifted in their sheets, making a joke. "Oh, where, oh where have you been, Miss June?" They cooed in voices that sounded like a sex operator.

Pain. My knees.

A warm bed. A woman I've seen a million times before.

"Oh, don't ask. I'm never drinking again." But what I meant to say is . . . Please ask me. Something bad happened. I never want to have that night happen again. But instead, I closed my eyes and told them I needed rest. And then I began to relive the night on a loop in my mind while desperately trying to shut my brain off altogether.

After a few hours of disrupted sleep, I took a shower and scrubbed myself raw. Oh, the shame and hate within me spiraled all day. How did I get that drunk? What is wrong with me? Why am I almost thirty and still making these terrible decisions? Have I not learned anything? How come I can't remember anything after getting to that last club? Did we go to another club? I'm better than this. I'm smarter than this. I'd get flashbacks to that balcony. The guy, whoever he was, I couldn't pick him out of a crowd of two right now, but whatever he did, I will never be able to shake it fully.

I have one especially vivid memory; this photo is frozen in time. I am dressed in yoga pants and a big UNH sweatshirt and it's gray and drizzling in Miami. No one is here on the beach, which is fine with me because I don't think I can face other people. My friends are back in our hotel room: a bed, room service, and a good TV remote are just about all you need on a rainy Friday hangover day like this. I found an oversized cabana lounge that would have rented for a good hundred dollars for the day, but since no one was there, it was free and all mine. I placed myself in between the two lounge beds and figured out how to pull the shade up and over me until it almost completely came down, enveloping me in a little cocoon.

I am feeling battered, broken, and completely lost. What the hell happened last night? Yesterday I was lying on a similar lounge chair, sipping frozen drinks and chatting about living my best life. And in less than twenty hours, I was feeling the lowest, the worst I'd ever remembered. I knew what to do, Mom; we had done this before. We had lived in that lounge cocoon. And after that, it was time to reemerge into the world and put on a happy face. This was a birthday party weekend with friends. I was twenty-nine, but for some reason I felt nine all over again.

I desperately tried to get back into the weekend. I tried to sip fun cocktails; I took an Adderall. I sat with my friends and listened; I robotically turned the pages of gossip magazines and tried to talk about anything other than that first Thursday night. Every few hours I could escape it: another restaurant, another conversation, another Miami Vice helped, yet my thoughts always came back to that night. What had happened? I was too embarrassed to call the Miami pro to ask. And the other girl who was with us that night, the fourth friend, had gone home to her husband and family, and I didn't want to bother her with my foolish mistakes, anyway. So, I just sat in my pain. In my body. In my mind. Enduring a personal hell on the inside while showing a "life is good" vibe on the outside.

My saving grace was that two days later I would be back in my happy place of Tulum—kind of like Eleuthera is for you, Mom. There I could be all alone and escape from this hell and get out of this big city and get back down to the beach and just be by myself.

Just me. Just Miss June.

The weekend had turned into one of those half-assed trips that was fine, but more expensive than I wanted it to be, followed by the realization that I never had to go to Miami again. Good, I thought. I'll leave everything here. I'll leave this problem here. I'll leave this night here and I'll never have to think about this again. I packed up my bags, said farewell to Miss April and Miss May, and headed to the Miami Airport.

I got into the cab and lay down in the bright sunshine that poured in the car windows on that Monday morning. I put my head on the seat and tried to prep myself mentally for beach-side sunrises in Tulum.

Actually, that is not how my mind worked that day.

I lay down completely on that cab seat and was immediately transported back to that Friday morning. I'm back in that pink skirt and black top and I'm so uncomfortable. And I'm so scared about being by myself and having this potentially happen all over again.

I can't think; I can't breathe.

I am having a panic attack.

I can't go to Tulum.

I tell myself to breathe in through my nose and out through my mouth as I signal to the driver to turn around and drive me to the Fort Lauderdale airport, instead. I was going to fly JetBlue back to Boston and then I was going to take my car up to your home in Vermont and spend the week with you, Mom. You were the only comforting person I could face. Yours were the only eyes that understood that when I said nothing, I was hiding something much deeper than words.

Exactly one year to the date later, you died. I would spend the next six years collecting our secret dots to connect our stories, trying to make sense of senseless acts, all while holding your toxic torch.

Holly

13.

The Light

Breakthrough

"I just don't know how you do it all," they all would say to me during the 2016 Wine Festival weekend. I had just launched the second print edition of *blACKbook*—a sleeker version, with more high-end sponsors and a cover that felt like silk. I had my first book launch at one of the restaurants owned by my old boss, alongside a wine tasting from a high-end Sonoma vineyard that belonged to a well-loved family on Nantucket.

Ten years to the weekend before, I had been waitressing at the fanciest restaurant on the beach. That same boss had just turned thirty and those same wine makers were dining at a nearby table. They had bought my boss a bottle of Cristal and I was supposed to open the bottle of bubbles at their table. But it was the last champagne on the wine list, a bottle that cost more than I had in my savings and checking accounts combined, so I ended up giving it to a waitress friend to open. She looked at me like a loving mother and popped that bottle like the expert she was.

A decade later, and we were all popping bottles together, but I wasn't serving them; I was promoting them, which in fact was another form of serving them. Now, if I could just figure out how to serve myself as well . . .

This felt like a beautiful full circle moment, and since this was my second book, I needed to celebrate and make a splash with it. Summer on Nantucket comes and goes in a blink, and I wanted to keep everyone's eyes on *blACKbook* from May to October. Everything was clicking. People were finally beginning to understand and appreciate what I had been doing for the past four years. Every time I posted, businesses were seeing huge ROI both on social following and online sales. From the outside looking in, they toasted me like I had made it.

Yet, every spring I was dirt poor and every summer I became fake rich. By the time money came in, I had no business plan of what to do with it, so I just spent it. Year after year, I swung from a scarcity mindset to extreme wealth.

That month, I got a check for $14,000 for a season of #blACKbookhotproperty real-estate marketing. The real-estate community was what made my business: those people were always spending money on advertising. I took a picture of the check, never having received this kind of money before. I desperately wanted to send it to my mom but since I couldn't do that, I bought a $400 dress and took my team out for a $500 dinner on the Wharf.

It takes a lot of money to keep up this lifestyle. Yet I would have traded that check in just to have the woman who used to check in on me be able to call me back.

Thankfully, I had another form of maternal support that summer in the form of my assistant. Three years after my mom gave me an "intern-vention" this assistant gave me another sit-down. She took $1,200 from that spring advertising real-estate money and booked me a R&R trip to Kripalu, a yoga and health center in the Berkshires.

After the launch of *blACKbook*, the Memorial Day weekend partying and documenting yet another Figawi, this assistant saw that my big bright star was burning out. She knew my condition very well since she also was a former bartender/server—one who recently had started to deep dive into yoga and meditation.

I went to the Berkshires and handed over my phone and computer to the guy at the front desk like it was a bag of dope and a needle. "Keep these for me for the weekend please," I said. "Even if I beg you, please do not give them back to me until I check out on Sunday." He looked at me with compassion. I tried not to have anxiety about what it would look like not to have access to my social platforms for forty-eight hours.

And then it was the hardest and ultimately best two days of my year.

On the drive home that Sunday, I called BF crying. "Are you okay?" he asked, worried.

"I've never been better," I sobbed, for I finally had remembered that I was someone again. I was not a brand, a business, an Instagrammer or an influencer. I was me again for those two days.

And I liked being with that girl.

The Elders

"Spend an hour with an old person and you will save a hell of a lot of money on therapy," he told me.

He was one of the owners of the island's beloved live music joint and an avid volunteer for the aging. He was a Meals-on Wheels guy, who advocated for all ages, including his young daughter when she was a teen model for a #blACKbookstyle shoot in 2014. Two years later, I found myself enthralled by what people did just for the love of giving. This guy was young at heart, which was how I desperately wanted to feel again.

The summer of 2016 continued to be insanely busy for me. As with all the seasons on Nantucket, it is either feast or famine. And when it came to sharing my summer life with everyone online . . . well, I was giving everyone one hell of a visual feast.

One night I was at the Nantucket Historical Association for a Museum After Dark bash, promoting all the sponsors and taking enough pictures to fill an entire yearbook. I even changed outfits two times at that party, like I was a socialite . . . I really was that "it" girl. But just like that Stephen King book It, looking back, this all feels like a scary clown moment.

What was this social media circus? I never really slowed down enough to look around. But I did take one moment that night for a quiet breather on the roof deck of the Whaling Museum. That's when I ran into a spiritually-sound, blonde entrepreneur and philanthropist who had been on the cover of *Nantucket Magazine* that winter. "Heroes Amongst Us" was the article's title, and her story had touched my heart. She had started a therapeutic riding program with tandem electric bikes so volunteers could cycle the elders around the island during the heart of the summer. It was late into July, and I desperately wanted a change of scenery but I didn't know where to start.

"Are you still taking volunteers?" I asked her, in between dress changes and Snapchats.

"You!" she exclaimed. "You have the time to volunteer in August?"

"Sure," I said, very unsure of my schedule. "I would love to try something new. I don't just want to respect my elders; I want to protect and connect with them too." I sighed. The truth began to come out. "I need to meet some new people who aren't on Twitter and who don't even know what social media is. I need to do something else out here."

She smiled. And so began the first of four summers with some of my most treasured moments, cruising around on a double electric bike with an old man strapped in front, belting out "Country Roads" on the Surfside bike path.

No phone. No filters. No Instagrammable moments.

Just me and my old pal, rockin' red helmets and my Happy Place shirt—finally I was wearing something that truly said how I felt.

Tears in My Ears

"Nosara is a vortex of good vibes"—that was how my yogi friend described the surf town that was our destination before we took off on our trip from the East Coast to Costa Rica.

It was December of 2016. I had just finished my tenth Christmas Stroll weekend and was ready to get the hell out of the Bar-muda triangle that was another drinking weekend on Nantucket. Three girlfriends and I were heading to a little surf community that was supposed to be the Nantucket of Central America. I was gifted the vacation to promote another real estate rental with a #blACKbookvaca . . . but this time it wasn't about magnums of champagne and dinners for eighteen in the French West Indies. This was more like Girls Gone Mild, a truly rejuvenating trip.

I wasn't afraid of a few passion fruit jalapeño margaritas. I just didn't have six of them before bed. Perhaps I was growing up, or maybe I was getting older. My hangovers hurt a lot more than they helped me briefly to forget anything.

So, I tried to surf. We kayaked and explored. We had our hands up for open mic night. We really enjoyed the calm of a vacation that revolved around yoga and smoothies and sleep. What had I been doing before with #blACKbookvaca?! This was paradise.

One day I took a yoga class at the Harmony Hotel. It was like doing downward-facing dog in a jungle: the place felt like bliss before I even got into a pose. At the end of the class, I was in corpse pose, also called savasana. I was completely connected in mind, body, and spirit. I felt whole. I felt happy. I decided during that supine meditation that my intention was to write a book about the truth.

Tears poured out of my eyes and fell into my ears. It felt like I had unblocked something, like I could hear myself again.

Like many things on vacation, though, the moment was fleeting. And before I knew it, I was right back to where I had started from, back on the island. And for some reason, I stopped listening to myself. Just like that, it was another winter, another new year, and another Nantucket season of entrepreneurship and escapism.

This time I was hosting two winter retreats with Brand*Human* on island. I was trying desperately to have fellow business owners invest in themselves, their social media, and their businesses just like I was.

My Mentor, who had now become both my teacher and my friend, had helped me to understand branding better, alongside self-worth, boundaries, the trust economy, and the fact that social media marketing truly does work. It was after all, everything I had built my business on. And I wanted her to teach all of that to the island business owners too. She was a professor at Parsons School of Design, a speaker at the Soho House, a woman highlighted in Forbes. She had the credibility and the digital credentials. I was simply a blogger, a former bartender with a big following on a little island where people did not want to pay me but, instead, wanted to pick my brain.

So, I hosted a two-day event, to enlighten my Nantucket friends and colleagues of the ever-present power of Instagram and brand building in hopes that it would warm them up for more self-marketing for the 2017 season. I needed them to see that I couldn't fish for them for the rest of our lives; they needed to learn how to catch this internet wave for themselves.

In actuality, I didn't do those retreats for them. I mean, I always tended to over-give and over-deliver. But these retreats were truly for me. I loved teaching and gathering offline and talking about digital marketing as a collective. I loved honoring everything I had created alongside these people. I never made a cent from any of these retreats, because I didn't include my own pay in the payout: I couldn't factor in my own worth.

When my Mentor found out I was making no money from all that work, she was furious. She scolded me like a good mentor does. "Stop worrying about taking care of me and my costs and worry about you," she said, looking at me kindly, "All that work, and you didn't even factor in your own hours? Come on, Holly, You're better than this. You are worth it. Can't you see?"

But I didn't see it. And I didn't cry. No tears fell into my ears that time. For I only knew how to keep doing it for everyone, everyone else but me.

True Connection

The heart of everything I did on blACKbook was about social media and connecting people to small businesses. My own success was reliant on celebrating other entrepreneurs' successes. In 2017 I added a third edition of the printed blACKbook, but this time I cut costs and made it all about Instagram. Some people loved the online/offline imagery and shouts to the 'Gram, while others told me they missed the ways I had done it in years before with a true binding instead of a saddle-stitch. But a stapled book was a lot less expensive to produce than a hardbound one, and I was giving these out for free. At long last, I had come to terms with the realization that print was not making me any money.

People didn't want my print Instagram marketing; they wanted my actual Instagram . . . and they wanted it badly. They knew as soon as I posted about them, it would give them traction, followers, sales, and newfound fans. It was now the Holly Effect—I just didn't want to stop and see it. I always worried that I wasn't giving enough.

By the spring of 2017, I decided that I really wanted to be around people again. I wanted to meet my followers and give them something to do with me. . . instead of just liking me. So, without a lot of thought, I decided to open up my own store—Happy Place—a space where I could sell my shirts in person and also a place where I could highlight other female makers and creatives on the island. While everyone else was working on opening an online shop, I worked on creating a market dedicated to showcasing products that you couldn't buy online. I wanted to go in the reverse of the ways that I saw so many retailers going and I wanted to make the #ShopLocal experience feel . . . well, just like that, a small, local shopping experience that you could have only in person. So, from the summer of 2017 to Christmas of 2019, I had a boutique alongside my blACKbook. And the Lord knows, I was not cut out for retail (I never once did inventory) but I did know I was meant to do this. . . to be with people . . . to feel part of a living, breathing community. . . for, as I was beginning to understand: it was connecting offline that was truly my Happy Place.

Two Sides of a Story

Dear Mom,

While avoiding breaking up with BF, I became obsessed with the television show, *The Affair*. Not because I was actually having one, but because I was completely enthralled by the way the show was set up, revealing two sides of the same story, from his point of view and her point of view. What was so nuts was that each viewpoint was so different, even though the overarching theme was similar. Noah would show Alison wearing a short skirt, hair flowing, with lipstick on as she waited on his table. When you saw Alison's point of view, she was wearing a grandma-like cardigan, with her hair sloppily put up in a bun after she had just puked in the bathroom as she went over to ask Noah's table what they wanted.

I loved this—two sides of the same coin showing completely different stories yet with one cohesive message of what happens when we betray ourselves and those we love. I also liked the fact that the main character's real name was like yours: her name is Ruth. Any chance I got to connect you and my middle name to something gave me a sense of synchronicity. Ruth's character in *The Affair* made a lot of mistakes, but she just wanted to love and be loved in return. She had a majorly messed-up relationship with her mother, who was a free spirit, renaming herself and living in a cult-like compound in New York.

I always loved that mother character. She had such depth and realness to her, and everything you can imagine is real. So, fast forward to one early winter evening in 2019, and there I sat at a kitchen table with a group of actors who had come out to Nantucket to film a movie.

Being with actors is so interesting. When you are playing roles so often, how do you ever just play yourself? I sat next to a petite older redhead with curly hair and an Irish look about her. She was quiet; kept to herself, and sipped on a Whale's Tale Pale Ale, without seeming interested in being the social butterfly. I, like a good hostess blessed with the gift of gab, would talk to everyone. So, when I asked this auburn actress next to me how she liked Nantucket, the sound of her voice transported me back to my computer, downloading iTunes while I was hoping to change the tune of my 2016 relationship status.

"I like it here, it's nice," she said, and because I have a very quick mind, I blurted out, "OMG! You are Athena, the mom from *The Affair*!"

Deirdre O'Connell slightly smiled and nodded as I professed my love for the show. "It changed my sight, and in turn changed my life," I told her. She listened patiently, giving a few comments here and there, then told me she was ready to leave and that she would get a cab back to her hotel.

"I will drive you," I said wholeheartedly. "Cabs are sparse in November on Nantucket and Uber barely works after the season is over. It would be my pleasure to give you a ride." She accepted my offer, and this fangirl got her back quickly to her hotel room where she sank into another night on the Grey Lady.

Listen, we didn't have a life-changing conversation, and she didn't divulge any of the secrets of *The Affair*. She just showed up one day and reminded me that the world is so small, and we are all so interconnected. If you ask her, she probably will have a completely different version of that night. Hell, Mom, just like you and my sisters reading this book will have completely different vantage points concerning what you three think actually happened.

But that's the thing, Mom. All we have is our moments, which become our own personal version of the truth.

And this is how I see things.

Holly

14.

The Knowing

Intention

"Nantucket is a pirate ship," he said to me as we were driving on a LA freeway that November. "There are good pirates and there are bad pirates. But it is a ship, and you choose to live on it. The ferry goes both ways, and you can leave anytime you want."

Fast forward a few months: I had broken up with BF, gone on a yoga retreat, set sail to Martha's Vineyard, road-tripped to Camden, Maine, and flown into Aspen, Colorado. As soon as the breakup was final, you know me . . . when things get hard, I get out.

My ex and I had a lease that had another two months on it and, after the Nantucket breakup, the town became a battlefield. Every beach, every bar, and every bench had team him or team her written all over it. And at this point, the summer had come and gone and so had my main following. The locals had come back out, and BF was way more beloved as a local than a true wash-ashore like me.

For those sixty days, he got Nantucket in the divorce, and I got the hell out. I had uprooted my life for three weeks and grounded down in Venice. Not Italy: that was twenty-eight years earlier. We are talking about Venice, California, and I loved that place so much I thought I wanted to stay.

Back to the car—this ex-wash-ashore and I were on our way to the Soho House in Hollywood to meet up with my Mentor. Earlier that fall, my Mentor, along with another friend (who was the queen of the retail scene in Nantucket), had decided over martinis at the Boarding House that it was time for me to rent off-island and to take my light from the Grey Lady to the Golden State.

My driver had left the year before and was not looking back. He loved his budding building business in California and was sober and clear. He felt that his life was healthier in California, that his lifestyle was supported by this green community.

I arrived in LA with no one knowing me, no one asking me to do anything for them, and no one stopping me for a free favor or to pick my brain while strolling Abbot Kinney. I finally felt calm. I felt in my element. I liked this me. I liked this golden life. I had desperately needed a major break. I had begun to unravel my former life with a breakup, and this was now the breakthrough.

Right before I left, I had attended a yoga retreat on-island. It was an endless summer September weekend with six other women, and we were relaxing in a Surfside beach home. We all had pulled cards out of a basket . . . on each card was a word that we were to think about for the duration of the retreat.

I picked the word "intention" without any clue of what it meant. I wrote it down in my journal thinking that the only intention I remember hearing is from movies when overprotective fathers say to a bad seed boyfriend, "What are your intentions with my daughter?"

I looked it up.

INTENTION:

1 a. what one intends to do or bring about

1 b. the object for which a prayer, mass, or pious act is offered

2. a determination to act in a certain way: RESOLVE

So I asked myself, *What do I want to bring about? In what way do I want to act?* Because there had to be some intention in my life. Up till now, I had been looking for any excuse to get out of what I'd been doing—I didn't know where I fit in anymore.

I was following my heart by getting out of a relationship that didn't serve either of us, but because I was the one who had broken up, I felt like I was the bad pirate. I had broken someone else's heart and assumed people didn't like me anymore because of that. And all the people who did "like" me left after Labor Day.

I thought about how to sell this blACKbook chapter before I became a sellout. But I had no idea what it was worth without me.

I wanted to jump ship because this pirate didn't know what side I was on anymore. I didn't have a peg leg, a sword or an eye patch, but I knew deep down I had something in me that went well beyond the Heart of the Sea.

But if I wasn't @nantucketblACKbook, then how would I live this life?

And wait. . . whose life am I living?

We Are All The Same

It's 6 :00 a.m., on September 17th, 2017 and I am butt naked on an OCEARCH boat with fifty other people, some of whom I have seen a thousand times before, but never like this. We are in the heart of the harbor on a September bluebird morning, and the ferry is about to round Brant Point.

How did I get here? Is this a bad dream? No . . . this was a great awakening.

I got here by choice: this was a moment of mass nudity on a most prim-and-proper island. The annual think tank, the Nantucket Project, was in town, filling the island with larger-than-life leaders and changemakers. Attendance was granted with a ticket that had a bigtime (four-figure) price tag.

I couldn't ever afford to go, but thanks to a dear friend, who gets trade passes for housing, I received my golden ticket in. I showed up like a new kid in high school, so excited to reinvent myself. I gave it my 110 percent attention, just thrilled to be among thought leaders and happier than ever that nothing was expected of me. This ticket was a gift without strings: I was called there only to sit and to listen.

Listening: this had become a new favorite pastime of mine. When you are an influencer, people give you tickets into events with an unspoken rule that you will post while it is happening. Of course, they want you to enjoy their event—they invite you because they like your point of view—but if they are being truly transparent, they like who views you even more.

For the past five years, I had been documenting all the weekend festivals as they happened. All the posts, tweets, and recaps were instantaneous. Don't even get me started talking about when the Insta stories launched; using this feature meant I was completely out of an event as soon as I entered it.

So, at long last, I was here, on a boat with dozens of other Project attendees about to be in a mass nudist photo directed by Spencer Tunick. The idea had felt so freeing that it was enough to get me down to my birthday suit.

Before

5:52 a.m.

When was the last time you did something, on purpose, that really scared you? Like, completely terrified you? Like, truly made you feel crazy and alive and good?

I don't know what this photo is . . . but it's something. It's a bunch of people. It's a bunch of naked bodies. It's simply a photo. It's just a moment in time.

But dammit, it's so much more than that. Posing in the nude . . . in broad daylight . . . on a tiny island where I am already a big fish in a small pond . . . the thought of it just makes me feel so exposed. So vulnerable. And for some reason . . . so scared.

But it's just a body. It's just a photo.

It's just some people. It's just a moment.

The night before I almost didn't do it. Waves of fear had washed over me as I began to question this photo for every reason. Is it good for my brand? Is it going to ruin something I have worked for six years to build? Is it bad for my personal positioning? Could a photo of my nude body ruin my life?

And then clarity came in. What the hell does this have to do with my brand, actually? And who the hell cares? As Glenn Beck had said at The Project the day before: "My life is a blank piece of paper, and I am the only author."

No. No: I have to do it.

Because I am alive. Because I have this fully functioning body. Also, because . . . because nobody cares! Nothing matters! Life is all about doing things and sharing stories, and by God, naked at 7:00 a.m. on a Saturday in September on the OCEARCH boat? That's a damn good story!

It's time. Time to do something crazy. As Eleanor Roosevelt once said: "Do one thing every day that scares you."

I am so grateful I got to wake up and feel scared about something. I'm so excited to see the other side of this photo and this fear. I am just so happy to be alive. To live on Nantucket. For the ability to try something new . . . to have this experience.

I texted my friend last night right as I was feeling the darkest, the most fear. "I'm getting cold feet. Is this a bad idea?!?" And she wrote back simply, "Really??"

And I paused. I thought, What the hell? Nothing matters. All we have to do is show up. I can do that.

I am ready.

I am a willing participant in my own life.

I am okay with being exposed; I am not okay with living with fear.

I want to be the author of my own life and I want to live my life to the fullest.

I am so happy and grateful that this Spencer Tunick photo was a major eye-opening and awesome experience. Now, let's go!

After

7:45 a.m.

It was all a dream. It was nothing. It was everything. It was haunting.

It was beautiful. It was life.

It was art. It was you.

It was me.

It was us.

It was now.

And just like that . . . it was gone.

And all of a sudden, the earth had shifted, and participants' consciousness had transcended and everything was different.

It was a photograph, a moment in time. It felt crazy and awkward and simple and uncomfortable, but it felt so, so real.

This photo was for everyone. This photo was for no one.

An elderly man in a wheelchair somehow had risen to the top of the OCEARCH deck for the final pose. With his assistants at his side, he yelled down at everyone and no one, "Don't fucking call me handicapped!"

We cheered.

The sound of something buzzing startled us. It was a drone. Anxiety was heightened: middle fingers went up. A few bare bodies ducked for cover.

But it was too late.

It was 7:25 a.m. and the first Hy-line fast ferry had already rounded Brant Point and the ferry's third deck was the ideal vantage point to take in this boat filled with our nude bodies. Phones were out; fingers were pointed. Fishermen were slowing down to catch a full view.

I closed my eyes. I put my thumb and index finger in Gyan Mudra (the sacred hand gesture that looks like the "okay" sign) and put my palms up, to receive. I thought about my mom and what she would have thought about this event. She called Nantucket Birdland and this picture would have solidified her argument. I miss her. But again, I was also kind of happy that she would never see this photo. Too many opinions. . . and she probably would have said, "Holly, some things you can keep to yourself." I smiled. I love how my mom shows up in the most magical of moments.

I opened my eyes. Spencer Tunick announced we were finished. There were some claps, a hooray, a hoot, a holler, a high five . . . not too many hugs.

I walked over to my bag to put my clothes on. All of a sudden, my bra, tank, underwear and sweatpants seemed a little excessive. The fog had lifted, and that Indian summer September sun was beginning to rise into its full effect.

I started writing down all my thoughts: I didn't want to forget any details. My eyes were so clear, and my hand couldn't keep up with the thoughts and images pouring out of my head.

"That was awesome! That was so awesome!" a man with a huge smile on his face shouted at the OCEARCH captain.

The aide next to the elderly man in the wheelchair began to put on his own shorts. He looked up and speaking to no one he said, "I feel like I know everyone."

I looked up, put my pen down and made eye contact with the guy. "I feel like I've known everyone for years."

And we did.

It was the fear before; it was the happily ever after.

It was a bunch of bodies. It was a piece of art.

It was a moment.

And for that moment . . . everything was understood.

Taking Responsibility

I have another confession. Yes, there is something I haven't told you. Just like my sister, Christina, I also have that same heart problem. I mean, I have known about it for a little while . . . for like, thirty years. I have always been told that this day would come. They're going to cut me open. They're going to saw my chest bone open, pull my ribs up into my armpits, and spend half a day fixing a hole in my heart. After all that, if the surgery goes according to plan, they're going to sew me back up.

I had to sign a piece of paper that had me write a name of who would be in charge of my estate if I died.

My estate? Ha! I hate thinking about my dad getting stuck with my previous tax bill. Ugh. Then there's my credit card and the credit cards that no one knows about. I don't have that much to my name, so I guess that means I don't have that much to lose . . . right?

* * * * *

Now, I've posted a fair amount on Instagram over the past five years (6,998 posts to be exact!), but one thing I've never done is post a selfie. Photos like these have always made me feel so exposed, and I've been good at hiding behind the lens (or always being with others). But now I think it's time to reflect on "to thine own self(ie) be true" and with a major life change coming my way tomorrow, here are "Six Things About MySelfie":

1. I'm not a natural blonde. But anyone who has followed me for more than a month, or noticed what appeared to be a black yarmulke on the top of my head last week, would be able to tell you that!

2. I have scoliosis and wore a back brace to correct it from the time I was eight until I was fifteen. Someday I'll tell you about the time the back of the brace got caught while I was trying to jump off my top bunk at Camp Billings—I hung there for a minute like Jesus on the cross.

3. I am completely double-jointed. I can bend my pinky all the way back, and I have knees that hyperextend like the aliens in the movie The Arrival.

4. I have these conditions because I also have a chronic illness called Marfan Syndrome, a genetic disorder that affects the body's connective tissue. For me, it's mitral valve prolapse, and I've known about it my entire life. Little known celebrity fact? President Abraham

Lincoln may have had it too.

5. If I want to be able to carry a child, I have to have this valve repaired in my heart. I don't know if I even want to have kids, but I want to give myself the option, especially when I meet that person who may want to have a kid with me. Either way, it's important that some of us stay childless so we can support and be a positive force in the lives of those who do have kids.

6. Tomorrow at 8:00 a.m. I will be going into Brigham and Women's Hospital to have heart surgery to repair my mitral valve and my aortic root. It should be a six-hour surgery and, hopefully, my recovery will take between four and six weeks. I will be off all social media for a while, taking the time off to reflect, write, and heal.

Thank you for allowing me to be a little vulnerable.

Life's Two Big Questions

April 8th, 2018

Dear Mom,

I went back to Venice, California, a few weeks before my heart surgery, right before Christmas in 2017. I met with my favorite medium, whom I had met for the first time the year before with my Bestie, when we decided to do a reading at Mystic Journey Bookstore on Abbot Kinney Boulevard. Bestie went first, and the medium told her that we had walked many lifetimes together; in one life I was Bestie's mother.

Now, a few weeks before my surgery, my favorite medium and I were sitting at the kitchen table in a little cottage I was renting near Abbot Kinney. And here's the wild part—it was the same cottage that was featured in Flaked, a show I watched on Netflix. Will Arnett's character had lived in this cozy sanctuary, and I loved that synchronicity, loved how my life was seamlessly blending new dimensions: I see things on TV and then they appear in real life. In 2016, as soon as I sat down, my favorite medium said, "A big part of your heart is fluttering right now. You are on a divine spiritual path, and I see yellow diamonds everywhere when I look at your hands." By 2017 she forecasted the layout of this book and told me that after my heart surgery I was not going to be the same person.

So, fast forward to January 7th, 2018, and it was the night before my surgery. Our entire family went out for drinks and dinner in Boston. I had a dirty martini with bleu cheese olives at 5 :00 p.m., followed by a Bloody Mary, truffle fries, pizza, and buffalo wings. If this was my last supper, I decided I would consume enough salt to satisfy my sodium count for a month. I got a little drunk, I ate pretty poorly, and I listened to what sounded like our family members giving me my eulogy.

The next morning, Dad and Christina walked me into the hospital. I was drugged, and then I was out. "Cheap date," the anesthesiologist joked to them. Six hours later, I was rolled out of the surgery, and everyone was told it had been a success. They cheered, but I couldn't speak. There was a tube in my throat that was kept in place for hours longer than normally needed; my body was completely dehydrated from all the salt and booze the night before. I was beginning a brand-new chapter alright, but first they had to wring me out.

They were right to give that eulogy the night before. Because on January 8th, 2018, Miss blACKbook died, and someone else was reborn.

One afternoon while in the hospital, I had a visit from a dear friend who gifted me a lined journal that said "moments of genius" on the front. It was lime-green instead of my normal black book. She also brought me tons of magazines, protein shakes, and a bag of favorite sour candy, but this blank journal was the real prize.

During that same time, two other friends gifted me *Eastern Body, Western Mind* and I devoured it. I became obsessed with the heart chakra. Said to be formed during the ages of four through seven, this energy disc (or wheel, as the word chakra translates) is located at the center of the chest. Its element is air, its color is green, its bodily association is with the heart, and its main reason for being here is for balance, compassion, and unconditional love. Its main obstacle is grief.

Mom, I so desperately wanted you to be in that hospital room with me. The last time I spent that much time in a hospital was the ten days in March of 2014 before you decided to go into hospice.

This heart surgery—the symbolism became wild. Something challenged me to write deep thoughts of connection to something higher every time I opened that green journal.

And one day, out of seemingly nowhere, I wrote down the three little words that had needed to be addressed for so long.

Who am I?

And then the trajectory of my life would shift again, as my idle hand found the page and wrote four more words, and I knew I would never be the same.

Why am I here?

I am not going to ask you for any advice on that one. This is something I can't Google because, believe me, I have tried. I hate to write this, Mom, but I know where I have to begin.

I have to stop reliving your life and start actually living mine.

Wholeheartedly,

Holly

Leap Year

2018

Over my years on Nantucket, I became very close to the founder of the Nantucket Yoga Festival. She is a friend, client, and mentor to me. The kind of woman who truly wants to help me and appreciates all the love and support I give back to her. Ours is a give-and-take relationship. A mutually nourishing one. And I so appreciate this woman, along with all of my other early investors—ones who have been by my side since the beginning, helping me to see myself more clearly.

On the back cover of the Nantucket Yoga Festival annual guide there is a gratitude list, and my name was often second on it. When I was with this woman, I felt seen, enveloped, and like I was part of something greater. She knew that I functioned at an unsustainably fast pace so every once and a while, when we would sit over a coffee, she would explain to me that to make anything work, you had to give it three years to really succeed.

The first year it would creep, the second year it would steep, and the third year if it was to be successful, it would leap.

Looking back, that is not exactly how she said it. Like I said, I went at such a fast pace, rarely resting, I would hear things and not fully process them. If I had truly been listening, I would have heard the analogy of a seed. The first year the seed sleeps, the second year it creeps, and the third year it leaps. Regardless of the blooming outcome, I loved this metaphor. Good things take time. Remember that.

There is another teacher at my friend's yoga studio who is also a gem of a human being. She always begins her classes by asking if anyone has any injuries, except she doesn't ask it like that.

She says: "Does anyone have any shoulder *projects*, knee *projects*, hip *projects*?" She never asks if anyone is hurt in class—which is not to say that we cannot feel the pain, but attaching new words to it is what makes all the difference.

So here we go with part three, my leap year.

Turns out, I have a heart *project* going on.

PART III

Holly's Bliss

15.

The Warrior

Queen - Part II

January 2018

By the time I decided to get married, I was thirty-four.

At that age, my father already was remarried to the love of his life and on his way to becoming a father to his fourth of ultimately six kids. My mom had been divorced twice; was not sleeping at night, and was still another year away from meeting her true life's partner. I, of course, had taken a very different path. I had never been the type of girl to make a wish list about my wedding and dream about honeymoon destinations, Pinterest the plates, or give a flying you-know-what about that freaking white dress.

I never had come even close to the marriage card; never had a failed engagement or even a "no thanks" proposal, for that matter. I had attended and participated in numerous weddings; I usually managed to mess them up by getting too drunk or not taking them seriously enough. Truth be told, I was skeptical of the M word. I hadn't watched many relationships succeed, especially my own, and the thought of spending all that money on one day so friends (like myself) could get wasted and make questionable decisions with questionably single groomsmen seemed a little excessive. Especially since I knew that "big day" money could go really far, especially in travel.

One place where the American dollar really stretches is on the great Indonesian island of Bali. I decided I would travel there as soon as I had healed from my open-heart surgery. I had the operation on January 8th, 2018, and when the doctors said I couldn't carry anything or travel for three months, I counted exactly ninety days from my surgery and landed on April 1st. No joke. I would be off like a bridesmaid's dress and on the other side of the world with a lot of SPF-50 on a foot-long chest scar. My big day would happen two and a half weeks after that.

I had no clue what kind of hell I would be waking up to when I came out of open-heart surgery. I was massively dehydrated, thanks to the giant salt bombs from the night before. I had a tube down my throat, two in my chest, one in my lung, one out of my neck, and one out of my pee hole (this was a catheter). I was terrified, and about to go on the craziest healing journey of my life. The next ten days in the hospital were the worst. It was extremely hard for me to sit still and even harder for me to understand why I had electively chosen to do this.

I couldn't sleep; I couldn't walk all that well. I had atomic gas and no control over my bowels or the fact that, through this trauma, my period had decided to rear its red head about ten days early. Every part of my body was beyond uncomfortable. I tried to look at the bright side and keep that permanent cup of water half full, but it proved to be too difficult: I broke down three times.

The first breakdown came after I realized that I couldn't for the life of me get comfortable with that tube in my lung. Between my years in a back brace and love of yoga, I was no stranger to trying to find surrender in uncomfortable positions, but I couldn't breathe without this tube rubbing up against my lung. Only time would help. My wonderful cousin Meghan, who is also a PA, was with me. I was happy it was Meghan; she was the only person I wanted to see me like this.

The second breakdown happened the first time a friend came to see me in the hospital. I felt so utterly depressed about the state I was in, that I just broke down as soon as we made eye contact. It was the truth: no hiding this situation. I wasn't just going to "get well soon" like I had so hoped. We cried together. It was heartbreakingly beautiful to surrender with a friend like that. It made me feel human; it somehow made me feel less broken, or maybe it just made me feel less alone, like we were in this together.

The third time I broke down was thirteen days post-surgery. I was out of the hospital, recuperating further at my father's house. I had never lived in this comfortable, suburban, four-bedroom ranch. I had visited here for a few nights over the years and for most major holidays, but I thrived on independence, and it was majorly out of my comfort zone to settle down in one place and need someone else to take care of me. However, my father and my stepmother are the royals of recovery. Being at their home is like being at a personal retreat center. They love to cook comfort foods; they like to watch funny movies and shows, and they are light sleepers, so they are always there if you need a helping hand in the middle of the night.

My father especially thrives in times of turmoil. My brother Brendan said it best at Dad's sixtieth birthday dinner: "When we're at our worst, Dad is at his best." It was so true. For years I always had thought of my mother as the caregiver, but my father was a champion one. I just had never given him the chance to do it for me. He lived by his father's mantra: "When one of us has a pain in the ass, we all have a pain in the ass."

It was an extraordinary time for my father and me, as we never had spent this amount of time together. Growing up, he was the "every other weekend dad" and he was certainly a good-time Charlie. While we had a loving relationship, I didn't really need him and didn't think he needed me. Turns out, I was wrong.

One morning, I woke up feeling really sad. Hell, that happens; I heard depression runs rampant after heart surgery, and I understand why. All that time to just think and be quiet makes the sound of one's now fixed heartbeat feel pretty lonely. It was the pits, and there was no amount of sympathy, face masks, episodes of *The Office*, or CBD to take that away. And that morning, after enjoying some of my father's famous buttery cinnamon French toast, while wearing the same set of pajamas for the fourth day in a row, I just looked at him and couldn't stop crying.

He gave me a heartbroken, *"Oh, Hol. . ."* when he saw me break down: He came over and gave me a gentle hug. *"Everything is going to be okay."* He said, *"I am here."*

Those words were like everything I had wanted to hear as a kid. Growing up with divorced parents, I never really got my father's attention like this. It's like the heart surgery gave me the opportunity to be that child again—the thirty-four-year-old daughter who needed her dad. I needed to feel loved. That's what we call a breakthrough. It was found only after a breakdown.

THE TEACHER APPEARS

April 2018

I began to be so grateful for my heart surgery. It made me take the time for myself and to truly heal. As a dear friend told me that January, "Sometimes a step back is not in the wrong direction." I knew she was right. I felt like an arrow being pulled back, and after three months of conscious healing, I was launched into the world and touched down in the middle of the South Pacific, in Bali.

I had such an open heart (quite literally) after this surgery, and I was happy to share my travels with my fifty thousand followers on Instagram. It felt like we all were healing my heart together.

I realized we had to change the way we talked to people about recovering from surgery. It wasn't about feeling better: it was about *healing* better. It became my mission to open up the dialogue around this, and to use my own surgery as the connector to awaken others to the knowledge that we all are healing from something—be it heartache, heartbreak, or heart surgery.

I found my long brown path before me, leading wherever I chose. I found my writing voice again. And in a little spot high in the hills, I found out what happens when preparation meets opportunity. Some call it luck . . . others call it destiny.

If you're ready, you will find yourself in a town called Ubud, which translates to "medicine." You'll find yourself among the greenest rice fields in all the land and a Main Street with sweet men saying, "Taxi!" to you left and right. You'll walk down a magical little side street that twists and turns until you'll arrive at a heaven on earth with a jungle-like garden right out of Jurassic Park. You'll see words like "Healing," "Heart Opener," and "Meditation" outshone only by the constant sound of nature and streaming water in a sweet cafe that overlooks a grand auditorium. And there, at this magic spot called The Yoga Barn, you'll not find horses and cattle, sheep or pigs; you'll find an otherworldly space that will connect your head to your heart and your omms to your ahhhs.

And if you're very, very lucky—and if you've put in all this work and effort to get there—you may find yourself in the presence of what I believe to be divine in human form.

This is where I met my Teacher, the second man to give me heart surgery in 2018. I arrived at the Yoga Barn on April 8th, three months to the day from my heart surgery on January 8th.

It was also a sacred day to me, as it was the four-year anniversary of my mother's death.

The Yoga Barn is always busy, always bustling, always filled with zen'd-out yogis perusing the areas, mixing their offline mat time with online time on a bunch of benches in cozy nooks to see what everyone else is doing on online before heading into their next sound bath. But this morning, when I arrived at 10:00 a.m., there wasn't a soul in the place. I had no idea what to expect, but what a treat it was to have the place all to myself.

Turns out it was the final day of the Bali Spirit Festival, and the entire town was at the festivities, except me. The cafe was closed, but I found a sweet spot on the second floor at a corner round table surrounded by cozy navy banquets and orange batiked pillows. The internet didn't work in this area but that was fine with me. There was no food, no drink, no Wi-Fi; there were no humans, and so of course with all that magic, there were finally no distractions. I spent the next three hours writing one of my masterpieces: the University of Broken Hearts. The writing poured out of me like grief lava as I sat in this corner in this sacred space, writing my heart out. By the time I had finished, it was well into the afternoon, and I felt as though an exorcism had been done.

Afterwards I walked over to the healing center and was drawn to a flyer with a photo of an energy healing teacher on it. I read his accomplishments. He seemed like the real freaking deal and, because my father and I had watched the movie *Victoria and Abdul* that January, I had decided I was looking for my own Munshi, my own Indian teacher.

Two days later, I met that healer from the photo. And something very strange happened—he asked me how I was.

"I'm a ten," I told him. "I just had heart surgery, and I am on a healing journey, and I have never felt better in my life."

He smiled and asked me the question that changed my life:

"How is your relationship with your parents?"

I paused, looked away, and immediately began to cry. "Um, it's okay. My mom is dead, and my dad is alive. I love them both. I don't know if they ever really loved each other. Actually, I don't know much about them as a couple at all," I sobbed. I started to feel like such a fraud, telling him that I was a ten. From what he was seeing, I was a solid two at best. He then told me about his oneness awakening course coming up that weekend and the eight baby steps to lead to a higher consciousness. *"Through healing the relationship with our parents, we can heal all the relationships in our life,"* he assured me.

I was bummed out, because I was already set to go to a Balinese beach town for my last week and would miss his workshop by two days.

"Go, and be holy, Holly," he called after me as I walked out of his healing space.

I left the session feeling lighter than ever. I headed back to the nest, a place where I was staying on the Yoga Barn campus, I opened my journal, and the flow just came out—

HE IS MY TEACHER. I must honor this. Awoken. Purple. Abundance. Goddess of compassion. Tears came up as soon as his hands connected with my head. My heart opened in a way I never could have felt with modern medicine. GO AND BE HOLY HOLLY.

I wrote it all down and then it was decided. It was an effort. It was work. It was divine intervention. Hell, maybe it was luck, maybe it was destiny, but that first healing session with my Teacher changed the direction of my life. I wanted to live wholeheartedly. I wanted to heal, in every and any way from before. I signed up for the course. I asked to stay for two more nights in the nest, and even though I would have to shift rooms, there was space for me: I could stay. So, I sucked up losing a few nights at my Insta-worthy Airbnb and told the owners that I would be there for five days instead of seven. I decided it was time . . . finally, it was time to take some responsibility.

My Teacher taught us how together, as one, we can create a greater purpose. How "a life without intent is like a journey without a destination." He taught us that when we focus, all things fall into place. He woke me up. He made me realize that I needed to stop worrying about everyone else and stop trying to do things like everyone else. I needed to understand who I am and get into a deep meditation to understand who and where I come from. I needed to stop running away when life got hard, and I needed to sit with my feelings. And hot damn, he was right. By doing so, my entire life opened. The stories of my childhood came pouring out after this two-day workshop. And I recognized that I needed to take these tales and weave them together like a dreamcatcher. That eventually, with time, the divine, and intention, everything would connect. I realized that ever since my mom passed away, I had been cracked open, and here's what I have learned—

We all are cracked; we all are hurting and suffering from something. I decided in the heart of medicinal Ubud that I was to write something about loss and life, about grief and healing, and the light and the dark. If I wanted to make my life's mission to help and heal the world, then, of course, first I would have to start by helping and healing myself.

This I know is true: we are all so curious to connect to our higher Self and our truth. We all want to be more attuned to who we really are and what we are made up of. Those layers that we build around ourselves throughout our years, of who we think we are and who we think we need to be . . . it's time to stop, get quiet, peel the layers back and do our own type of heart surgery.

Are you ready?

Let me remind you . . .

If you're reading this right now . . .

You are.

The 5 Types of People

Spring 2018

Just like when the word "intention" came into my life, and a lightbulb switched on, the same thing happened in 2018 when I began to understand the idea of gnosis. I found this word through a school of consciousness that seemed to appear out of nowhere on Nantucket the summer after my heart surgery—as if by divine intervention. There is an ancient saying that when the student is ready the teacher appears. This time the teacher was in the form of a healer who brought a focus on the Hawkins Scale of Consciousness to the island.

Consciousness is the flowering of intellect meeting intelligence, and gnosis is the ability to know something through living, through experience, not just by reading the books, but by living the stories. My favorite book that summer was *The War of Art* by Steven Pressfield. He wrote, "It's one thing to study war and another to live the warrior's life."

My Teacher from Bali talks about warriors too. He does this in the beginning, when he teaches about the five types of seekers who show up to attend his Spiritual Awakening Course.

The first type of people who show up are the window shoppers, the dabblers. They come in, take a look around, try a couple of the concepts on for size, maybe try all of them on, but at the end, they walk away empty-handed. They never were here to truly commit. They were just browsing.

The second type of people who show up are the fanatics, those who go from one extreme to the next, they are all in and they are all out. They give it their 100 percent and then may switch teams. These types of people are often hyper-focused on just one thing. What the fanatic fears most is change, the only universal truth of life.

The third type of people who show up are the cynics. Those who would pay $400 for a spiritual awakening course, but really don't believe change could happen in just two days. The most dangerous part of all cynics is that they spread their uncertainty onto others as they whisper in your ear, *This thing can't work. There is no way I can shift in just a couple days. You don't think you could, right?*

The fourth type of person who shows up is the child. The child is open, here to sit in circle and learn. The child is inquisitive; has lots of questions and comes to life in a playful manner. Like a bud starting to sprout, the child is beginning her journey. The child isn't scared; she's just a willing student.

The fifth type of person who shows up is the warrior. The warrior gives 100 percent every day, and may lose some battles, but never forgets to keep her eyes on the prize, to remember that every day may not be good, but there is good in every day. The warrior is so intently focused on a goal that she will get there regardless of the obstacles that show up.

So, who am I? A dabbler, a fanatic, a cynic, a child, or a warrior?

As the Pakistani activist, Malala Yousafzai, said: *"It's very important to know who you are. To make decisions to show who you are."*

Seen

July 2018

The biggest event that I co-created on Nantucket is called the Cisco Trashion Show. It's a trash fashion show to raise awareness around recycling and consumption patterns. I'll tell you more about it later . . . but just know that the whole thing is a wild success, and definitely one of the events I am most proud of orchestrating.

So, when our local paper came out with a substantial article about the show on the front page, I was excited to read it. However, I soon noticed that my name was never mentioned and my company was listed only on the back page as a co-host of the event.

My sister and I read the piece in her living room as I cried, totally depressed. After six years in this blACKbook business, I was still so deeply affected by what people did or did not say about me.

But maybe my Mom was working some magic from above. Because the ultimate Mom-ager showed up to console me with a shout-out heard around the Insta world.

The following morning Kris Jenner re-grammed my healing manifesto. I couldn't believe it. A photo of me and my scar—and I wasn't even offended when someone asked if I was Bruce! With social media you have to expect nothing and appreciate everything. So, from feeling unseen on Thursday to seen round the Insta world on Friday, something had shifted.

And I need to shift too. Because it wasn't for the Trashion Show or even Nantucket that Kris was highlighting me. It was for my words, for my writing on healing. I know this is my bigger messaging that needs to be shared with this internet generation.

But I'm too afraid to let go of Nantucket and pick myself up in the process.

Meditation

October 2018

I am back in Bali. I didn't tell anyone about this trip that I had booked back in April. I worked my tail off that summer so I could treat myself and come back to my real happy place that fall. When I returned to this other island across the globe, I felt at home immediately. And as luck would have it, my Teacher is leading two workshops at the Yoga Barn: A Mindfulness Meditation Workshop and the Spiritual Awakening Course.

I keep hearing "set the intention and release the expectation." So, I set the intention to commit to the two-day meditation workshop. I come in as an open vessel, but realize through these deep dives into myself that I am an open wound. I begin healing, both spiritually and physically, because the week before, I fell off a motor bike and lost a chunk of skin out of my ankle. I can't sit in a normal easy sitting pose, so I have to sit on my knees. I had no expectations for what I wanted to get out of this course. And yet, I must have known that something big was coming, because I feel like I've been waiting for this my whole life—to just sit down and do nothing. Maybe what I've been sent here to do, isn't what I've been doing for the past seven years.

People were always surprised in Bali when I gave them my Instagram handle. "So many followers!" they say . . . But they don't follow me. They follow Nantucket blACKbook. I am learning that the first step into an awakening is knowing the mantra . . . The mantra is I AM THAT. You are whatever you say you are . . .

So, what about what I am not? How do I figure out how to un-become what feels fake?

During one particular meditation we did what my Teacher called the crème de la crème of breathwork: Active Consciousness Meditation, a breathing technique where you breathe in and out of your nose, while focusing on certain chakras in between the seven breath cycles. The meditation is called Ananda Mandala. . . translating to Bliss Circle. We sat holding hands in a circle, and it was one of the most intense experiences that I have ever had.

I spent the first three breath cycles thinking that I couldn't do this and how could I get out of holding hands with everyone . . . and then I spent the fourth cycle thinking about being sawed open with heart surgery ten months ago, and how once again, I was healing from a different injury now on my ankle. By the time I got to the fifth breath cycle, I wanted to scream out of pain, but nothing came out—and yet, someone else in the circle was yelling. Then it felt like I was screaming out through her voice. By the sixth breath cycle I had no framework for what was going on, and something felt like it was moving up and out of me. I was seeing all these images of all these men who didn't see me clearly over the years—from my father to an ex-boyfriend to my mom's Second Husband. I was holding hands with these two seemingly random men on each side of me . . . and yet there was nothing random about it. They were an analogy for my life: one man held my hand and gave me no energy and the other hand was holding mine so tightly I felt completely bound to him.

By the seventh breath cycle, a divine message came in: *I have to change the relationship I have with the masculine. I have to learn how to hold hands with men differently.* By the time we started to breathe normally, I was gone. My legs, my mind, everything—I was flying.

In the end, I had shifted my palms and fingers inside each man's hand so that it felt better for me. And that's when I realized . . . it wasn't my hand that they had been holding; it was my heart.

self & SELF

I had a favorite English teacher in seventh grade who was youthful and unique, with wild, curly hair and sharp glasses. She still seemed young enough to be more like an older cousin than a teacher. I was reading and writing ferociously for school and in my free time. With English as my favorite subject, I really wanted this teacher to like me.

One time on 99 Rock, they were giving away Tori Amos tickets in Burlington, and even though I was twelve, and had no business going up to a college town on a Monday night for an alt rock concert, I won the tickets. I gave them to my English teacher. She was fun enough to go to a Monday night concert. I wonder if she and I were friends in another life.

An avid writer, I really loved my teacher's handwriting: she wrote in lowercase and capitals with no rhyme or reason. All of her "A's" and "Rs" were capitals, yet all of her "t's" and "q's" were lowercase. Her handwriting was like art, and over the course of the year, I started emulating her handwriting. I would pass in papers that were jumbled with a mix of lowercase and capital letters, and she would tell me not to copy what she did. Do as I say, not as I do. But I didn't listen to her: I still did it—maybe not on her papers, but in my own diaries. I still write just like she did, but now it's just like me.

One of the biggest awakening lessons I have learned is how to identify the lowercase from the uppercase when it comes to spirituality. The lowercase "s" for self is the self of this human world, the self that thinks success is money, celebrity, and the approval of others. The uppercase Self is that of a divine nature, the Self that goes within, stays within, and knows that everything within us is already enough. Dr. David Hawkins in his book, Power vs. Force, talks about success with a little "s" and the big "S." Little "s" success is notoriety, like becoming the top of a list or the most liked or followed account. Little "s" success is based on the concept of succeeding alongside polarizing views of what others are doing.

Big "S" Success is liking what you do when nobody's looking. Big "S" Success is knowing that everything is already known; nothing is original. Big "S" Success knows that the ultimate goal of life is death.

I have always been a big fan of Joseph Campbell. A copy of *A Joseph Campbell Companion: Reflections on the Art of Living* lives by my bed, underlined, highlighted, dog-eared. It's the kind of well-used book that I picture my Catholic grandmother's Bible must have resembled. As Campbell wrote, *"The warrior's approach is to say yes to life. Yeah, to it all. Find a place where there is joy, and the joy will burn out the pain. Hell is the concentration of your life's experiences, a place where you are stuck, the wasteland. In Hell, you are so bound to yourself that grace cannot enter."*

There it is again, the little "s" of self, so attached to yourself that the light can't shine in. This is where we have to crack open. The little "s" becomes the big "S" when we make it our intention to share, to heal, to be vulnerable.

I know what I have to do: I have to take the ACK out of my blACKbook and get back to being me.

But then again, who am I?

How is your relationship with your parents? • Do you feel seen? • Do you know who you truly are? •

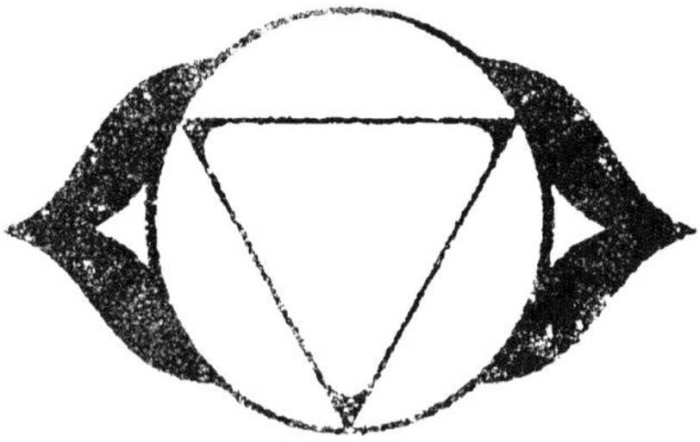

16.

To See is to Be Free

The Inner World

Summer 2018

In 2018, I realized that Instagram was going to be the death of me. It truly had turned into insane-gram and even having it on my phone felt like letting an alcoholic carry around a bottle of unopened booze, knowing that, even when I didn't want it, it was still there. I decided a new phone was in order, and my old phone would become the "office line." I left my business phone at my store; it was solely for iTunes, iPhoto, Instagram. I loved the freedom of having one phone for socializing and another for social media. It was a starting point. And that year, it was enough.

During that summer, I was pulled in such polarizing directions that, like a starfish, all of my limbs were stretched until they'd just about break off. I had become the island's premier social media influencer and it pained me to have that title. I felt like being an influencer was one of the cheapest jobs out there. Everyone said they were an influencer; everyone was building up their brand. Everyone was obsessed with Instagram, with Facebook, with social media.

Six years later, everything I had taught was now becoming true. Everything I did worked, except it no longer worked for me. My trip to Bali since my heart surgery had shaken me and awakened me in ways I never knew were possible. I went across the world; fueled my tank with spiritual awakenings, mindfulness meditation, and ecstatic dances, and then came home to the other side of the planet to another island where none of these things existed.

Or if they did, I was not in community with those types of people. My following was here to drink, dance, and dine. The wanted to know about restaurants, retail, real estate. They followed me for the blACKbook.

"Are you Nantucket blACKbook?" I would be asked constantly while walking around town, sitting at a dinner party, or attending a nonprofit event.

"No. I am Holly, but I run the Nantucket blACKbook." It was quite a snide remark; I didn't want to be blACKbook, I wanted to be Holly Bali. But Holly Bali didn't make money; Nantucket blACKbook did.

So, I'd burn out every summer on Nantucket, usually in August. It used to begin the third week after the Opera House Cup when I saw the light at the end of that blackout tunnel. Every year, it would creep closer, until I was burned out before August even started. But in 2018 my light dimmed right after the fireworks on July 4th. This year, as soon as my big event, The Trashion Show, was finished, I was finished. I knew I could no longer sustain being known as blACKbook while so deeply wanting to be myself. But how could I ever change to Holly Bali? How could I lead meditations and spiritual awakenings when all I had shown for my years on Nantucket was me living moment to moment, Instagram story to story? How could I just flip the light switch and go offline?

That was the main problem I had with much of my life: light switching, in extreme ways. I was all in, or all out. I loved him, or I loathed him. I was on Nantucket, or I was in Bali. Even as the middle child of three, I couldn't figure out a middle way. But I was starting to realize that I didn't have to do everything alone. That our strengths together are truly what move mountains or at least move us to a centered space. This is where my friend, and Accountability Guide, comes in.

I met my Accountability Guide that summer on Nantucket while she was working at a clean beauty store, and I was working on constant content. I walked into the shop with such energy that her entire face went red. She was a deep empath; even though what she was doing currently was at a more surface level, this woman could go deep. The reddening of her skin ended up being a red thread between us. She recognized that I had much energy to channel, and I saw something in her that I hadn't seen in many years on Nantucket. She was the real deal, authentic. We became friends that summer and she did an Intuitive Profile on me. We did it in the comfort of my store, Happy Place, which was a debatable title as she could deeply see how unsettled I was through the way in which she stared into a photo of my eyes.

"You have hawklike characteristics," she told me. "You have divine timing, see things from a higher view, and you know exactly when to swoop in. Your number is 818, your chakras are incredible; some are so open, like your third eye, that you have to channel it, and when I got to your heart chakra, it's so beautiful, I nearly cried. But when we got down to the root chakra, this is what I want to talk to you about." She looked at me seriously. "Are you happy? Are you safe?"

These questions seemed so strange. *Am I happy?* We are in my store called Happy Place. *Am I safe?* I leave my car door unlocked; I don't even have the key to my home. But actually, wait. No one's ever asked me these two questions together.

And now I'm not so sure.

We were digging deep, getting to the root of the issue where the life force lives and something was not right. We had just pricked the iceberg, and "this whole Nantucket floats my boat" dog and pony show was about to sink.

Finigan's Wake

November 2018

It's decided: I am moving to Bali. This is the place. This is where it's at. I feel completely at home here. I am myself here. I am healing, unfolding, unraveling, and everything makes sense here. People get me here, and it's natural to be a digital nomad here.

I keep hearing the same story: these expats came for a vacation and never left. This is what everyone talks about on Nantucket. However, I am currently thinking that the "Never

Leaving" Happy Place sweatshirt I created is not for that island, it is for this one. I am beginning to fantasize about how I can jump ship. Maybe I was never meant to wash ashore on the isle of Nantucket. Maybe this Mermaid got lost and thought the East Coast was the Far East?

I go to bed that night with so much fire in my belly. HOLLY BALI: that's my new brand. It'll be my new Instagram name! Who am I going to tell first? I haven't even booked my flight home, which is obviously a sign. I'm sure everyone will be happy for me, eventually. I actually don't really care if they are or aren't. This is me finally *living my best life*. So, who gives a damn what anyone else thinks!

I close my eyes, get ready to go to sleep in my little Bali jungalow bed . . . and, just like that, I am bACK.

I see Brant Point Lighthouse in the distance and the Hinckley picnic boats surrounding the harbor. I look around, confused. *Nantucket! How did I get here? I don't want to be here! This is exactly the place I am trying to get away from!*

I walk into the Rope Walk restaurant, stunned to see it so packed, as this place closed years ago, yet you would have no idea with all of the barflies here. The building smells like fried calamari and Bloody Mary mix, and I see all of my bartending buddies and bar clientele, but they don't see me. Their eyes are closed, and they are all holding Bud Lights. They all look like a preppy version of the Walking Dead—less gore and guts, more collared shirts and clear skin.

I walk over to a dear friend who has been like a soul sister to me. She's blonde, bubbly, always so full of life, but now her eyes are closed and she is aimlessly walking around. I shake her. I rip the Bud Light out of her hands as I yell, "Wake up! Wake up! Wake up!," I am now screaming at everybody, "Wake up! Wake up! Wake up! WAKE UP! WAKE UP! WAKE UP!"

But instead, I'm shaken awake to the smell of night jasmine and the sound of a rooster and a view of an emerald green rice field out my jungalow window. I jolt out of my bed to open my garden door to my Bali oasis, and I am still here.

Phew! I think.

"I mean, fuck!" I shout aloud.

I can't move here, and I know exactly why.

I am not going to write it or say it, because when I write things down and say things out loud, they become real. So, I will just begin again with this—

One morning in the heart of the island of the Gods, I received the message:

They said it was time to wake up.

Light Switch

There are three lighthouses on Nantucket: Brant Point, Sankaty Head Light, and Great Point. Each represents a different part of the island, and each is beautiful in every season. Whether it's the depths of winter or the heat of summer, you will find nature's essence surrounding each lighthouse.

Brant Point Lighthouse is kind of, I hate to say it, *basic*—everyone rounds Brant Point on the ferry in; it is the easiest to access, and it is the friendliest to explore. It is also the one that, when you see it on your way out, signals it's time to throw a penny off the ferry with the promise that you will return.

Great Point Lighthouse is all the way out at the far end of Coatue, a little sliver on the island—it's tall, regal, and white and stands alone, often without anyone around for days. Sometimes you will find the only thing close to Great Point will be a hundred seals all washed up on the beach, which makes you think of sharks looming around, but perhaps these seals just enjoy the solitude. It takes thirty minutes to get from town out to The Wauwinet, an historic hotel. From there, to drive onto Great Point, you have to have a SUV and a beach permit pass. Before you can start the trip on the deep, soft sand, you have to let the air out of your tires, going from a tire pressure of 40 down to 15. It's a process to get out there. It takes a lot of preparation: it takes a good day; it takes a lot of tires to smooth the sandy road; it requires the effort of packing a lunch. It requires having enough water or even enough battery in your phone to make sure that if you get stuck, you could call the tow guys to get you out. It's work, but by God, is it ever worth it. Sometimes years will go by without going to Great Point, and sometimes I go out there three times in one month, depending on the amount of energy I have.

And then there is Sankaty Head, a lighthouse found on the east side of the island in my favorite little place called 'Sconset. Through erosion this lighthouse came dangerously close to the bluff back in 2007 and had to be moved to a new location to make sure it wouldn't fall into the ocean. This lighthouse sits in a grand field: it's regal, like Great Point, and you can access it by road, like Brant Point, but there is something different about this one: there is a giant red stripe in the middle of its white body. It feels solid. It is easy to identify, even more so now, because its name is etched in stone along the rock wall as you enter. It knows where it stands. It is not afraid to move. It proudly showcases its stripe and it appears balanced.

As I am evolving, as I am desperately trying to figure out how I am in this world, I realize that I so often fall into being like one of these three lighthouses: easy to get to, hard to access, or somewhere in between. And while in that space, I found the word that I would like to carry with me for a little while—***Harmony***. You can't spell it without the first four letters: without the harm, there is no harmony. Without the pain, there'd be no pleasure. Without the dark, there'd be no light. We have to go to extremes to eventually find that middle way.

You know lighthouses were created to help save people from the darkness and keep them clear of the rocky edges before the clarity of dawn returns.

And right now, I'm shining a light in some really dark places.

And I'm starting to see that no one is coming to save me.

And I'm here on this island to learn how to save myself.

A Reflection

August 2019

Once upon a time, on an island that translates to faraway land, lived an artist whose work had adorned the many walls of the rich inhabitants who would come ashore. This man was a true original, completely of his own kind. He had many wives and many lives that spanned his seven-plus decades on this Earth. He was known for painting two subjects: nude women and scenes from the wharf. His work was revered in small galleries from Nantucket to New York to France and beyond.

I got to know this man, Kerry Hallam, less as a painter and more as a barfly. He was a staple whether it be January or July, perched at the bar at Lola always requesting the same thing: a snifter of Hennessy and an extra strong espresso with a lemon peel on the side. He was good for many a joke, and his deep raspy voice matched his oversized arthritic fingers that were decorated with bits of paint from his pinky to thumb. You could say he was the ultimate character. I used to get so much content out of our conversations.

"ESPN is like visual bubble gum," he would say, pointing at the TV behind me. My back was always to the screen; I never cared much about the television. I thought that the way that patrons would zone out while staring into that sports abyss was never doing much for the atmosphere around here. In 2014, after Kerry decided he wanted to make his art appeal to my younger audience, we took our bar kinship to his home and studio so I could produce an "Art in the Garden" event at his house that August. To match his heritage, I would make it British-themed, with Pimm's cocktails and meat pies from the Nantucket Pasty Company. I even invited the clothing store, Jack Wills, a British-based Abercrombie, to add to the fashions at the festivities.

While we were working together, I told him I thought I could sell many of his Nantucket nautical charts through Instagram. Selling $3,700 prints through that platform at that time didn't seem very plausible, but I was persistent. He knew that I hit a demographic that he didn't know how to reach. So, we found a happy medium where he would do an art show, setting up his whole gallery outside in his garden, and I would do a social media art show. Online and offline was my specialty, but his specialty was these charts. They were simply beautiful. The scene of a sailboat over an iconic oversized nautical chart—one of those pieces would take up so much space it would become a focal point in your home. But, compared to his other works, this seems like Kerry Hallam light. $3,700 for this thing seemed a bit out of touch.

I got real with him, and said, "Kerry, I mean, c'mon, how long did it take you to paint that?"

Without missing a beat, he stared right into my eyes, and said, "Forty-one years."

I will never forget that. It was so true. There's no shortcut to building a legacy. It takes decades to hone one's craft.

Now that he has passed away, I find Kerry's words even more profound. It seems so unfair for artists to have to die to become valuable: inevitably, his art will start to become more precious and will have a higher price tag than it did during his seventy-eight years alive. The same was true of James Joyce back in the 1900s—no one took his work seriously. It took him sixteen years to write Finnegans Wake; his books were burned, and he died penniless.

One August morning, about five years after Kerry Hallam's "Art in the Garden" party, I found myself in the 'Sconset garden of a dear friend's home where I had come to connect with her and her mother. It was year seven into blACKbook, and I still didn't know how to make this business work. I had become an expert in marketing for others—selling Nantucket reds, and the Nantucket experience to tens of thousands of followers online—yet I was experiencing total burnout. I wanted to burn this blACKbook down to the ground. If you looked at my financial situation, I wasn't penniless but in crippling debt year after year: dirt poor in April and fake rich in August. It was always feast or famine, and even though I had a few bucks in the bank, I was spiritually broke.

As I drove down Milestone Road to meet up with my dear friend and her mother, I felt like I was going back into the womb. I was coming back home, as 'Sconset had always truly been my Happy Place. When I arrived at their sweet cottage in the center of West Sankaty, I took one sip of coffee before I broke down. Seeing this mother/daughter powerhouse who had such endless love and support for each other triggered a deep longing for my own mom. If she had seen me over the past half decade, she would have immediately known something was not right. But I had perfected the face on Instagram; the filter of living my best life was one I shined over myself daily. Fake it until you make it, right? NO! I don't believe that is right. I actually believe that's how so many of us live out a lie and become completely out of alignment in our mind, body, and spirit. I was sick of faking it.

My friend's mother is a total dynamo as far as women entrepreneurs are concerned. She started "85 Broads" that brought together the women of Goldman Sachs to discuss ways in which women in the financial world could be both fierce and feminine, be caring mothers and badasses on the stock floor. It was a Facebook-like group back in 1997, before Facebook even existed. Her venture capitalist firm was called Milestone Capital Management, which was crazy, since I drove down Milestone Road to get to her. If she added me to her womens group, it would become 86 Broads: in the restaurant world "86" means something that is out of stock, sold out, done for the night. That was me, the 86th Broad—about to drive my car into the ocean and never look back.

But they saw what everyone saw. "I was crushing it," they said. "Best [illegible] island. No one did it better, no one's story was more authentic." They knew firsthand: I had promoted my friend, the daughter, and her art business back in 2014 as well. She was the modern artist; she was making herself known through Instagram while offering traveling art lessons for children where she became both a big sister as well as an art teacher. Her art was sweet Wagoneers with her dog, Willis, at the Nantucket lighthouses. When I promoted her business on blACKbook, her entire career opened up. She became highly sought-after and now was booked a year in advance for her lessons. She also loved to give the credit back to me. Her mom had taught her the importance of the saying, "Never forget who took you to the dance."

But there was no dancing, no swaying, sashaying, or waltzing into what I was about to say to them. The jig was up.

"I want out," I confessed. "I don't want to do this anymore. I am so miserable. I hate being online. I hate watching people on their phones. I hate this blACKbook thing. And the worst part of all, I hate that I have nothing to show for it."

They waited for me to cry it out. Then, taking off her sunglasses, my friend's mom kindly looked at me and asked for another meeting, for me to bring my P&L sheets from the past three years. "Let me take a look at your numbers," she said, "and see what is really going on." I nodded, knowing that I had some major work to do.

First up, remind myself what P&L means. Second, talk to my accountant (also my friend) who used to tell me regularly to save more, spend less. A few days later, after I had printed out my 2017, 2018, and up to September 2019 profit and loss statements for the first time in seven years, I compared the past three years of my business. I couldn't believe what I saw: in 2017, I had netted over a quarter of a million between my blACKbook and Happy Place space. In 2018, I had brought in $200,000. But three-quarters of the way through 2019, I had brought in only $90,000 and I didn't have plans for bringing in any more money that fall. What had happened? Where had all of that passion gone? And more importantly, where the hell were the profits? This could have been called my loss sheet. When I slid the sheets across the table outside a little shop called Yummy that Tuesday afternoon, I felt completely yucky about what I was seeing. Apparently, she did too.

My friend's mom skimmed through the sheets, kept her sunglasses on, and said firmly yet with a sense of sadness: *"You so grossly undervalue yourself, it's scary."*

I nodded, tears streaming down my face. I didn't see myself clearly.

I knew how much I had cheapened myself since day one. I'd used being less expensive while being the best as my trademark—a total paradox in self-worth and the world in which we live.

Many men had tried to tell me this over the course of my lifetime of blACKbook, beginning with my father. "I don't get it, Holl," he would say to me, "you are sitting on a goldmine." The only other Nantucket internet marketing group in 2013 telling me to raise my rates. Yet for some reason, the only time my lack of self-worth ever came through, was from a queen, a sage, a mother, an entrepreneur, and a total badass.

"First things first," she said, "you have to get rid of that Happy Place store. And next, I am going to write you a check for $10,000. It's not a gift; it's a loan, but hopefully it will give you enough time this winter to sort your life out.

"You are a writer," she stated firmly. "Go own your words."

I am a writer. And writer's write.

Sometimes I come back to how long it has taken me to write this book. How to find value in all of these stories. Then I see my dearly departed friend Kerry and remember that although this book may one day launch out of nowhere, it took me thirty-nine years to write it.

And I know that I cannot go into this next chapter so grossly undervaluing that.

Lifting the Veil

December 2019

I often get sick around Christmas. For the entirety of my twenties, it was usually because I was hungover. After my mom died when I turned thirty, I used to get the sickness that comes with being burned out. I would over-busy myself for twelve months a year and then without fail, my mother's birthday would show up on December 20th and stop me in my tracks. As soon as I slowed down, I became ill, or perhaps I had been sick all along, but never allowed myself the space to heal.

Christmas Eve also doubles as my half birthday. On the eve of my thirty-six-and-a-half birthday, my face started to break out. At first, I thought these bumps were zits, bringing me back to a horrific time during my junior year in high school when I got bad acne all over my forehead and burned it all off with retin-A. Yuck. My forehead dandruff sloughed off in such a way that I can no longer understand how anyone thinks that stuff is okay to put on your skin. But this wasn't acne twenty years later. This was something that I couldn't hide: a rash above my left eye wrapped its way around the side of my face, reaching the top of my hairline, all on the left side only. It didn't really itch, but my eye had the feeling of an eyelash stuck in it. I started to WebMD myself and self-diagnosed myself with shingles, which is a rash on one side of the body that sort of looks like it might blister. A few extreme Google images did the trick for triggering a full-on panic attack.

You know what's so interesting about getting a rash on your face? It's that moment when you can't hide that something is not right with you. Usually, a rash might reveal itself somewhere that you could cover up, like some bad eczema on the elbows, or even an itch down there from too-tight leggings or a prolonged time in the bathing suit. But alas, here I am, on the eve of the big holiday that is supposed to be filled with good tidings and toasts to the most wonderful time of the year, and I feel like (and personally know that I look like) a big piece of burnt coal.

It comes as a bit of a surprise to me when I go back to what led me here. About six weeks earlier I had felt on top of the world. I, of course, was not home, I was in Bali where the weather is a balmy 80 degrees, where the restaurants are fueled by vegan-friendly food, and where the time comes and goes like the tide and the days mash together into one beautifully blissed-out holiday. I am not sure how or why this happens, but every time I come home from Bali, I get sick. Not just this one time with a rash, but the year before with a staph infection and a hemorrhoid. Or the second time when I came home with a UTI, or even the first time when I arrived back home with an altered state of consciousness. I couldn't handle getting back into my island life.

Every time I went to Bali, something shifted in me and every time I came back, whether mentally or emotionally or physically, something was released out of my system.

At this point I had been spending the last two years living at my sisters summer house on island. As the eldest of us three girls, Christina has a memory like a steel trap and often remembers way more than Sanna and I ever would. Being the first born is kind of like being an "elder"—and Christina had become a mother figure to me while I lived in her home. My sister is oh so generous in her offerings of truth, while once in a while, her delivery can leave much to be desired. I have heard it's not what you say but how you say it—tell someone to go to hell, in a kind way, and maybe they'll look forward to the trip. Christina does not offer that comfort ride on the road to the fiery den. She will often give it to you straight, with no chaser, and for a sensitive soul like me, her word medicine can go down like a warm shot of gin.

Christina's main topic of conversation this time around was that my rash was a made-up reaction to finding out from our aunt that our mom had herpes during our childhood. This news literally made me break out into a painful rash, and when I looked at WebMD for guidance, I intuitively chose shingles, not because I am so familiar with them but because shingles was also known as the *herpes* zoster.

The mind is a very powerful thing, they tell you. Could just hearing about a skin dis ease your mother had, cause you to break out in your own rash? I have an incredible knack for focusing on one thing until it drives me crazy or makes me crazy successful. After going to the ER twice on Christmas Eve, it turns out I was right.

It was shingles.

And I called that 2019's Christmas my Shingle Bell Rock.

But something was happening beyond those blisters, on a deeper level, in my mind, body, and spirit. I sensed a seismic shift coming; I just couldn't see it clearly yet. The whole left side of my body was breaking out in hives. My half-birthday present from the universe was lifting this veil over my left eye, for the year 2020 was to bring new clarity in ways I could not ever have imagined.

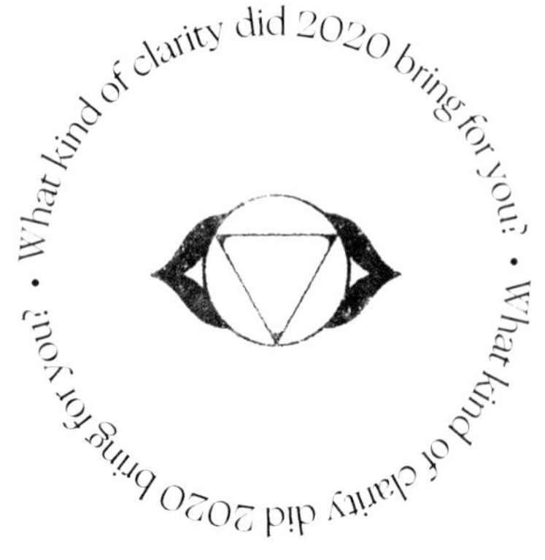

17.

Whatever We Resist, Persists

The Power

October 2018

The first time I realized I was powerful, I was thirty-five. It was almost Halloween, and I was in Bali wearing a white lace kimono, white bodysuit, and short jean shorts with my long blonde locks all beach-waved-out from being in a high bun for the past two days. I was dressed as a free spirit, and this was perfect, because it wasn't a costume. It is who I am at my core—a liberated woman on a spiritual journey in the heart of Ubud.

I was taking the Spiritual Awakening Course with my Teacher. I had already taken and passed this class back in April, but sometimes a little divine intervention shows up in the most familiar of places. I happened to be back in Bali six months later, continuing my healing, writing this book, and still trying to find myself. The two-day course happened to fall in the time that I was still at the Yoga Barn and the course just happened to be half-price if you had taken it before. I had asked my guides, during my two-day meditation course in the days prior, what to do. They told me to keep learning; keep being the student; keep doing the work. I took this as a sign to stay on the path and take the Oneness course again, to keep awakening this sunny spirit of mine.

I arrived with thirty other seekers—healing souls of all kinds trying to rid themselves of suffering. These were people from around the globe who told the same story in a different language: problems with mother, problems with substances, a life that had completely fallen off the rails, a father who had died, a relationship that had ended, a career that had to change. Something, dear God, *something* had to change. They didn't realize what they were in for during this Spiritual Awakening Course, but I did.

I had done the work back in the spring and it had changed my life. It was the message that I went home with: you have issues with your mother, you'll have issues with partners, both in life and in relationships; you'll have unnecessary health issues; you'll have connectivity problems. Problems with your father? Well, then you'll have issues with your self-worth, your career, and your finances. I had both: problems with my mom, who had passed on, and problems with Dad, a man who was very much alive.

The good news, my Teacher said, is that love can heal relationships at any stage: you can heal relationships with parents whether they are dead or alive. Love, it turns out, truly is a miracle.

During the first day of the course, we went around the circle and said our names, stated where we were from, what we were doing there, and why we were ready to spiritually awaken. I loved listening to everyone's stories. I had become quite detached from them, but still held such empathy for everyone alongside space for them to speak their truth. Once you get over the fact that everyone just wants to be seen, heard, understood, acknowledged—whatever it is—you realize we are all one. We are the same.

When it was my turn to speak, I felt like a pro. This was my third time introducing myself at one of these circles, and I'd prepped my mind to use my voice with alliterations to make my gift as a word artist stand out. I was addicted to the feelings that came from learning from my Teacher: my main reason for being in the class was to show him that I was a dedicated student, and I would do anything to take him and his teachings and his bright light to a little place across the pond called Nantucket. I knew that it wasn't enough to be on my own healing journey . . . it wasn't fun being in this light house all alone . . . I wanted him to illuminate everyone else, especially my family.

My Teacher told me the whole world was a family.

I smiled to seem like I agreed, but didn't buy that completely yet. I said that my three best teachers were my past, my parents, and him. They were what had changed my life. He smiled, but always kept his ego in check. There weren't enough compliments to make him forget that the most important words were the ones he told himself, the ones he spoke with his divine.

On that day, there was an active consciousness meditation, one that aligns the chakras and gets the root chakra to ground down so that we could all ground down in the space, crack open, and be able to align with our own truth, our own true light. I had done this before. I was the only returning student in the class. If you asked me, I had already passed with flying colors. That's the thing about learning . . . when you love the material, it doesn't matter what the class is and what you get in it . . . it only matters that you know that the knowledge changed your life. And a refresher course never hurt anybody, either.

Before the hour-long meditation began, my Teacher asks the class the same sequence of questions.

"Is anyone pregnant?"

The obligatory male class clown raised his hand, and my Teacher playfully asked how far along.

"Does anyone have any respiratory issues? Any asthma?"

The room went quiet. I thought about how my mom had three quarters of her right lung removed from one of her many tumors. Would she have raised her hand? Everyone in the class looked around without trying to make eye contact as not one of them raised their hand.

"How about heart conditions? Does anyone have any cardiac issues?"

I paused. Was it worth it? Did I want to raise my hand? Single myself out? Show that I have a leaky heart valve? Even though it was "fixed" in January, I was told that I would never fully heal from the disease, that it was a chronic illness. That "chronic" might have meant little or nothing to some, but for me it meant that I had a shadow of a heart disease following me around from start to finish.

Or did I?

I decided to raise my hand. I knew my Teacher knew. I understood that raising my hand was more about alerting the class than alerting him. I knew that raising my hand wasn't merely to call attention to myself. It was that my heart's rhythm was different from that of others. I had to be careful; show a bit of vulnerability. My most vital organ would be forever beating to a different drum, and that was okay.

My Teacher made eye contact with me as I put my hand back in my lap. He nodded, and then paused as he looked back at the class and said, "You know, Holly is very powerful."

My eyes watered and my heart pounded as the class members smiled and nodded their heads in agreement. They didn't know me from Eve . . . but he did. And he was the most powerful healer I had ever come into contact with. The mere touch of his hands to my head had made tears flow out of my eyes. The first question he ever asked me caused me to unravel my entire family's storied past and painful secrets. From much of my adult schooling, I knew two things: genius sees genius, and teachers like mine don't say things that they don't mean.

I decided at that moment that I was ready to adjust my healing journey, to pivot and take the new yellow brick road wherever it might lead. I was given a clue . . . a gift by another very powerful Teacher . . . that I am very powerful too.

I just have to figure out where this power is coming from.

The Voice

July 2019

Nantucket is home to one of the first green landfills. The way we sort trash is an art. In town, we have not one, but four trash barrels that live together in clusters. Each bin has a different colored hard hat that reads: glass, food/paper, aluminum, and plastic. You get very used to separating your garbage on this island. So much so, that when I travel and there's no recycling, I can't physically put a plastic water bottle in a trash bin. I will set it to the side of the trash bin. I guess I would rather go against the grain than go against what I actually believe in, which is high consciousness, especially in places of high consumption.

Back in 2016, one of the founders of our beloved island brewery approached me to ask if I would be interested in bringing a trash fashion show to Nantucket. The brewer had been in Kona, Hawaii, checking out a sister brewing company, when divine timing led him to witness what a Trashion Show could look like. Hawaii, like Nantucket, had to be extra careful with the ways it consumed.

As I have grown older, I have become fascinated with sustainability and how microcosms and resort populations keep their happy place clean. This work is not glamorous: it's not sipping magnums of Domaines Ott while beachside at the Galley or savoring littlenecks at our oyster bar, Cru. How we use those bottles and shells the second time around had become of high interest to me, although honestly, this awareness only came to serious light after I was illuminated by the brewer's experience in the Aloha state. The brewer knew that I had years of event production under my belt—from fashion shows on the beach, to pop-up fashion shows in art galleries, to organizing and executing numerous sipping and shopping events. He knew that I was the person who, in a very short time, could make his Trashion Show dream into a summer reality.

Anytime someone believed in me and the power of blACKbook, my ego soared. And when my ego soared, I could get literally anything and everything done. I could put a brick on the gas pedal and rock and roll at a rate that would make your head spin.

My three-person team plus the general manager of Cisco Brewers created the first Cisco Trashion Fashion Show in just three months' time. I persuaded three different salons to do the hair and makeup for a dozen models; we had a dozen outfits made from scratch to be worn on a makeshift runway in a red, white, and blue Americana beer boxed catwalk.

As usual, I had to over-deliver, so I committed to making two of the outfits as well as organizing the entire event. Our theme was plastic water bottles and Styrofoam. By the time my girls and I were able to create wearable trash, after executing the Trashion Show every single step of the way, I didn't have it in me to go all out with our look. So, we bought a case of water bottles; drank the water, then took off the labels, and grabbed a slip dress to connect all of that plastic. And the Styrofoam dress? Let's just say that was half-assed at best. I went to Stop and Shop, bought Styrofoam cups, and the girls and I took them apart to create another simple dress that we had copied from Pinterest.

The show was a huge hit. Everyone loved the concept. Some of the outfits were insanely creative and some of the looks were, let's just say, subpar; we will call those ours. And yet, the message was clear, it's time to wake up to our consumption patterns. It's time to get more conscious around how we recycle.

I organized the Trashion Show for three more years. Every summer that show became a bigger production. Every year, there was more coverage. Celebrities walked: El Pres from Barstool Sports made appearances in 2016 and 2018; a future Sports Illustrated Swimsuit cover model sported a blACKbook collage skirt in 2017. We added beach cleans prior to the Trashion Show: we would connect at a certain sandy shore on a Sunday and find trash on the beach that we would turn into outfits. After a few of our subpar designs, we had created a new rule by 2018: 80 percent of the outfit had to be made from recycled materials, hence the beach clean; 20 percent could be artificial or store-bought materials.

In 2019 things were shaping up to be our biggest year yet. The local magazine read worldwide had said it would be a sponsor and would write a feature about the Trashion Show ahead of time to build momentum for July's event. I was always especially pleased when another publication talked about what I did; much of the local media had looked at me like competition and would rarely write about what I created.

I waited anxiously for that summer issue to debut, thrilled finally to be getting coverage after years of hard labor. When it came out, I wasn't even on Nantucket—I was in Montana at a wedding—but I knew I could still get it online. Sitting at a small dive bar outside Big Sky, drinking margaritas while eating a greasy cheeseburger, I opened my email and saw the magazine had launched. My Partner was not on Facebook, not on Instagram, not into press, not into influencing, and still had an old-school email he made when he was eighteen, so he sure as hell was not into taking his work on vacation with him.

I, however, still had trouble separating work and play.

This Trashion Show was my best work on island, so I wanted to read what the writer wrote. When I found the feature, though, I had a sinking feeling upon first glance. From the title to the first photo, to the words that were strung together, something felt very off.

The header in bold letters said GETTING TRASHED, and under that title it stated "From Garbage to Gucci, Cisco is making recycling trendy again." The cover model, a gorgeous local girl who had been in all three Trashion Shows, was on the catwalk sporting a skimpy bikini covered in balloons found on the beach. The article described how the event began and gave credit where credit was due—to Cisco, and me, and our beloved emcee who was a teacher. But the writer wrote a sentence that pained me more than the sex-sells cover, more than the headline that was more trashy than classy. She said that, our first two years, we completely missed the point by making outfits out of new materials and acting like they were recycled. I couldn't get angry at her for including that information, as I was the one who told her that, in a casual way over coffee with the manager of Cisco. And this is how we learned the lesson of the 80/20 rule. But the way that the writer wrote the passage made me feel like I was being called out.

Because I was being called out and rightfully so. Because I don't always practice what I preach.

I sat in Big Sky with big tears coming down my face while my Partner, utterly perplexed, looked at me. "Why do you care?" he asked. "You know the event is amazing. You know it's more than these photos or off-putting headlines. *Why do you care so much about what other people write about you?"*

However, something very surreal happened a month later. It was the fourth annual Trashion Show, my senior year. All the outfits were senior superlatives; we had sold out of our tickets early; the day was blazing hot, and the models never looked better. This full-scale production was something I never had known was possible. I also knew that if I had been hit by a bus on the morning of the show, it would all fall apart—that was how indispensable I had made myself.

That was how much my ego was glued into every crevice.

After the show, I was on the mic doing my obligatory thank-yous and sharing my love for what we had created since 2016, when something moved its way up my throat and started speaking through me.

It was like an out-of-body experience: this voice within started saying things that weren't on my script. My circuits were scrambled, yet my voice was clear, firm, and completely empowered.

"This is my last year doing this show," I said. "We are definitely going to need some help for 2020. So, if you want to get involved, please let us know."

And that was it. I saw the brewer in the audience with a look of confusion on his face. Everyone else was giving a standing ovation, but he seemed stunned. The general manager came up to me after I had finished speaking and, putting her arm around my back, she said, "That will go down as the day that Holly broke up with Cisco on stage in front of everyone."

I nervously laughed and left quickly. Usually, I would stick around for a drink or two, but I was exhausted and elated, full of uncertainty as to how the hell that had just happened. Cisco Brewers is like the coolest kid in high school on Nantucket, and maybe I was one of the coolest girls alongside them, but that Trashion Show prom-like breakup wasn't my finest moment. What was coming out was what happens when you don't value yourself over the years. You get to a breaking point, and you lose it. Or in my case, you gain it—your sense of worth, your value in this world.

That next week I found one of the last letters my mom wrote to me. It was from six years before in July of 2013, and during that time I was into my second year of blACKbook. I was still bartending four nights a week and the blACKbook online platforms took up every waking hour of my life. My mom had written to me to tell me how proud she was of me, and she even wrote out the definition:

> PROUD
> 1. capable, good valiant feeling or showing pride such as
> a. having or displaying excessive self esteem
> b. much pleased
> c. having proper self-respect
>
> *("That's the best!!" Mom wrote after c.)*

A-ha! Proper Self-respect. That's what my voice was conveying.

It had become high time to toss energy out of my ego and trust my inner voice that had been lying dormant in me for so long.

Say What You Mean, Mean What You Say

November 2019

"You are going to have to say what I say and not think about it," the Healer told me as I lay on the bed in her healing sanctuary in Canggu, Bali. "Don't think about it. Don't put a story with it. I am just going to do this clearing alongside you, and I will hold space for whatever spirit needs to move out." The music got louder—an African drumming beat that felt tribal, that felt just as intense as what I was about to go through. Earlier, the sweet girl at the counter had told me that this Healer had just returned from a retreat and was extra powerful this week; I could feel it.

We had met the year before while I was in Bali on my first healing journey. After I wrote the chapter around the hardest thing that had happened in my family, I had a reiki session already scheduled with her. It was divinely timed, as if the Universe knew I was to be writing one of the most painful stories of my life. Moments after the writing was done, I was sent straight to the healing room.

My Healer gave me a beautiful session where I felt my body go limp after so many years of holding trauma in. She brought life from her palms into my body, and when we were finished, she let me rest as she looked at her notes. She told me that my throat chakra had just started to open up, but there was a lot of gray, murky vomit that lived below that cluttered my first four chakras. The 5th chakra had just opened a crack, but there was a lot of work still to be done.

She told me the words "teacher, teacher, teacher" kept coming up during the session. "You know you are a teacher, right?" she said. At that point, I didn't even know my left hand, let alone the left side of the body, represents the feminine, or that my right side representing the masculine had been completely out of balance, out of whack for my whole life. I thought of my favorite quote from *The War of Art*: "It's one thing to study war and another to live the warrior's life." I was a student of life; I was getting educated at the University of Broken Hearts. This was no four-year accredited university. This was a lifelong school of hard knocks.

That reiki session stayed with me, so, a year later, when I was back in Bali, I decided on my last day in my Happy Place that I would book a session with this special woman. I didn't ask for any particular treatment, I just left it up to a grab-bag offering. Turns out, I would be having a Shamanic womb clearing—one that I didn't ask for, but was spiritually destined to have. I arrived at her healing space wearing my favorite gold dress with no underwear and a bathing suit top. The dress skimmed my ankles and always made me feel feminine, and free.

As in many of my Bali days, I was at home in myself. I spent most of my days on these dirt streets walking aimlessly with no destination, truly being present in this journey. I loved Holly Bali. She embodied self-care, and she wrote and wrote and wrote and healed and healed and healed. So, when I went to see my Healer on that final Bali day, she had me on her table and had her hand over my womb space over that golden dress.

"You have to just trust me," she said. "Just say what I say over and over again until it moves from your womb and out of our mouth."

I felt a bit uneasy, as if she'd taken me to an edge of a cliff and said, "Close your eyes and jump: trust me." It's like, who the hell are you again, and do you have a parachute? But oftentimes during spiritual moments, you realize that you have the parachute the entire time—you just have to believe it. So, I took a few deep breaths, closed my eyes, and followed my healer's words.

"I hate you," she said, which startled me. "Say, 'I hate you.' Say it. Keep saying it, 'I hate you, I hate you, I hate you!'"

I have always been good at following directions, so I did as I was told. I said it quietly, almost methodically, like I was putting an equation together. I + Hate = You. She pushed me: "Scream it like you mean it, 'I hate you, hate you!' Get it out! Get the rage going! Feel the anger!"

I did as I was told. I got that fire in my belly through my nose-only breathwork as my voice shifted and became more defiant. "I HATE YOU! I HATE YOU! I HATE YOU!" It was like a wheel spinning, totally out of control, no brakes on this one. The bellows came deep from within my womb, traveled through my stomach, piercing through my heart, almost dry heaving out of my mouth as I screamed it in a way that would wake neighbors.

"I HATE YOU! I HATE YOU! I HATE YOU!"

My eyes burst open and lava-like tears spewed out; my body convulsed as the words left my mouth, and I felt as though I had been through another exorcism. By the time I had calmed down, I was sobbing, feeling sick and light at the same time. The tribal music changed to "A Beautiful Chorus"—the harmony settling in after the harm.

One of the things I prided myself on most as a kid was that I never told my mother I hated her. Although I had heard both my sisters say it, I could never say those three words out loud to her. I actually couldn't remember a time telling anyone I hated them.

So, wait: *then where the hell is all of this hate coming from?*

18.

Wholeheartedly

The University of Broken Hearts

April 8th, 2018

I opened a Facebook message from a girl I had not spoken to in years. She wrote, *"I finally get it. I know what you've been talking about now. I lost my mom."* And then she wrote something that connected my heart to my head . . . from this earth to another place:

"I've come to realize that we teach people how to birth babies, but we don't teach people how to deal with death, which is strange, because death is a birthing of sorts—from the physical world to the spiritual one."

So, it's now that we have to go back to class, to the school of grief.

My mother's last words have been haunting me since the day I heard them. I came up from Nantucket to Vermont on April 7th, 2014, and barely recognized her. She was a mere shell of herself, yet seemed so clear as she called me into her room and asked, "Did you write something?" And as I shook my head, confused, she paused and said, "Don't worry, you will."

She passed away the next morning.

Below is one of the hardest pieces I have ever written and one of the most heartfelt truths I have ever found. So, for all those who have ever lost someone, and especially to those who have lost a parent, I dedicate this to you.

After the profound death of a loved one, you are unknowingly accepted and unwillingly enrolled into a School of Hard Knocks. Like all of those before you, you arrive to this campus anxious and disoriented, angry, and feeling a new sense of the word sad. And I'm sorry, but we can't harp on what happened to get you here... school is about to start and time stands still for no one.

So welcome, students . . . to The University of Broken Hearts.

FRESHMAN YEAR: THE YEAR OF FIRSTS

You arrive at the University of Broken Hearts, well, broken. And this place is just as awkward as it is uncomfortable. You are constantly crying at the most inopportune moments, and you are feeling a serious disdain for people who just keep going along in their days, acting as though all is well and nothing has happened. (Don't they realize that the most important person in your life just died!?!)

A heavy sadness has found its way inside of you and even if you tried, you could not explain this weight to anyone. This is one thing that can only be deeply felt. Your freshman year is dedicated to going through the motions. Many freshmen choose vices over classes as numbing our pain becomes like a shortcut to pass the time. Other students choose to not talk at all . . . hoping to blend in, affirming "I'm fine" so many times every day that even they end up believing it. Most undergrads at the University of Broken Hearts can barely show up for Grief 101. The idea of having to go through a full year of firsts without their person just sounds impossible.

But the year of firsts begins before you even realize it's happening. First Mother's Day without sending her a card. First birthday without her voice singing on your voicemail. First Halloween without her telling you how much she hated that holiday. First Thanksgiving without being able to tell her how thankful you were for her health. Her first birthday is quickly followed by your first Christmas without her. The first grandchild born that she doesn't get to greet. And finally, we arrive at the first anniversary of her passing. It is only then that we take comfort in the fact that enough time has passed, and we realize we are still here.

We are still alive.

And it's a Christmas miracle.

We toast with tears as we try so hard to push forward. That excruciating year of firsts is now behind us. Life went on . . . and somehow, so did we.

And the best part is that you never have to relive that year of firsts again.

SOPHOMORE YEAR: THE MERRY-GO-ROUND

Our sophomore year arrives, and we are familiar with the University of Broken Hearts campus. There's a large merry-go-round in the center of the school, and we just walk by and work around it. We busy ourselves to drown out the overwhelming feeling of loss we still find inside us.

Our sophomore slump creeps up on us when we realize that the heavy weight inside of us is the shadow of our lost one. We have survivor's remorse and are so preoccupied with death that we are forgetting to live. Grief 202 focuses on how to rid yourself of that heavy weight and teaches us how grief is like a wave . . . you can stay put and continue to let the waves almost drown you . . . or you can release that weight, head to higher ground, and get on the merry-go-round with everyone else.

We start seeing the need to build up a community around us again. We realize that living is not as much fun to do all on our own. We begin to change the people we spend time with. We recognize the incoming freshman class and give them a shout that things may suck for a little while . . . but they'll get past it. (And then we feel grateful knowing that our own year of firsts is far behind us.)

One spring day at the end of your second year, an upperclassman sees you on the sidelines, reaches out her hand and pulls you up. All of a sudden, your view has changed, and everything seems a little brighter. Before you can digest the kind act, you're spinning round . . . You're back on the merry-go-round! And damn, does it feel good to be among the living again.

JUNIOR YEAR: LIFE AFTER DEATH EYES

By your third year, your classes have intensified, and as they teach you a deeper understanding of loss, you begin to see life with more clarity. During your junior year, you start to simply be grateful for the time you had with your loved one and you begin to shift your perspective regarding what it means to experience profound loss. Even though you still deeply miss that person every day, in Grief 303 you are recognizing that their death was not your end. That even though they may be gone, somehow, in a spiritual way, they are very much still here and have just been transformed.

The University of Broken Hearts has formed some of your biggest opinions on the world . . . and it's helped you to become more open. So much so, that you take some of your junior year abroad. You go and see and feel and experience the world again. You can't believe it, but while away you realize the University of Broken Hearts has now become your comfort zone. Through your junior thesis on time, you recognize that life is precious, and every day is a gift, not a given. You now know that growing older is a privilege denied to many and you are here and that is what counts. One morning, you wake up and everything looks different. You quite literally have new vision. Somehow you begin to see a yellow butterfly everywhere.

You've been granted life after death eyes and through this superpower, you can see that the one you lost is actually found, for they live everywhere. They are listening to you. They are watching over you. They are protecting you. That's why you get these new eyes. You learned how to change your perspective. This is your gift for completing your junior year. For sticking through it. For keeping on the path and for holding on to hope. For continuing to show up in this world, and for showing up for yourself.

SENIOR YEAR: A-HA!

And here we arrive at our senior year, four years post a profound loss and, gosh, look at ya. Still alive. Still kicking. Still keepin' on, keepin' on. You don't fully realize it, but you are nearing the end of school as you can't stay at this university forever—you're actually beginning to outgrow it. You've passed all the Grief courses and could go through your Year of Firsts with your new eyes closed. It's time for your final exam.

They ask you but one question.

How have you healed?

Hmph. That's a doozy. Let me think. Well, there's a lot of empathy and compassion for myself as I reflect on my Year of Firsts. (When I used to drown my sorrows in bottomless wine glasses instead of hydrating my mind and fueling my soul.) I don't spend nearly as much time on the Broken Hearts campus, but every once in a while, I find it my civic duty to mentor a freshman or to give a hand to someone who needs to get back on the merry-go-round. I've found joy in being of service to others—I've found my purpose in that. Death is still a total mystery to me . . . but now I'm not seeking to crack that riddle. I'm learning to love the unknown.

I look back, thinking what a true gift my time at Broken Hearts was—how lucky I was to love a mother so deeply that it took me four years to figure out how to wholeheartedly move on after her death.

Aha! There it is.

Wholeheartedly.

My whole heart. I'm feeling it again. It's no longer broken. I took the time for life to process. That yellow butterfly that's been chasing me this entire way was her! Letting me know that when I'm ready . . . I can start my new journey and fly away too.

GRADUATION: THE BIG REVEAL

It's graduation day at the University of Broken Hearts . . . and today I get to be with everyone again. I now see the world with my Life After Death Eyes, and when I look up at the bright sky, I see my audience is all my loved ones who have passed on. They are beaming, so proud of me for persevering. As I look up at everyone, you, Mom, hand down my diploma. And it reads: "I hereby declare Holly Finigan a graduate of the University of Awoken Hearts."

That's when I realized there's no such thing as the University of Broken Hearts! In fact, after a profound loss, each and every one of us is lovingly accepted into a College of Healing. Turns out, the University of Broken Hearts was just a nickname given by some sad freshman a long time ago . . . a story no one truly remembers but a name that the college chooses not to shake for the way it puts the new kids at ease.

So today and from here on out . . . I decide it's time to fly on . . . wholeheartedly.

Here's lookin' at you, Ruth. And thank you . . . for everything.

P.S. I hear you.

You're saying you're scared.

You're saying this pain is all too much.

You're telling me that you don't think that you'll be able to make it through this school. And to that, we say . . . *"Don't worry, you will."*

Awareness is the New Wellness

October 2019

"You are never too old to be unaware," the woman said. Her whole left side was bruised. She had fallen down a flight of stairs while looking down at her phone. Instead of missing a text, she had missed a step and tumbled down the cement, landing hard on the floor. She was lucky to be alive. When she showed me her stomach, my knees got weak.

We had been sitting for eight hours a day in our Grand Master Reiki Class with our Teacher in Bali. She was older, German, and worked as a nurse. Maybe that was how she was able to withstand the pain. She had been so attentive all week. I saw her shift in her seated position once in a while, but never once heard her complain, even though her body had been battered that whole time. Even though she had been practicing Reiki on others, I wished I could have had her sit on the bed and given her that energy back. This was it—*the universal life force energy, Reiki.*

I was taking a five-day intensive course given by my Teacher. It was my fourth time in Bali in just eighteen months, and I had no idea why I was taking this course, except for the fact that I would have taken any class my Teacher offered.

Reiki is an intuitive healing experience—a spiritually guided practice with the intention of healing. It uses the hands as extensions of the heart to share universal life force energy. What we first have to understand is that we all have this life force energy. Anyone can learn to use it, and it can never do harm. Reiki is passed down through attunement, and when you are giving, you will be guided, as Reiki has a mind of its own. You become the hollow bone through which the energy flows. The heart, the crown, and the palm chakras open and you just want to share that love. Reiki is for those who want to be joyful, loving, and free—just know you have to ask permission before you give it.

Reiki enhances meditation; it illuminates clarity and aids focus. It dissolves emotional blocks. They say one hour of Reiki is equivalent to three to four hours of deep sleep.

Over the days of my training, I discovered the gold thread to understand why I was there. I could *write* with Reiki, and thus honor this process, knowing that the greatest gift I could ever give the world was through my hands . . . by writing loving truth.

But first? I needed to practice what I preached. I needed to learn awareness and have patience. I had to put down my phone, look up, and remember that you are never too young to start becoming more aware.

The Graceful Dismount

December 2019

And then one day, I just stopped. Like it was something out of *Forrest Gump*. You remember that one, right? When Tom Hanks was running and running and running and then everyone started to run with him, and he did all the things and saw all the places and was so simply deep with his thoughts, like the bumper sticker "shit happens." And then one day, after running for three years, two months, fourteen days and sixteen hours, with all these people running and following him, he just stopped. Turned around, and looked at everyone and no one as he said, "I'm pretty tired. Think I'll go home now."

This is how I felt at the end of my blACKbook career—aware of the idea that there was an end of me online as I knew her. One day, I got heart surgery and something in me awakened. *I'm pretty tired. Think I'll just embody my actual body instead of living out a digital one.*

One of my mentors and dearest friends on Nantucket is a thirty-plus-year restaurateur on the island. I worked for her back in 2010 at her restaurant Corazon Del Mar, which translates to "in the heart of the sea." During that time in my life, I was drinking enough tequila to kill a gorilla. Because of that, she and I had more of a working relationship than a friendship. But after my mom died, after my heart surgery and the ways in which my own heart flowered, this extraordinarily talented woman took me under her wing and talked me through how to leave things.

"It's all about the graceful dismount," she'd preach. "All about leaving on your best day." In the restaurant industry you rarely see this kind of exit. Usually, people on Nantucket don't know how to gracefully dismount, so they leave the island with guns blazing, their middle fingers up in the air, promising never to return.

I had been desperately trying to reinvent myself after heart surgery, but how? How can I get out of being @nantucketblackbook and start actually being me? She coached me on the transition. It was slow and steady work with a tried-and-true visionary. *I had to leave on my best day.* I couldn't just drop everyone who had been following me; *I had to take them with me.*

But what happened when I finally changed my name on Instagram? When I finally stopped being @nantucketblackbook and actually became @hollyruthfinigan?

I lost five thousand followers almost immediately.

But you know what? *None of that mattered.*

Because what I lost was nothing compared to what I was about to gain.

For after all that running around, blogging, Facebooking, tweeting, pinning, and 'gramming . . . there I was, finally ready to come home— and home is where my heart is.

Forgiveness - Part I

January 2020

When I was twenty-five, I got Maui'ed. By that, I mean my Kiwi boyfriend and I moved to Hawaii, as it was perfectly equidistant between his home in New Zealand and mine in New England. Sometimes when I tell people about how I lived my life in my twenties, I almost can't believe how brave I was to spin the globe constantly and fearlessly insert myself into new locations.

I have always known Nantucket is a tough place to break into. The only thing that makes you successful on this island is time, and even on one of the wealthiest islands in the world, no one can buy that. But if I thought it was hard to become a part of the Grey Lady community on the East Coast, I had no idea how difficult it would be to become part of this little western Hawaiian island. From the beginning, people were weary of me when we moved to the whaling village of Lahaina. As soon as I said I spent my summers on Nantucket, my coworkers knew it didn't matter how much Aloha I tried to exude: it was clear to them I would be going back home eventually. But for the five months that my Kiwi and I lived there, it was like a honeymoon for us—so effortless, that I felt like Maui had been my home in another life.

Years later, during my meditation teacher training in Bali, I learned Ho'oponopono, the Hawaiian forgiveness meditation, and felt an immediate connection. . . almost as though this wasn't the first time that I had learned this prayer. To do the meditation, you picture someone in your third eye who needs your forgiveness and then you say:

I Am Sorry.
Please Forgive Me.
I Love You.
Thank You.

So, as I intentionally dismounted from the Nantucket blACKbook in 2020, I took a piece of this Ho'oponopono with me. With a new year on the horizon, as I consciously decided to break up with one of the most intense relationships I'd ever have, I sat on my favorite beach in 'Sconset and did what I always did: I wrote a letter. So, without further ado, a letter of admiration, gratitude, and forgiveness to my first digital love, to my blACKbook—

Dear Nantucket blACKbook,

I am sorry. I am sorry for putting so much power in the hands of other people who don't have our best intentions. I am sorry that I abused you too much in the beginning, and I am sorry I left you out to dry to be alone in the end. I am so sorry I didn't see all of our power clearly until now.

Please forgive me. Please forgive me when I let people disparage you on comedy stages and Facebook pages, and I didn't stand up for you when I had the chance. Please forgive me when I used you to get out of my relationship. Please forgive me for when I changed our name on Instagram and for when that guy took your handle and tried to make you into a parody account.

I love you. I love you for giving me the ability to share my love of Nantucket with the world. I love you for helping me perfect storytelling through 2200 characters in an Instagram post. I love you for helping me grow a thick skin, and I love you for making me realize it doesn't matter what anyone else sees of me as long as I see myself clearly.

Thank you, blACKbook. Thank you for being there for me when my mom died. Thank you for getting me out of the bar business. Thank you for helping me see the power of global connection on the internet. Thank you for helping me see the world. Thank you for Bali, for Virgin Gorda, for Anguilla, for Saint Barths, for Kennebunkport, for Newport, for Stowe, thank you for Doha, Qatar. Thank you for the opportunity to give so many other people joy on a daily basis with #blACKbookthoughts and for the ability to raise up so many brands and businesses and non-profits over the course of eight years.

Thank you for us, blACKbook. We are a great team. And it doesn't matter what anyone else says.

Because I believe we are gold, blACKbook.

Solid gold.

Forgiveness - Part II

February 2018

Have you ever had a past love whom you needed to thank, but you didn't know how to do it? BF and I got together after my heart surgery, and I felt like my heart broke for a second time after we connected. But was my heart breaking? Or finally coming back together again? Love works in such mysterious ways.

* * * * *

We met up . . . eighteen months post breakup and the coveted ninety minutes together flew by in ten. The laughs were genuine, and the conversation flowed like a river with an occasional quiet moment that led my conscience to react: is this it? Are we done?

Not yet, I thought. Just let me ask one more question about your mom. And get one more recap about your best friend's wedding. Let me tell you quickly about my Bestie and her baby. Let's have one more skip down memory lane . . . please, I'm not ready to go back to doing this all by myself. Not just yet.

But eighteen months later, it's too easy to focus on all the good times. Too easy to feel a sense of longing after and not hard enough to question everything that happened before. It becomes too easy to stroll down that terribly inviting (and ultimately crippling) road called "What If."

But that is not why I asked for this meeting. You don't catch up this far along down the rocky road for a cheap fix, a quick hookup, or even to talk about the way it could've been. You do this with the best intention for each other. Hell, I promise I'm not trying to put an axe into your current stability.

But damn, it felt nice to see you. It made me so happy to share in moments of sincere laughter together. And hey, there's no denying that you look good. Sure, a bit older, but with hints of your fountain of youth. In my eyes, you're still that same sweet guy that I picked up straight off the slow boat, eight years ago this April.

"I need to thank you," I started. We were veering toward the end of our conversation. The hour-and-a-half was coming to a close and I needed to make sure I told you what I had felt every day for the past year. But as soon as I said thank you, those silent tears began to slide down my cheeks . . . and when they came, you didn't speak. You were always so good at that—being able to say so little and make me feel so much.

I couldn't finish my gratitude. Each tear shed was like a testament to every moment you stood by my side. Through the hardships of the beginning of blACKbook. Through the loss of my beloved mother. Through the busyness that I drowned myself in for years after, incapable of slowing down for the fear of having to face my shadow. Each tear was for every memory that you made with me as we journeyed toward each becoming our own person. Tears that taught me how we had been walking on an unmarked path for so long that we got lost, and in that darkness, we parted ways.

But silly me to even try to just say thank you. That type of gratitude can never be spoken or even defined. It can only be felt within the heart.

Our oh-so-familiar minute-long hug hurt just as much as it healed. Our meet-up was so easy while it was happening, yet felt bittersweet when left. How can such short moments in time be so double-edged? You can't make yourself feel what I felt. Those years of our lives as a couple, dedicating our time together in hopes of bettering the other person . . . it was all a gift.

So, in closing, let me try this again. I just needed to say . . .

I am sorry.
Please forgive me.
I love you.
And thank you. . .
For everything.

FREEDOM

November 2019

"Take what you need," the flyer said, and three little pieces of paper hung below. It reminded me of what a twelve-year old girl would put up for her summer babysitting services, her number to be ripped off the bottom. I was at Bali Buddha, like a boutique Whole Foods, in the heart of this Indonesian island. When I travel, I love to be both completely out of my comfort zone and surrounded by a thing or two that keep me extra comfy. So, shopping at this pricey grocery mart brought me back to the feeling of being at Erewhon Market in Venice, California, a time in my life where I felt completely at peace and in my element in November of 2016.

Fast forward two years. It's November of 2018 and I am writing this book while righting the stories of healing the relationships with my past and my parents. Being the middle daughter of a divorce made me into a sunny and funny, likable kid who could adapt easily. But it also made me the ultimate people pleaser, trying to satisfy both my mom and dad on every other weekend. I grew into a high functioning adult, with my circuits scrambled, thinking that only when other people were happy, could I be happy, too.

Back to the sign . . . the three words below "Take what you need" read: STRENGTH, PEACE, and FREEDOM.

I immediately went to pull on STRENGTH; courage and strength were what my mom asked us to pray for right before she passed. But I guess I wasn't feeling it that day as I didn't even have the strength to rip the word off properly. I looked at the next word, PEACE, and thought about when I gave my mom the Proust Questionnaire and asked her how she wanted to die. She answered, "peacefully."

Shaking myself out of that last image, I remembered that last scene with my mom, when a bright light shone into the room, the moment that she took her last breath. It seemed a sign of something higher, a light illuminating from above, a story of endings and beginnings, a chance to start over.

All that was left was that sacred F word that I had been seeking for so long.

As I ripped off the word FREEDOM, the shiverees came back into my body; the sun shone bright on the crown of my head, and it was there that I felt it.

And I know what I have to do . . .

I am sorry, Mom.
Please forgive me, Mom.
I love you, Mom.
Thank you, Mom.

19.

This Shit Happens For You

The Shitty Truth

You know what's so often excruciatingly uncomfortable but at the same time extraordinarily satisfying? A huge bowel movement.

This is what we call a release. It's a purging . . . so you can purify. Before, you feel like it's all bottled up and about to explode. After, you feel so much lighter and satisfied. And no, I can't sugarcoat this: the truth of BMs is they literally do stink.

You feel like sometimes you might both cry and puke right before it happens. You may have to go out of your way to find a place to release, and that place may not be your number-one choice, but sometimes you can't have the number-one choice when it comes to the truth of the number-two business.

I once saw this meme that read: "People say love is the best feeling. But I think the best feeling is finding a toilet when you have diarrhea." Or, as my old boss said to me, walking by the bar after he destroyed the single-stall washroom at work: "Honey, I don't eat roses." But let's leave the thorns and get to the flower of the matter . . . that feeling of knowing it's out of you. Ahhh, that is what we call the blissful bowel. And guess what? The same blissful feeling comes after a big emotional release, after you have talked about the hard stuff. Because the truth is we can't avoid the truth. No matter how hard we clench our butt cheeks and try, eventually what's in us will find a way out.

I remember watching *Schindler's List* in seventh grade and, aside from the entirety of the movie, which would stay with every impressionable mind at any age, I will never forget the scene where that sweet little boy, trying to outrun the Nazis, jumped into the outhouse. He literally escaped a hell by being willing to sit in everyone else's shit. I wondered, is this also what it feels like to release the stuff no one wants to talk about? Is this what it feels like, releasing the shitty truth from when you were a kid?

It happened in other movies too, like when Tim Robbins was willing to crawl through a half mile of sewage to escape prison in *The Shawshank Redemption*. Sure, it was tough to stomach as the audience watches him puke while crawling through the tight tunnel, but the ending moment, when he finally got spit out onto the land during that rainstorm with his arms outstretched—that was one of the most emotional connections I've ever had to a film. It showed me what freedom looks like from the other side.

Or how about that scene in *Bridesmaids*, when they all ate some spoiled meat and got so sick at the high-end bridal shop that they terrorized the place with their bowel movements? From the toilets, to the sinks, to the bride escaping that scene in a wedding dress only to find herself going #2 in the middle of the city street? Sure, it was horrifyingly funny, but also heartbreakingly relatable, because that's life. Life can be pretty shitty, but, hot damn! Life can be pure laughter until you cry for joy, too.

When my three-year-old nephew has to go to the bathroom, he takes his tiny Superman briefs off and sits on the porcelain god like he's going to battle. A minute later, he may find himself in some constipated discomfort. "Sumthins hurtin' me," he'll roar as things start to shift. "Sumthins hurtin' me!" He'll get really impatient. He'll scrunch his whole face together and put his hands into fists as he yells, "Come on! Come on!" And when it's all over, he simply smiles. "Raise your hand if you want to wipe my butt!" he yells cheekily to anyone in earshot. He gets off the toilet and with no sense of judgment, stares deep into the bowl filled with his perfect BM. As he joyously flushes it all down, he grins like he's won first prize. "Big Daddy poop," he declares. Never once does he bring that BM in the bathroom back up. He leads his life wholeheartedly until it's time for the next bodily battle, which he never denies.

That, my friends, is a blissful bowel.

So, are you ready for a big pile of shit? Ready to swim in some unfavorable truths? I gotta warn you, this may make you super uncomfortable. This might make you angry, and it may make you cry.

But let me tell you, after you deal with the stories and the trauma, after you sit in your regret, forgive yourself, and accept the filthy truth, it is then that you'll know the feeling of bliss.

Let's take a break from movie night, and all this bathroom talk, and let this story air out. I have a question: does the shitty stuff in life happen to you or for you?

Let's begin again.

The Unconscious Mind

May 2021

Dear Mom,

I am writing this from a playroom in Concord, and you know this neighborhood; you had a playroom in this town as well. You raised us girlie girls here until we were three, six, and eight. Being back here is kind of surreal because now, thirty-two years later, baby Sanna has just moved back to this town, and she lives a hundred yards from where we first did. She now has two kids. They are one and four, and sometimes it makes me feel very sad that you never got to meet either of them. But alas, no dwelling on the facts of life. I mean, we all still carry a bit of each other. Older sister Christina's daughters are Ava Page and Hope Ruth; one shares your middle name and the other has your name as her middle name. I am so grateful that you at least got to meet Ava. You said your favorite occupation was being a grandmother, which is great, because oftentimes the things that don't pay us any money are the things we are meant to do in life.

Speaking of life, you know I have been taking all of those courses with my Teacher in Bali—those eight baby steps to a higher consciousness. My Teacher is often-times childlike in the way that he laughs and makes fun of himself. Yet, at the same time, he goes very deep with each and every one of us, making us take responsibility for our lives and recognize how to make the unconscious conscious.

Did you ever know about the unconscious mind, Mom? It's so much more powerful than the conscious mind. From the way it stores memories and how fast it works, this supercomputer in the mind is known for three things: a repetitive, compulsive, destructive thought pattern. The conscious mind is repetitive and compulsive as well, but its thoughts are constructive. During my Teacher's course, the fourth baby step is the most important: it's a deep-dive meditation into healing the relationship with our parents. It's where the unconscious mind becomes conscious. I deeply connected with you the first time I did this. My Teacher takes us on a guided meditation around letting go of whatever it is we are mad at our parents about.

When I saw your face, tears poured out of my closed eyes, and I shook, and I finally spoke aloud . . .

Mom, how could you ever have let him back into our house?

Everything flowed out after that: the anger, the sadness, the words of the traumatized nine-year-old child that had been living in me for so long—afraid to say the one thing to you that had trapped me in my unconscious for twenty-five years. But that's the thing, Mom . . . as soon as I said it, as soon as I let it out, a feeling of freedom and lightness washed over me.

You know I have been trying to write this book for almost a decade, but it is so painful to bring up these stories from childhood. I used to say, I couldn't write this book because the story would kill you. In some weird, wild way, I am figuring out that it kind of did. But, Mom, my Teacher also loves to ask: what is the purpose of life? He will present the question, then, as people answer happiness, love, family, to find yourself, he smiles and nods at each one, always asking, is there anyone else? Often, he will stump us all.

"The purpose of life is to live!" he'll say in a joyous and life-affirming way. My Teacher says that he is playfully serious and seriously playful. I love that about him; I aspire to be like that.

So, as I said to you in the beginning, I am writing this from the playroom of your grandson's house. I have to do it at 6:30 a.m. because James Jack will wake up at any second, and he has been looking forward to having his auntie, Holly Ruth, to play with. You know he is four years old, just about to enter into his heart chakra growth period. I want to make sure that he lives with an open one.

For I think it's my real, true occupation in life, to help people live from the heart. I'm not sure if there's any money in that. But it doesn't matter, because, just like being a grandmother, it's priceless.

Wholeheartedly,

Holly

Snaking The Drain

The only regret I have when it comes to my mother is one that happened on her fifty-eighth birthday.

This is quite strange because she had been dead for three-and-a-half years, and most people's regrets with others seem to be about the things that they did while living.

My only regret when it comes to my mother is the fact that I didn't share her regret when I had the opportunity to do so. I was in Venice, California, and it was December 20th. I always loved to pay tribute to my mom on the days of her arrival and departure. I liked giving people a subtle reminder that life is so precious we should appreciate what we have while we have it.

One day late in March of 2014, I was reading the back page of a *Vanity Fair* magazine in the hospital and pulled out the Proust Questionnaire—twenty or so questions that the magazine asks some smug, hilarious, or enlightened celebrity each month. I wanted to give my mom the same questions. I had heard from our hospice nurse that patients were at their most clear at death, so I believed there was no reason for her to lie. Her answers were strikingly simple and, later on, quite profound. I loved her responses because they put so much into perspective for me and reading them three years later in 2017, I decided to share them with my Instagram and Facebook following in hopes that people would see how kind and inspiring and beautiful my mother had been, in hopes that I could keep that perfect memory of her alive.

But my regret. Oh, yes: take this to the grave, I cannot. The one question that I omitted from that post was the most important one to her and to our family. "What is your greatest regret?" I had asked her.

She looked away from me after I spoke and stared out the window. Without hesitating, she responded, "My second marriage."

This was, of course, her regret. It was, if you ask me, her cancer. I told myself I didn't put it in the post because most people would think she was talking about my stepdad, her life partner, Steve. They had been together for twenty years and were the best of friends. I didn't want to have to explain it was not him; most people didn't know that Steve was my mother's third husband, that between my dad and Steve there was her Second Husband.

That's because we were never allowed to talk about her Second Husband.

That's because he is a child molester.

That's because our mother was so guilt-ridden by the action of marrying this man and bringing him into our lives. That's because she was so ashamed that she allowed him back into the house even after my sister told her about the sexual abuse, and shamed further because she silenced us, making us promise that we wouldn't tell our dad in fear that he would take us away. That's because our mother waited to divorce her Second Husband until six months later to let the dust settle.

I believe these guilt and shame emotions manifested in her . . . in the form of cancer. It began in 2002 in her uterus and left her with the first punishment: a full hysterectomy. You put your kids in danger? Then you shall have no more kids. After that, for eight years she was "cancer-free." Still no talk of her regret. By 2010 it was a grapefruit-sized tumor on her right lung. The next punishment: you don't tell the truth? Then we'll be removing half of that lung. Now every time you breathe, you will think of this, spirit was telling her. And then for years after that it was small tumors that erupted like pesky reminders: an egg on her back, a golf ball on her rear, another egg on her thigh. Deal with it, the cancer was saying. Let it go. Don't hold on to that shit anymore. But my mother—I don't think she had it in her to face the guilt and shame. She just had the courage to tell me on her deathbed that one thing that she never accepted, that she never forgave herself for.

And I wasn't brave enough to share her truth when given the opportunity to do so. She had finally admitted it to me, but it took me another five years to truly accept it, to forgive it, to tell the truth.

So here it is.

Our mother unknowingly married a child molester. He sexually abused my sister and then he haunted us like a living ghost for years. The only person who was protected after the shocking event . . . was him. Twenty-nine years later my mother's regret was to be passed down to my sisters and me like a torch.

But that's the thing about regret; it doesn't scare you as much once you wholeheartedly admit it. It becomes just another truth in your book of suffering and healing.

So, it is with great love, forgiveness, and acceptance that I share with you for the first time ... my mother ... in her own words.

Here's to you, Ruth—

What is your idea of perfect happiness? Ten Bay beach with my daughters.

What is your greatest fear? Dying in pain.

What historical figure do you most identify with? Oh, jeez, that's a doozy. I'd like to have a thoughtful answer.

What trait do you most deplore in yourself? Over-kindness.

What is your greatest extravagance? This Izzy & Fresh lipstick.

What is your favorite journey? The one on which I am about to embark.

On what occasion do you lie? To spare someone's feelings.

Which words or phrases do you most overuse? Hot Dog.

What or who is the greatest love of your life? My children and my husband.

When and where were you happiest? Paddling up the Assabet River in Concord.

Which talent would you like to have? I'd like to be great at dancing.

What is your greatest regret? My second marriage.

What is your current state of mind? A little anxious.

If you could change one thing about your family, what would that be? Nothing. Nothing.

What do you consider your greatest achievement? Winning the 1976 badminton all-star championship. But seriously, raising three of the most wonderful women in the world. Bright, funny, good women.

If you were to die and come back as a person or thing, what would it be? I'd like to come back as a piece of beach in Eleuthera.

Where would you like to live? Woodstock, Vermont.

What is your favorite occupation? Grandmother.

What is your most marked characteristic? The cleft in my chin.

What do you most value in your friends? Honesty.

Who is your favorite hero of Fiction? Holden Caulfield. Oh no, I mean Owen Meany. Rats!

Who is your hero in real life? Oh, that's a doozy. Tina Turner.

What is it that you most dislike? Insincerity.

How would you like to die? Peacefully.

What is your life's motto? To Thine Own Self Be True

What regrets do your parents have? • What regrets do you have? • What is your family's shitty truth? •

Forgiveness - Part III

Dear Mom,

This will be the hardest letter I've ever had to write and one not nearly as fun and light-hearted as in my camp days when I used to send you notes about archery and arts and crafts. No, I'm not a ten-year-old girl anymore, and twenty-eight years later I am a woman more into active meditations and raising consciousness than anything else. Because of this, my life has been cracked open in painfully beautiful ways that I never knew were possible. With bright light and awakening, I have to share some of the darker sides of our life as well, things in our past that we've been hiding from for years, things that I know you have needed to heal from for a very long time.

But first, I must express an apology from twenty-nine years ago.

I am so sorry that I didn't tell anyone from the very beginning about your Second Husband and the molestation that happened during our childhood. But how could I? I was nine years old—just a kid—and I didn't know what had truly happened; I just knew it was your husband. You told me what he did was bad, but then you let him back into the house for months after the abuse.

Mom, withholding the truth from everyone taught me a number of dangerous lessons: that sexual abuse should not be talked about, that men can get away with bad things, and that secrets around childhood trauma are not only tolerated but accepted. You then trapped me in the lies, always telling me that I was "a good egg" and that you could "always count on me" . . . so I never disobeyed you.

But what you did was not okay. I am so sorry I didn't have the maturity or the courage to tell Dad or anyone else about the abuse on Dogford Road. I now know that this was when I became so good at holding in secrets. My life has often felt like a string of white lies—telling people that I was fine when in actuality, I was deeply suffering.

I wish I could write to you saying the abuse ended for me there, in that A-frame house deep in the New Hampshire woods in February of 1993.

But twenty years later, on the night of April 4th, 2013, I was raped in Miami. I was out celebrating with friends. I was having fun; I got drunk. I went to a club with another friend where everything looked white and then everything went black. I awoke to being raped on a balcony fifty floors up in an apartment building that I never remembered arriving at. The only reason I was jolted back into this nightmare was that the pain was so unnatural and so intense that it literally shook me awake, brought me to tears and to my knees, and then I passed out again. I know very little from that night. I just knew that when I woke up in the morning, the stranger next to me tried to put his arm around my waist, and my whole being rejected the touch from him. Every muscle tensed and the shiverees stood up on end. I couldn't hide the disgust and utter violation I felt by his presence.

The body does not lie.

I left that building as fast as I could, thinking that I didn't know what to do. I had been drunk. I was so clouded by fear and shame and guilt for putting myself in a situation like that. I was almost thirty. College-educated. Traveled the world. So smart, I thought. How could I ever have been so stupid? I didn't want to bother my friends with my poor decision-making, with my mistakes.

So, alas, that scared nine-year-old girl living in that twenty-nine-year-old's body didn't have the strength to tell anyone. Unfortunately, instead, I had the conditioning that bad things happen to good people, and sometimes you just gotta deal with it and sit in it. So, I sat in your secret for twenty years, and then I suffered in my own body and mind after my rape for another five years after that.

And one day, after heartache, heartbreak, and heart surgery, I realized the only way to get out of this hell was to go through it. To admit it. To say it out loud. To accept it. To take responsibility for my life. To tell those I love and who love me about it.

To finally blow out this toxic torch of holding all this crap in.

Because I don't want to keep it in me anymore. Because it was sexual abuse, and I don't want to live my whole life caring about what anyone else has to say about it.

Because I forgive myself for it . . . and that's what counts.

I love you, Mom, and I forgive you, too.

And if you could be so kind, could you please try and forgive yourself? Dying with regret was tough, but living without ever forgiving yourself?

Oh, Mom, that must have been so much harder.

Wholeheartedly,

Holly

20.

To Heal it, Is to Feel it

The Mother Wound

Dear Mom,

I've always loved the number eight. When I bartended on Nantucket, people would often order the local spirits, from a distillery called Triple Eight. Apparently eight is a pretty lucky number and three eights in a row must be exceptionally blessed. In the spiritual world, the number eight symbolizes abundance, wisdom and most importantly . . . *love.*

Spirit and spirits ... two things I have so often been working alongside.

You know, eight is such an important time in a child's evolution. Beginning at age eight until twelve, children are in their throat chakra, the energy disc that is a powerhouse, known for truth, communication and speaking things in to existence. If we get caught with unresolved trauma in the throat, it means we may stop voicing our feelings and learn how to lie and get really good at keeping secrets.

Did Amie ever tell you about one of the first memories she has of her mom? It was from when she was eight. And it would break your heart.

Do you remember in 1996, when Amie went to the doctors and didn't tell anyone? I mean, I am sure you guys did this a lot, but remember when Amie went in to the hospital because she was having tingling in her hands? They found out she had an aneurysm in her brain and shortly thereafter she went in for surgery. Amie never wanted to ask for help, so they even had to hire a nurse to sit with her as she was healing. She had a shunt put in to her head and one time, while still in recovery and left to her own devices, Amie got up to go to the bathroom and literally ripped the shunt out of the crown of her head.

We come from very powerful women: I cannot deny that. But I also must remind you, Mom, that Amie has always had a hard time asking for help. She is so private about anything that's going wrong or could be seen as unbecoming. And I don't get it – because you told me that asking for help was a sign of strength.

So, I am not sure how to teach you this . . . and *yet*, I'll try.

I am the product of you. And you are the product of Amie. And she is the product of her mother, and all the mothers before her. And many of these mothers have been closed off, kept quiet and stuck in their unconscious minds for centuries.

Mom, I understand why you had such a hard time telling your truth and feeling your feelings . . . because as a baby, you were born to a woman, who at the age of eight, had already closed down her voice and shut down her heart based on her own mother's trauma.

Keep reading. Your heart knows what I am talking about . . . even if your head hasn't caught up ***yet***.

Wholeheartedly,

Holly

The Sacred Space

October 2019

"Women have switched off from their bodies," said the teacher at the divine feminine workshop. "They are not listening."

"When we shut off from our Yoni, we shut off our power." She was preaching different ways for women to stand up for themselves. "Practice using your voice, ask for what you want, don't just love me, worship me. Get into full body consent. Sex should not be painful. Discover your sensuality, turn on Yoni consciousness."

I sat on the floor as she gave this talk, which was exactly where I belonged, as I was floored with everything I was hearing. I was at the Bali Modern Women's Festival divinely timed for the first week I was back in October of 2019. This was a three-day festival all around celebrating and empowering the female mind, body, and spirit and . . . the Yoni, which means sacred space in Sanskrit. Though I had never heard of a Yoni massage, the powerful process that this woman was explaining had everything inside of me tingling.

We talked about trauma, whether it had been from birth, molestation, rape, and how the Yoni held onto the trauma and in turn, turned off our pleasure points. But the teacher preached that it didn't have to stay this way. Through Yoni massage, you could activate different spots, G Spots, P Spots, all the spots. You could come back into your body and feel safe again. After my rape in 2013, I don't think I ever processed how much I had turned off my Yoni. Sex had become methodical, almost like part of a to-do list: put the boyfriend's name in a checkmark box right in between laundry and Instagram. There was a massive disconnect before and after that weekend in 2013, or perhaps it was more like a death.

This was a rebirth.

"Vulnerability makes us feel alive," she said, *"Write down your wants."* We did this right after we had all taken our mirrors or phones and stared deep into our Yonis—every single one of us in our own process on our backs like bugs trying to stare deep into the exact place where we came from. I tried to tell my sisters about this process that evening. "Yoni massage? Yoni gotta be kidding me!" they said. They thought I was falling off the deep end, losing it, but in all actuality, I was finding something, the power of the Feminine. The ability to look deep into myself and to love myself from the inside out.

There was another teacher during that festival, a beautiful bright blonde angel of a woman, whose course was just called "The Self Love Journey." She taught us the gift of having a daily practice. And how do you get there, you might wonder? You slow down to the moon cycle. "Every month, we are given a chance to renew," she said. "Self-love is knowing your worth, your value, and having awareness. She brought it back to the idea of our period or **Our Moon** as she called it. "Do you ever just let yourself bleed?" she asked. "Do you ever just do nothing during your Moon, let yourself go into the art of feeling?"

Attune to your moon cycle was her message. She designed this journey with nature in mind:

Week 1: Your Winter. Think of your moon as a cleansing, a hibernation, and the bleeding is your process. It's winter, so go within. Be quiet. Be still. No sugar. No carbs. No booze. Just be. Let yourself feel what is releasing.

Week 2: Your Spring. Become like the maiden and gently reconnect with society and begin to let others back in. Do it slowly and consciously. Don't rush this process. Let it unfold.

Week 3: Your Summer. Queen it. Tap into this energy. This is when women ovulate—when you make love to get pregnant. This is when you feel your best and look your best; your clothes fit right; your skin glows and your energy flows. Use this energy to your advantage.

Week 4: Your Autumn. Begin to wind down, as you transform and prepare for winter. Set yourself up for your moon by finishing what needs to be done and putting your next big meetings and in-person events back into your spring week. Make soups and stews and create space for the following week, so you can begin your hibernation once again.

Here is a Post-it I would like to pass to the patriarchy: Why were we taught extensively about war and his-tory, yet we were never taught as women of her story . . . the story of why we bleed and how to honor our cycles? Why have we been conditioned to use tampons as a way of plugging up our periods, pretending that they are not happening? Brands like Playtex Sport give women the idea that you are supposed to move consistently with a super-plus roll of toilet paper up your Yoni.

There is power in our blood. There is divine femininity in this process. Every month, we are given the chance to slow down, feel and renew. Every moon we attune to, gifts us the knowledge of our mothers, our grandmothers, and all of the powerful Yonis that came before us.

At the end of that day, from Yoni massage to the Self-love journey, I finished my sessions alongside a tall birdlike teacher who preached about feminine magnetism and how being in a feminine state as a state of receiving helps us feel safe. "As women, we need to learn to ask for what we want," she said. "Practice a pleasure list of what fills your life daily. Practice Self-appreciation. Receive. Receive. Receive." At the end of her course, she had us chanting aloud, *"I reclaim my Divine Feminine!"* knowing it was never lost, knowing we had always had it, allowing ourselves to soften and come into flow.

Vulnerability is my truth, it is my ability to be seen and heard, it is my journey to wholeness. I am not coming of age . . . I am coming of being.

By the time I was thirty-five, another healer had shown me the teachings of the Hawkins Scale of Consciousness and helped me understand that the lowest level of consciousness is *shame*. Through deep meditation and this healer's emotional intelligence teachings, I realized I had been living in sexual shame since I was nine years old: from the molestation to the years that I was told to keep that secret from my father; from the shame I felt after my first UTI to the years of developing an STD phobia but continuing to put myself in the same situations because I didn't want to have the shameful sex talk with partners; from the night I was raped at twenty-nine to the five years it took me to forgive myself and accept every decision; to the truth that sometimes our body knows better than we do all the shame and sadness that the women in my family have been carrying for generations.

I needed to learn that the one thing that needed to be healed the most was an ever scarred and oh so sacred relationship with my body. The relationship with my encee, as my mother called it. My vagina, as they name it in sex education.

I decided I would finally give my femininity a name that it so deserved by calling it something that made me happy. I would honor it. I would stop taking this incredible opportunity of being a woman for granted. This fine gift of being in my feminine . . . this divine honoring of myself and my body . . . for all that it's been through. For all that it has healed from. For all the women who brought me here and all the women who went before me and for all the women who will come after . . . This is for letting go of all the shame that I used to associate with it. For the first time, I decided it was high time to start and forever be living, loving, and healing the relationship with my Yoni, my sacred space.

Because Yoni know what?

Being a woman is a very powerful thing.

And if we could understand even an ounce of how powerful we truly are, we wouldn't be afraid of anything.

What's *Within* A Name

January 2021

Dear Mom,

I am writing this to you from another Amie's house—the home of my island mother and my island father, who live in that beautiful rustic beach house at Surfside. You know this one; we stayed here with Amie in August Of 2008. I know the exact day, because you both wrote thank-you letters so beautifully in their guest book. That was also the last time Amie came to Nantucket during my seventeen-year stay.

As usual, your mother made a lovely impact on those she met. Amie has such a ladylike demeanor, with a kind and caring way about her. The morning we were set to leave, Amie was beautifully dressed while standing at the kitchen sink, not just doing the dishes, but cleaning the sponge and reorganizing the fridge before the owners were to return that morning. I had bartended the night before; got home a little late and pretty buzzed, and was still asleep in the main bedroom. You were reading out on their deck and listening to the waves. My island parents caught an earlier flight than planned that day and returned home while I was still fast asleep in their bed. Luckily, that was not their first impression of me.

Amie met them in the kitchen and introduced herself as Dorothy. I awoke and reintroduced her as Amie—a nickname, pet name, to which my island mother took a liking. A year later, when her first grandson was born, my island mother decided to rename herself Amie after your mother. Nine grandchildren call her Amie to this day.

Speaking of names, I often thought it was strange that you named my sister Christina after your aunt's daughter Christina, who died in a car crash at just seventeen years old. And I always wondered why my great-grandmother Dorothy named her daughter after herself. On my father's side, the Finigan male name was set to be a legacy, but I had rarely heard of, in those I've met, the passing down of names on the matriarchal side. Many *dots* of my life started to connect once I began healing my relationship with you, Mom. After a few deep meditations and parent healing processes, I began to climb up the maternal ladder and recognized that the issues I had with you would ultimately seem like small potatoes compared to connecting the *Dotties* before me.

When I got home from Bali in November of 2018, I was spiritually open in ways I never knew were possible; I was receiving messages and downloads far faster than my human body and mind knew how to handle. Since I couldn't call you, I called Amie. Your mother has forever been a private person, never speaking much of her childhood. However, as a born storyteller and a trained journalist, I have always known how to ask the right questions, how to pull one sweater string and unravel the entire cardigan.

I began by asking Amie about her sisters. Just like my sister Christina, Amie was originally the eldest of three girls: Dorothy, Polly and then Deborah. I kind of knew the story of her middle sister, Polly, of how she also had died in a car accident. It was the mid 1930s and Polly was just three.

From what I pieced together over the years, the story was that my great-grandmother, Dorothy, called to her daughter Polly, and as she did, the small child ran into the street and was hit by a car and died.

Tragedy brings families together or rips them apart. In this case, it obliterated Amie's family unit. Amie's parents divorced and sent her to an orphanage at six years old, while Deborah went to live with family.

After I got home from the Far East that November, I called Amie and began like this: "Amie, was your mother pregnant with you when she got married?"

She sighed and responded, "Yes, and it was very embarrassing for our family— especially for my grandfather, who was a minister."

More questions: "Amie, why did Great-Grandmother Wyman name you Dorothy?" Another sigh; another quick response.

"My grandfather told my mother that I was to be named after herself, as a reflection of what she had done."

Everything buzzed in my body. So much shame for being pregnant before marriage. A man commanding you to name your first child after yourself. A daughter in the womb ingesting all of this guilt before she even exited the birth canal. The shame-naming of the daughters, the death of a child, sending another child away after tragedy like, acting like things never happened, like, implying that now we can't take care of you.

I pressed the issue, knowing I had opened up my often-closed grandmother.

"Amie, what is your first memory of your mother?"

She went quiet. "I don't have a lot of good memories of my mother," she said. "My first memory of my mother, I am eight and she is telling me that she hates me."

There it was. I HATE YOU. I HATE YOU. I HATE YOU. The clearing out of my body . . . the words that had lived in too many women for far too long. I truly believe my great-grandmother did not hate her daughter, Dorothy. I believe she hated herself for what happened to her daughter Polly that day.

This is quite the name game, and a lot of Dotties for you to connect. Amie turned ninety recently, and things aren't working as quickly for her as well as I know she wishes they would. When I tried to bring up many of these stories, Amie would often tell me the tales, trail off on a tangent, and then stop altogether once she realized she was going through a dark tunnel. "There are some things I tend to put out of my mind," she would say when I pushed her to get to the light.

Yet here's the truth, my dear friend, my mother and my grandmother: *the only way to heal it is to feel it*. The only way to get out of this hell is through. For even when things aren't on our minds, they are still in our hearts.

Because this is bigger than history and her story and my story and your story.

This is about releasing and forgiving all the old stories that no longer serve us, and in doing so, sharing the light that comes by connecting the dots before us.

Mom, I know we wrote this book together. I know we wrote it for grandmothers and for mothers, sisters, daughters and friends everywhere. We wrote this to let them all know that they are so loved.

That, in fact, they are love.

Because the true name of every baby born is Love.

Wholeheartedly,

Holly

21.

The Innernet

Fearless

February 2019

"Remember to live without fear." That was the last line of the last letter I ever got from my first love. I had broken up with him months before over the phone when he was in England and I was in New England. Even though he was from New Zealand, and I from New Hampshire, we had such a strong connection, after very little time together, that you might think we had known each other in another life. He gave me great gifts over our brief year and a half of being together, and yet, this was the present that truly stayed. It resonated for me ten years later, rereading it. That letter meant little to me when I first read it and now, it felt like everything I needed to hear. It represents everything I want to be: consciously fearless to speak and write my truth even when it hurts like hell getting it out.

And yet nothing petrified me more than an event in February of 2019. After a deep meditation teacher training and sitting in my Self for a solid month, I decided I had to tell my dad that I had been raped in 2013 in Miami. This was the scariest thing I had ever done because thirty-five-year-old Holly was both telling her dad about a rape and having her first real conversation about the molestation that had happened twenty-five years before as well. My poor father . . . for over two decades, I had been hiding things from him.

After that Facetime with my father, after sobbing through the story from Bali, after hearing the love and concern in his voice and seeing the tears in his eyes, I realized just how important it was to start letting go of these stories and awakening to my truth.

I've learned that becoming fearless is having the courage to take myself apart and put myself back together again.

And where to begin?

Healing the relationships with our parents.

This is the never-ending story of where we start, where they end, and where all of us get to begin again.

The Four Baskets

May 2020

During the Pandemic, since no one could travel to Bali, I took Bali to my community by putting together my Teacher's first three-day online Spiritual Awakening Course. I did this with one goal—to get my parents to take the Eight Baby Steps to a Higher Consciousness workshop alongside me. I had to use the growth formula: in order to get what you want, you need intent, effort, and divine intervention. My intention was to get my dad to do the course. My effort was being the example and doing the work myself so as to show that if I could evolve, so could he. And then there was that divine intervention.

When COVID 19 closed down the airports and all travel plans had to be put on hold, the chance to put the course online easily presented itself in May of 2020. People were desperately seeking connecting during this time and a weekend on Zoom with a random group of others seemed truly appealing. I put an Eventbrite together for a Friday-to-Sunday course, and my father and stepmother were the first to sign up. My childhood Bestie and ten other friends, who had heard me rave about the program over the past two years, completed the baker's dozen in our first online group. About a half-hour into the first session, as my father learned about the unconscious mind and the power of taking responsibility, he looked at my stepmom in disbelief and said, "You know, I thought we were doing this course for Holly. It turns out we are doing this for ourselves."

"Duh, Dad," I laughed. "Of course, this is for you." This is for all of us. We all need to do our own work. We all have some major relationships to heal, and here was our chance.

But why I was really there was that I needed a chance for my father to hear the fifth baby step: healing the relationship with a child. And in doing so, he would learn the teachings of an ancient Vedic tradition of The Four Baskets—how it's so important to think about a seed of intention before we become parents and to decide consciously how we want to bring a life into existence. The four baskets represent the four consciousness levels of a baby from the womb to the world.

The first basket is from the moment of conception until two months in the womb. It asks very important questions like, how was the baby conceived? Was there the intention to make a baby or just to have sex? Was the baby created out of love? Or a rape? What were the adults thinking about what they were truly doing while they were making this child? Were they drunk? Were they conscious? Did they even want to keep it when they found out the mother was pregnant? Was the family supportive when they heard the news?

The second basket is months two through eight while the baby is in the womb. How is the mother doing during this time? And how is the father? Are they engaging with the baby? Are they listening to music and dancing? Are they talking to the baby together? Does the baby feel loved? Does the mother feel safe? Do the mother and father have a pleasant relationship during this time? The child is ingesting everything that is happening, both inside and outside. Some spiritual teachings advise the avoidance of intercourse during this time so as not to harm the developing embryo. It's a great time for the child to learn, as it can't go anywhere; even when the mother is asleep the baby is still awake. The child is, in essence, the mother. And if the mother is not taking great care of herself or if the father is not present, the baby feels all those feelings.

The third basket is the delivery. We must remember that as rough as the birthing process is for the mother, it is also rough for the baby. This child, after being in a warm belly for months, is now getting pushed down a tight tunnel and entering cold air for the first time. The third basket asks questions like, how was the delivery? Was it natural? Was the child delivered by

C-section? Did the baby have any hardship trying to get out, like the umbilical cord around its neck, or was the baby breeched? Recognize that the trauma was not just the mother's, but the child's as well.

And finally, the fourth basket represents the first six hours that the baby is out of the womb. It asks questions like, how was the baby welcomed into the world? Was the child able to get skin to skin with the mother immediately to feel a sense of safety? What was the vibration of the others in the room? When the baby was announced . . . it's a girl! Was there excitement? Was there disappointment? The baby is a living buddha at this moment and it is taking in all the reactions and emotions of the room, whether they were voiced or not.

And when it came to my own four baskets, this I know is true: when my mother said that I spent the first six months attached to her hip, I felt safe and loved by her. And I know there was a disconnect between my father and me from the get-go. Even the fact that he said that his first memory of me was when I was two was a sign. I believe that when I was born, the second child and the second daughter to a man whose name was set to be a legacy, I saw disappointment in my father's eyes upon our meeting. I believe it was unconscious on his part, but I felt it just the same.

After learning about the four baskets, I realized that I had to heal from those first few moments with my father while we both were still here on this earth. I then had to remind myself that my father did not ask to be named after his father. This re-naming of a male heir was a tradition passed down to him that wasn't his choice. So, I began to have much more compassion for him: he was just following the leader—doing what he watched his parents do.

I had to remember that we are all a product of our upbringing and every day we have the chance to start anew. For my father and I are so much more than a boy and a girl and a Finigan. We are, in essence, holy spirits having the human experience . . . and here's the truth: we humans can heal and we spirits can begin again, whenever we want.

At the end of the course, my Teacher told us that we can use this internet as a tool to gather, as long as we remember that our most important connection is to the one inside of us, the connection to our Innernet.

Ahhh, there it is.

The word that I had been seeking all these years. After a decade as a digital entrepreneur, I came full circle online to the truth: to own who we truly are, we have to embrace our shadow and get back to the root. We have to inhale courage and exhale fear and do the work to heal our primal relationships.

This is how we connect to our Innernet.

And trust that underneath all the stories—beneath the guilt, the lies, the fear and the shame—lives a bottomless well of love in each and every one of us. Trust that the love we have for our parents is so strong, that we have it in us to heal every trauma at any age.

Trust that it's never too late.

A Parting Gift

March 2022

Dear Mom,

The last present you gave me was a bookmark. I mean, compared to your first present of life, this may seem like a little gift, but as they always say, the best gifts come in small packages. This was no ordinary bookmark that a bookstore would throw in with an address and social media links on it; this wasn't brand-new or manufactured like that. This bookmark was a hand-me-down, for it was the bookmark that you received from your mother. It was a foot-long red satin ribbon that on one end had two intertwining silver hearts and on the other an inch-long letter cutter with R.P.M., your initials, engraved on it.

I had just turned thirty and was living into my tenth summer on Nantucket. You had decided to give up calling the island Birdland and had learned how to fly and ferry over and just savor the place alongside me. You knew the power of islands: you had always called Eleuthera your happy place and realized that this rock, thirty miles out to sea, was mine.

Since you couldn't be with me on June 24th, 2013, you simply mailed a package out to me with a card and some money. And if I'm being honest, the $100 check seemed to be a big present. I didn't know then that your red bookmark was the true gift. See, this bookmark was part of your sanctuary. It was a constant in books by your bed. John Irving was your favorite, but Wally Lamb and Cutting for Stone were often a topic of admiration and conversation. You loved to read and were always impressed by my ability to put the pen to the page. You would say, "Writers write, Mermaid" in a way that irked me. I felt like you were always just trying to get me to stop bartending.

Hindsight is always 20/20. I now know you were letting me know that no one else could or would do this job as a writer for me. I didn't know it at the time, but your bookmark was a clue on this journey to awakening. You would leave us nine months later. I now realize that there had been so much of you preparing me to get into my write state of mind. I thought we were always writing stories. You knew I had to right your story first.

During your last stay in the hospital, I was there with you for those ten days and ten nights. I didn't plan to do it—it wasn't like you can plan to do this—but Christina already had a daughter, and Sanna worked in corporate America, and Steve couldn't physically do it . . . so I did it. I sat with you and tried to radiate positivity while showing you New Yorker cartoons and looking at old family pictures. But you were not attentive to this story hour; for much of our time together in the hospital you were violently throwing up. From dry heave to heavy pull, you quite literally showed me all the toxins inside of you. You gave me a first-hand account of what it looked like to try to extend a life with chemo and radiation: a release of those drugs was now your only way out.

I listened as you made yourself throw up into that plastic wash bin. I did it with a pillow over my head until I finally stopped dry heaving myself. Eventually, I'd hold back your hair, or come out from behind the curtain so you knew you weren't alone. I'd never seen more vomit come out of one person. You weren't even eating, and yet your body still kept purging. How much of this crap was in you? I had to look fear in the face. I had to get over my pukephobia during this time as your caregiver, bringing you ice chips, bubbly ginger ale, and a willing smile with a joke to say, "Well, thank God, that is out of you!"

You always said I was sunny and funny.

And then there was your actual bed. You had one decorative pillow in the middle of your perfectly made California king; it was a square red needlepoint cushion that your mother had made and given to you. It read Truth with the T extra-large, and the Ruth written below. "Tell the truth, Ruth," your mother used to say to you—apparently you had been good at keeping secrets and telling white lies during your childhood. Like mother, like daughter. The pillow was signed "DM" in the bottom-right corner for Dorothy Mori. It read 1980 in the left corner, the last year before you became a mother. Another beautiful last present from mother to daughter. "Keep the memories, lose the things," my bright therapist had told me a month after you died. When we went to clean out your room, I didn't raid your drawers; I simply took the Truth pillow from your sanctuary. It called to me.

When you gave me your last words, I knew that there was something more to it. "Did you write something?" you asked. When I shook my head no, you responded, "Don't worry, you will." This became part of a bigger treasure hunt. You left me with another gift—you knew I always had something in me, that eventually a great story would unfold out of my hands. And, if I had the patience and really put all my love into it, like a field of dreams, the readers would come.

Oh, and the last gift, that sweet red bookmark, aligning me to the tRUTH and the hearts of the matter. The best part of that present isn't just that it gives the gift of reading, but that it gifts another side to the story. For whenever I flip over the silver R.P.M., I'd see H.R.F., my own initials, engraved on the back.

This bookmark became the first page of my brand-new chapter: the fact that your life would always be part of me and like a red thread, I would always be connected to it. And yet, eventually, I would have to let go of all of your narratives . . . and start my own story.

And what I've learned is this:

We can't live by our parents' stories.

We can't die holding on to their regrets.

All we can do is forgive them and love them.

And that, my mother, is enough.

Wholeheartedly,

Holly

P.S. Did you know, Mom, that, in the state of New Hampshire, a victim of sexual abuse has up to the age of 40 to prosecute her perpetrator? I'll write to you when it's all over—the final note in this bittersweet symphony.

The Rebirth

February 2022

From 2018 to 2022, I began to get curious about what happens when we get quiet. After years of being online, I started to really enjoy just sitting, without any technology around me, while tapping into something deeper.

In March of 2018, I was deep into a full moon manifestation meditation with six other spiritually-sound women on Nantucket. Since my heart had been cracked open that January, my body craved stillness. My mind would shut off during these moments of rest and I saw clearly what was going on both around me and inside of me.

During this guided meditation, I asked my Divine for help with the conclusion of my book. It was there where I heard, "Do the work." Disappointed with that answer, I then heard her again. She said, "Look at your hand." There was a big heart on it and I heard, "See? Don't just do the work. Love the work."

I jotted those lines in my journal and then spent the next five years remembering them as I wrote this book.

Yet, by 2020, I did not want to do blACKbook work and I didn't love the digital business I had created, either. I was exhausted from promoting Nantucket on social media for years and I knew I had to make a change.

With so much unrest in the world and online, I didn't post during the month of June and, without any real goodbye, I closed down the blACKbook with an Instagram right before my 37th birthday that summer. As I wrote in the end of that post:

"My next chapter will be more conscious and educational. It will be genuine and inclusive. I am ready to serve my community in a new way."

That July, during this first summer living in a resort town dealing with a global pandemic, I began to think about how restaurants were getting hit the hardest, especially since I had been a bartender for nine years on Nantucket and knew how much we service industry folks relied on that summer income from Memorial Day to Labor Day. I recalled how my mom had said asking for help is a sign of strength, so I teamed up with two summer residents who both had backgrounds in marketing along with one of my first interns and her dear friend who had created an Instagram account dedicated to sharing restaurant information. We transformed the Nantucket blACKbook into the Nantucket Dining Sourcebook and created the island's first 100 percent inclusive restaurant guide enhanced by a partnership with Flowcode technology. Flowcode is like everything I'd always been searching for in my early days of printed blACKbook, and as "the Tesla of QR codes," as it was described by Nantucket summer resident and founder Tim Armstrong, it made it easy to take people from the sourcebook page to a webpage to show a restaurant's most up-to-date information for seating, reservations, take-out and beyond. The book was a crowd-sourced fundraiser and, with the help of twenty-four summer residents, we were able to create this book at no cost to any of the restaurants while gifting back 5,000 of these books to visitors and year-rounders alike.

That same summer, I shifted careers in another way, too. They say timing is everything and like that hawk, I often know exactly when to swoop in. The love of my life and I got together in November of 2018. It's a relationship I hold sacred and I choose not to share it publicly. And yet, I feel inclined to share this one thing, because oftentimes, our partners see ourselves and our power even before we do. My Partner told me that I needed to be doing real estate. I was amazing at it, he said, and I had done it for everyone else for years. Now was the perfect time to do it for myself. He also promised me that, if I got my license, he would give me my first listing—his seven-bedroom contemporary Madequecham beach home that he had just finished custom-building that summer. I got my license that August; joined an entrepreneur who had a boutique real estate firm on Centre Street, and together we launched my man's Madequecham home on the market right before Halloween through a video that made me feel like I was the host of my own MTV Cribs. My Partner's home had a 90 percent offer in the first week and the deal closed right before the holidays. And yet, the real Christmas present was tapping into that real estate market with all my blACKbook knowledge right when I did, because we sold almost $25 million in homes in my first year.

Things continued to look up as I linked up with more humans at just the right moments. Divine timing is something I wholeheartedly believe in. I still kept up my summer intern programming, even after I had closed down blACKbook. I never searched for interns, they just started coming to me.

One of my 2021 interns used to work at an iconic downtown tee shirt shop and suggested that my Happy Place clothing brand could live on in her store. Since closing my shop in 2019, and not creating much in 2020, a high pent-up demand for the Happy Place logo had developed, and yet, I didn't have the true interest to run a shop again. So, as fate would have it, the woman who co-owned the store with her husband told me that she was asked if she had Happy Place shirts all the time. She admitted that it would make her life easier and more enjoyable if she had the shirts in-store and offered to take the brand in-house and sell the tees for me. That summer, we started having the merchandise back on the shelves in this store that was literally known as the company for Nantucket Clothing. It was, as they say, a perfect fit.

And there I was, evolving just like what happened during the blACKbook days, with my collaborative businesses in restaurants, real estate and retail, and yet, there was something I knew I still needed to do. Not for the money, but for my heart.

In the spring of 2020, with all the free time that I now had without blACKbook, I decided to start leading meditation for two moms, who each had three young kids. I had known these women from my early days on island, when we were all waitressing and bartending, and when our spirits were more into late nights at the Box than mornings spent in meditation. What began as the two of them coming over to meditate outside, became a group of six moms who would get together weekly for the next year with a sharing circle. The O.M.M.M.s (Our Mom's Monday Meditation) would sit together from 12:30 to 2:00 p.m. every week as I would lead them in a breathwork practice while holding hands. It was my way of being that mother's helper again—an opportunity, as a woman without children this time around, to hold space for these mothers during the pandemic.

I started to hear the stories of these moms who were having to navigate so much daily uncertainty and pressure with children and masks, health regulations and vaccines, and the constant "are we or aren't we" with online schooling. I knew they needed a way to be there for themselves just as much as they needed to be there for their families. Sitting with these women as they processed their guilt and grief, I'd ponder, *what if my mom had had a group like this to be with? Would she have been able to heal? Would she have been able to release her pain?*

These women became sisters to me. I never charged them for these circles. We made these connections donation-based, with all funds raised going back to random acts of kindness to help others in need.

And by loving these mothers . . . I began to see that I was my own mother.

Because I have done all this work to rebirth myself.

And now, I don't just do the work.

I love the work.

How The Story Ends

Dear Mom,

I am writing this to you from the middle of the Atlantic Ocean—a perfect last letter from your mermaid daughter. No, I'm not shipwrecked or even swimming. I'm on the fast ferry heading across Nantucket Sound back to the island after, in typical fashion, my flight from Boston was canceled and I had to hop on the Peter Pan bus, then onto this rocky ferry home to Never Never Land, to that little Grey Lady thirty miles out to sea. You always said that places hardest to get to were the most worth it when you arrived. After eighteen years of living on Nantucket, I have to agree.

As the waves bounce us back and forth, and while the lady next to me keeps her head down from sea sickness, the guys to my left down their bloody marys, the dogs bark, the children cry, and the bathroom line with green faces grows longer, this remix of a classic reggae song keeps coming on my EarPods. Its lyrics keep me smiling as it tells me, don't worry about a thing. It sings that every little thing is going to be alright.

Can you name that tune? Because this song leads me back to you: you and I in the car listening to 99 Rock. You and I walking down a path in the Vermont woods, me crying about how I didn't know how I'd pay for a trip I wanted to take during college. You and I walking the beach at Surfside while I tell you I want to break up with a boyfriend. You and I on the white sands of Eleuthera, me telling you how I didn't know what else I was good at besides bartending—I was trying so hard to figure out what I was going to do with my life. Like your cards to me would read . . . *I know you'll figure out what you want to do* . . . Back then, I needed to hear it from your voice to believe it . . .

And can you believe it? It's been eight-and-a-half years since you passed over that rainbow. So many shifts. So many changes. I sometimes wonder if you'd even recognize me. Lord knows, there are days when a "time hop" photo on Facebook will show up and I'll barely know who that girl from 2014 was. I was so lost, so disconnected from my Self and so plugged in to so many things that didn't serve me: Facebook Followers. Instagram Likes. Twitter Retweets. Google Analytics. These apps consumed me; literally ate away at my brain, my being, and my sense of belonging. Over the course of five years, I dug myself out of that dark world wide web hole and began to see the internet for what it was: a teaching to get us back to our Innernet and an extraordinary way to connect with the world. As my astrologist loves to say, "Earth is a school and we come here to learn lessons."

> And that's when it becomes so crystal clear.
> These lessons in loss became a master class in the Heart.
> It made me into a teacher.
> That is who I *will* be.
> You always said, "Where there is a will there is a way."

Except when you died, there was no will. I don't know why you did that; maybe because you didn't think you had anything to pass down, or perhaps because you didn't want to put anything in writing. Oh, and that writing—those last words to me: "Did you write something? Don't worry you *will*."

It's like your will was this book. You always knew that there was some gift within me. What I did not realize then was that you were leaving us with unfinished business.

You were showing us first-hand what the unconscious looked like in a human form. It looks like emotion stuck . . . which is a lack of energy in motion. E-Motion.

It looks like cancer.

You know, without your "will" there was one piece of jewelry that Christina and Sanna and I would pass around over the years: your engagement ring from your life partner, Steve. The ring was big and beautiful: two diamonds sparkled brightly and the large emerald felt unique to you. The gold was heavy; when we wore it, it felt like we were holding your hand. Christina had it on her finger when she gave birth and so did Sanna. I would wear it on days when I wanted to feel like you were with me.

One day recently, thanks to a dear friend who is a jeweler, I decided it was time to take that ring and spread its love so that finally Christina, Sanna and I all could enjoy it together. I had my friend take the emerald, diamonds and gold apart. She made the emerald into its own necklace and the two diamonds into their own necklaces. She took the gold and melted it down into a new ring so we all could hold you close to our hearts in our own way.

The emerald went to Christina—the big one for our big sis. It's also green, the color of the heart chakra; after you died, Christina became like our mother, always holding us close to her. She's been through a lot, that sister of ours; she makes us think about what we are doing and how we are holding ourselves and others accountable. She, as you said, has always been good and strong.

As for me, I had this deep need to keep holding your hand in a new way. So the jeweler took that gold and melted it all down. Together we designed the ring into a coiled snake, like the kundalini energy it represents, moving up and out of my hands, even as I write this. That ring is a reminder that my hands can do hard things, that I am here for a big reason: to do the work and to love the work. And to remember that, yes, like you said, I am sunny, and, yes, I am funny, but what I really am is an alchemist, because I took all of that shadow and turned it to gold.

Oh, and Sanna is quite the magnificent one, too. She now has three kids and works full time and still manages to do it all and love everyone in the process. She was even able to do something else during the time while she was pregnant with her third child, her son. She held a light up to something that had been in our shadow for far too long.

Sanna brought justice to the molestation that happened to her thirty years ago. She brought your Second Husband into the court system to hold him accountable for what had happened in 1993. Yes, that six-year-old, who had both courage and deep understanding of right and wrong from a young age, brought that aggravated felonious sexual assault case back to the police, three decades later. Sanna then pressed forward; she used her voice and took this story out of the darkness and back into the court system.

How did it all turn out? Well, on October 26th, 2022, your Second Husband, who pleaded guilty to everything, by the way, was sentenced to twelve months in a House of Corrections. In his seventies, he will be listed as a sexual offender for the rest of his life. The story became a front page article in your favorite local newspaper the day after his sentencing.

Divine justice has truly been served.

Sanna got both diamonds for that one, Mom. For doing the work for herself, and for the work that will be done by sharing this story with others. You always knew she was motivated and resilient, and now, oh, Sanna! She is an inspiration to us all.

That's when I remembered—*your last words.*

I now know what they *really* meant.

You were asking . . . did we ***right*** something?

And to that, your daughters say, together—

Don't worry, Mom.

We did ***right*** *something.*

We did.

Wholeheartedly,

Holly

A Revelation

Did you ever hear that limerick, "There once was a man from Nantucket?" It's said to go something like this:

> *"There once was a man from Nantucket,*
> *whose d*** was so long he could suck it.*
> *He said with a grin*
> *as he wiped off his chin,*
> *"If my ear was a c*** I would f*** it."*

Isn't that disgusting? Foul. Offensive. And for some strange reason, people find it funny.

At the tee shirt shops on island, you will find hats, shirts and even baby onesies that read, "I am the man from Nantucket." They have been around for so long that they obviously must be a good seller. And yet, it frustrates me that this is the rhyme that Nantucket is world-renowned for. The island's fame should not be vulgar and all about the men on Nantucket—the whalers, the sailors, the adventurous gents who went out to sea to kill. It should be about the women out here too. The women who are still here. Hell, the island is even called The Grey Lady. This slice of sand, thirty miles out to sea, has been run by women for centuries. Petticoat Row pays homage to all of the ladies who kept this beautiful island thriving while the men went out and came back like the tides.

For the majority of my thirties, I have been watching the patriarchy unravel and make a seismic shift. The revolution called the internet created during my youth was male-centric. The connections that came from it were all outside of us. The ability to be on technology morning, noon, and night and have no boundaries around our phones, our computers—none of this stuff was thought about. The social media platforms were not created by women or with women's highest good in mind. And this was no fault to one person or one gender, but as collateral damage to an unconscious culture constantly seeking approval, likes, followers, and connection outside of ourselves.

The #MeToo movement brought anger to light, brought out the shadow that lay dormant in so many women for so many moons. It raised hell, and in doing so, it raised consciousness. But the idea of smashing the patriarchy? It's just about as masculine an action as it comes. It's not about beating or hitting or warring something to death. It's about burning something down that no longer serves a world and together rising up, like the phoenix.

One of my favorite mentors on Nantucket talks often about how a rising tide lifts all boats. This is a great analogy for the Nantucket restaurant scene, where this little island has become a cuisine capital of the East Coast. And yet, this analogy applies to the whole world. For I believe it's time as a world to rise up together.

So here is my whale of a tale, a poem that I would like to share. It's not about being online, but offline. Not about going viral, but getting vulnerable. And it's not a revolution, it's a revelation, so listen to my declaration:

We are
in the middle
of the beginning
of a conscious revelation called
the Innernet,
and the future is bright.

This time, we
Grey Ladies
know everything
does not have to be so
black and white.

To the patriarchy:
please listen,
follow us . . .
as you'll see . . .

That from our wombs
to our words,
we know
the next revolution
will be led
by the matriarchy.

PART IV

I Am

22.

The Awakening

The Golden Serpent

"Children learn best from stories," my Teacher likes to say. As we are young students of some old wisdom, my Teacher does his best with metaphors: story hour is always a favorite during his course. One of his best tales is that of a golden eagle who, as an egg, was stolen from his nest by a hunter and dropped onto a chicken farm. The egg hatched, and the golden eagle grew up believing he was a chicken that couldn't fly. My Teacher loves to talk about this around the issue of conditioning. How would an eagle see himself properly, if the fifty billion other chickens in the world around him were into hen's pens and clucking around? It wasn't until that golden eagle's mother, who never stopped searching for her missing egg, finally found her son on the chicken farm and convinced the golden eagle that he could fly. I have heard this story told in other ways as well.

In *A Joseph Campbell Companion: Reflections on the Art of Living*, his story was of a pregnant tiger who was starving and came upon a flock of goats. The pregnant tiger pounced on the goats with such energy that it brought on the birth of her baby tiger, and the mother promptly died herself. The goats adopted the baby tiger who grew up thinking he was a goat, completely malnourished and ultimately a pretty miserable creature. It was not until another tiger came upon the flock, and saw the baby tiger living as a goat, that things changed. The elder tiger brought the baby tiger to the water's edge, showed him his reflection, and said, "You see, you are a tiger; be like me." Joseph Campbell calls that some real Guru stuff.

I have a different story. Same same, but different. This is a tale of the golden serpent daughter who was born to sleeping bird parents. When her egg hatched, her parents, with their closed eyes, assumed she was just another baby bird. So, the golden serpent grew up believing that she was a bird, jumping from tree to tree, nest to nest, never really being on earth, and always thinking there was somewhere else to go. She saw things from so far up that she almost floated away.

The serpent would have dreams about other big snakes knocking at her door; she'd watch horror movies with snakes as the villain, and hear from the men in her life about how fearful of snakes they were. She would learn that extreme fear of snakes is called *ophidiophobia* and that over half the population has it. So, this serpent daughter lived in a Birdland, fearful of snakes, until one day, she road-tripped from the northeast to the vast southwest and stayed in a land where there were no bird sounds and really no sounds at all.

One night, while connecting to land, the daughter went belly to belly with Mother Earth who told her, *"Listen my child, you were born to be of this earth. Stop resisting your life on this sacred ground. Stop flying everywhere, tweeting all of the time while desperately trying to Google this mystery called life."*

Mother Earth's command was great:

"Be here now. Sit on my land and, in silence, your inner eye will awaken and you'll

see who you truly are . . . for you, my dear one, are the life force energy. You, my golden serpent, are exactly who they tell you to be afraid of."

And the girl awakened to see that she was a serpent. She had spent her whole life dreaming of herself, fearful of herself, realizing that many would be scared if she and all of the other serpents came into their power. She remembered that the golden serpent represents the Kundalini. It is coiled three-and-a-half times and lies at the base of the spine, representing the life force energy that lives equally present in each and every one of us, oftentimes lying dormant in most people for the entirety of their lives. The daughter realized her body had been prepping her for this revelation all along. Her curved spine, her connective tissue disorder, her heart's dis-ease, her blocked throat, her closed third eye . . . it was all just waiting for that life force energy to move up her and awaken her to her innernet.

For what was within her was far more powerful than anything outside of her.

And how did she stay awake? While sitting on the land focusing on her breath in meditation.

For it is in the silence while on Mother Earth that we finally see our true Self clearly. Breath is your spirit. It is the breath that has the power to wake every serpent up and to move that energy from root to crown so we can finally let go and surrender to what we are so afraid of...

Of being here in the moment.

There's no stopping this awakening.

I told you from the beginning, by holding this book, you were ready.

The collective is awakening as you read this.

All right now.

The First Step

I would like to begin again with the quote: *"A journey of a thousand miles begins with one single step."*

And the first step in a spiritual awakening is knowing the mantra.

The mantra is *I am that.*

Let's try it out . . .

If you say, *I am tired,* consciousness says, so be it; you will continue to be exhausted. If you say, *I am upset*, so be it; you will keep feeling unsettled. If you say *I am happy*, so be it; consciousness agrees, and so you are content. How strangely simple this all is, right? You are so powerful that whatever you say you are, you are.

As for me, after doing all of this work, after having a grand idea for this book and thus sharing my Truth . . . I recognized during my favorite 49-minute chanting meditation, the three things that I am.

I am Existence, Consciousness, Bliss.

And if I want to be free, then I gotta be me.

So, who am I really?

I am my father's daughter.

I am my mother's child.

And most importantly . . . just like every other baby born . . . I am love.

We Are All One

In January of 2020, I entered back into the Nantucket community and began sharing this book and my writing in person again. I had become sober curious so I don't use liquid confidence anymore to perform in front of an audience. And I also don't come here to be seen. In fact, the first time I reappeared, I showed up wearing my pajamas and UGG slippers. Over the course of the next six weeks, I began to put myself back out there offline, not at a bar, but at a little winter hideout called The Corner Table Café.

These days, I don't try to escape the winter; I embrace it. Now I simply show up, put my name down on the Open Mic Night list and don't get any special treatment. Every participant gets seven minutes, no more and no less. The comedian/host loves to mock me as he introduces me. "Here she comes, Nantucket's very first influencer. Now put me on the hot list!" he demands. We laugh: I make fun of him and tell him that he has become an expert at duplicating the only other comedian's jokes on the island. I am an easy target, but I have thick skin. The more they hate on me, the more they love me. I don't need mail or a male to remind me of that.

I position myself on the stool, this book in my lap. Nervous energy rumbles from my stomach and makes its way out to my hands, as my voice gets a bit shaky, and tears begin their descent out of my eyes. Right before I speak, I pause and take a deep breath, and remind myself not to be afraid of the void.

And I finally feel at home... not just on Nantucket, but in my heart.

At that moment, it is just me and my little black book again. Sharing what we have heard... and what we have learned... and remembering how everything is connected... and that we are not alone.

For alone means all one.

The Heart Of A Lion

April 18th, 2018

OMG! My wedding day! I almost forgot to tell you guys about this.

That's what happens when you're in love with the whole damn world and wanting to make this earth a better place: you forget about yourself. It's a wonderfully liberating feeling. But I told you in the beginning of my Bliss section that I would share my marriage story... so I'll take you back to my big day.

On my last morning during my first trip to Bali, I was at Crate, my favorite cafe in the center of Canggu. I showed up in a deep V, multi-striped, one-piece bathing suit that proudly displayed my scar, my favorite jean shorts, Converse sneakers, no makeup, and messy beach hair from a morning dip in the ocean. I ordered a Mango-Licious smoothie bowl and a coconut milk iced latte that had Instagram written all over it... but not today: I just enjoyed it. I sat at a communal table across from a Swedish food blogger. We chatted about how much we loved Bali and how much we felt at home here. I told the blogger I was leaving that night to fly back to the States. The blogger told me that she didn't want to be sad about leaving Bali during the last of the time she was on island, so she booked her return ticket while she was still here. That way, the blogger could return "home" knowing she would come back home to Bali eventually.

It was brilliant: best advice anyone had ever gifted me. It changed the direction of my life. So, I connected to the "life is crate" Wi-Fi and booked a one-way flight from NYC to Bali. I would arrive home to Nantucket on April 18th and would arrive home again to Bali on October 10th. I would get through another Nantucket season, and then I would go back to Bali before I knew it. It was sorted.

That morning I had taken out an extra $100 from the ATM and, in Bali, that is a lot of Rupiah. I was kinda bummed out that I had withdrawn all that money because my cash flow was a bit low after the weeks on vacation. But everything happens for a reason, including that ATM. I walked over to the pop-up Crate Concept shop after breakfast and with all that Indo Rupiahs burning in my pocket I browsed through their beautiful bodysuits and bikinis. I lusted over their kimonos and put my hands all over the soft, white, lacy fabrics. They were perfect: I wanted to wear them all. Then I arrived at the jewelry case. I found layers of gorgeous pieces, delicate and feminine, the type of jewelry you want to stack and wear forever.

And then I saw it: the one—a simple gold band with the face of a lion.

It was perfect. It was everything I never knew I had ever wanted. When I tried it on, I realized it was just a bit too big, but that made me like it even more, like the ring was something I would grow into.

And at that jewelry case, in my version of a bridal shop, in that perfect venue, over a two-course meal of lattes and smoothies, with the last Rupiah I had to my name, and right after

I had booked my October Bali honeymoon, I bought that lion ring. When I slid it on my left middle finger, I realized that I had at long last found the one.

And I married my Holy Self.

And it was just like they always said:

The best day of my life.

Self-love

Dear One,

"Be the right person and then the right person will show up," my Teacher stated during his consciousness course.

I posted this quote and so many others, but I did it for everyone else, not recognizing what these words really meant for me.

I had gone to so many workshops, retreats, and ceremonies trying to figure out who I was. I was constantly waiting for someone to tell me what I was worth. I had Instagrammed so many words about loving yourself and being kinder to yourself and appreciating yourself... but did I?

After my heart surgery, I sure as hell had been trying. I had been doing the work. Been showing up for myself and putting in the time.

One morning, I woke up and my Divine told me I was so close, but she first needed to know what I had learned from all this heartache, heartbreak, and heart surgery. I needed me to answer one very important question.

What is Self-love?

Hmph. That's a doozy. Do I know? Do we ever really know? Are we ever really ready to fully love ourselves?

Well, here goes something—

Self-love is becoming the best version of yourself so you can help empower others. It's falling in love with yourself so you can fall in love with the world. It's honoring yourself and by doing so, understanding what honor looks like to you. And if you don't feel properly seen... that's because you don't see yourself properly. For Self-love is that mirror just waiting for you to look into it and say, "I love what I see."

It's the great acknowledgment that all of life is a mirror. That genius sees genius... you see beauty because you are beautiful. You know she's smart because you're smart. You know what feels wrong because you've been wronged. You know what feels right because you have been right. But Self-love is not about right and wrong... it's about dropping the judgment. It's knowing that every single person on Earth has something that triggers us and makes us feel less than—and that every single one of those exact same people is here to gift some teaching. Self-love is the treasure hunt to find the beauty in everyone and everything.

You have to remember that when it comes to Self-love, no one is going to do it for you. No one can change your life like that. Teachers, coaches, and mentors can help you get started—they can even inspire you and assist you to understand how you want to change your life—but no one just shows up one day and Self-loves your life for you.

Because Self-love is waking up one day and saying . . . Something's gotta change. And it turns out that something is someone . . . and that someone is you.

Self-love is remembering that at our core, we are all the same. It's about knowing that we are all just trying to figure it out . . . and no one has a magic guide that you weren't magically given. That's because Self-love is a journey, and you are the only guide that can lead you there.

Self-love is knowing that you don't have to worry about finding the right person . . . *because the one you want to find is you*. Each and every one of us is already ENOUGH and Self-love shows you that you can truly have it all, just not all at once or when you want it.

Self-love is recognizing how we all need people to show up and support our big accomplishments—but first, Self-love teaches you that you need to show up and do the work yourself.

Self-love is like that very important reminder they give on airplanes: first, put on your own mask so you are safe, then you can help put others' masks on too. Same goes for the ultimate message of life: we have to love and care for ourselves so we can then love and care for others. We have to be brave first; we have to be brave enough to do the inner work, to see the love in our true outer selves. We have to hear what our body tells us, and then we have to be careful and kind with what stories we tell that same body daily.

I love you and I am listening, we say to our partners, our parents, our kids . . . but do we ever say that to ourselves?

And don't worry about changing others; they will follow in their own time. As Gandhi so eloquently put it: *"Be the change you wish to see in the world."* Change your sight and change your life to see that a Self-full life of loving yourself the most is how you connect the dot, dot, dots and the dash, dash, dash. You'll see that there was a Self-love seed planted in you a long time ago. And in time, it will sleep, creep, and leap into a flower.

* * * * *

My mom used to tell me that if a man really loved me, he would sing, "Oh! Darling" by the Beatles to me. She also asked me the same thing about all of my boyfriends during my twenties. As things would get serious, she would pose the question: *"Do you love him so much you can't stand it?"*

I didn't ever know the answer to my mom's question. Because I actually didn't know myself, so how could I ever know my boyfriend? I didn't see myself, so how could I see myself with him? I didn't take time to understand myself. To be myself. To tap into myself. To know what it meant to love myself. So how could I ever properly love anyone else?

And through a painfully simple and seriously solo process called meditation, I began honoring a practice that has changed me and so many before. I finally sat down in the mornings and started the day by doing something just for me. It was so tough in the beginning, to just sit. I had a hard time just being in my body. I had difficulty feeling comfortable alone. I had trouble getting out of my overactive mind. I'd try to sit perfectly . . . and then would stare at my bunions and wish I had different feet. I would put my hands on my knees in *gala mudra* and open my eyes too quickly and then glance at my nails and wish I had gotten a manicure. A minute in, I would hear a big fly around me, swat it away and then curse myself, wishing I could just pause and sit in it and let that pass. Hell, most mornings, I'd sit down, get three minutes into my Insight Timer, and then nature called, and I had to, once again, put my practice on hold to go and release something else.

But what happened next is the gift that became the ritual. I would show back up to the present. Into the practice. Every day . . . for years. For my life. Around the globe. There'd be days when I would look at my feet and think, *these bunions are in BALI! They get to sit and meditate with me. Lucky bunions!* Or, after a long flight home, I'd admire my strong, sturdy legs that made a thirty-seven-hour trip in four different airports. *Now they get to kick back and be upright so all the blood would drain from my cankles. Lucky strong legs!* I'd stand up straight. Work on that flat back—and I'd remember my back brace and what it felt like to be so constricted, and how this beautiful tool was helping me to see that nothing would ever fix me completely. How my slouch, my curved spine, would always be a reminder that healing is a forever job . . . and meditation would teach me that standing up straight is something I need to do for myself daily.

Then I would gaze down at my hands, see the dirt under my nails, and remember how good it feels to do hard manual work. I admired my hands for all that they have been through, perfectly imperfect, weathered from all those years in the service industry. Look at my fingers and recall how many people have been touched by the words I've typed. A friend once said that my hands are an extension of my heart. Ahhh yes. And that heart. My big heart that feels and loves and beats for me every day of my life without asking for a thing. And that beautiful body of mine that functions automatically, only asking for the occasional release in return—be it a long walk, an ecstatic dance, a physical connection, or even just an extra-satisfying happy bowel movement. I'd relinquish control to that body that breathes in and breathes out. Yes, always coming back to that breath.

BECAUSE I HAVE BREATH! Because I have life!

I have the ability to tap into my spirit just by sitting in myself, focusing on my breath and slowing down. And by sitting in myself and understanding the power of the mantra *I AM HERE*, I am able to unwind into my meditations, stop doing and start actually being.

Because that, my friends, is awakening to our true nature, to be here in our bliss body and to embody our divine right for unconditional love.

And one day, it all clicks. And I shout to the sky: "Mom! Mom! I got it. I finally understand what you were saying. My heart is my happy place. My true love is my Self. The one I've been waiting for my whole life... was me."

And now, I am ready.

I, Holly Ruth Finigan, take my heart, Holy Truth Begin Again, as my Self-love partner. To have and to hold from this day forward, for better or worse, for richer or poorer, in sickness and in health, until the moment when we part.

* * * * *

So now, dear reader, we have but one question to end.

We're going to sit this one out, because *we do*.

Because this question, oh darlin', this one's for you

Wholeheartedly,

HOLY Holly

Holly ▼ HOLY

Ruth TRUTH

Finigan BEGIN AGAIN

Dear Reader,

For me, the Chakra System has been an incredible road map and tool for Self healing and spiritual awakening. Every chapter title and image in Part Three of Holly's Bliss has a connection to a specific chakra from the crown down.

The Warrior	The Crown Chakra
To See Is To Be Free	The Third Eye Chakra
Whatever We Resists Persists	The Throat Chakra
Wholeheartedly	The Heart Chakra
This Shit Happens For You	The Solar Plexus Chakra
To Heal It Is To Feel It	The Sacral Chakra
The Innernet	The Root Chakra
The Awakening	The Kundalini

Over the next few pages, I give a brief outline of the seven energy discs. It is my great hope that the Chakras will inspire you to go on your own treasure hunt.

Wholeheartedly,

HOLY Holly

An Introduction to the Chakras

(Sanskrit meaning "wheel" or "turning")

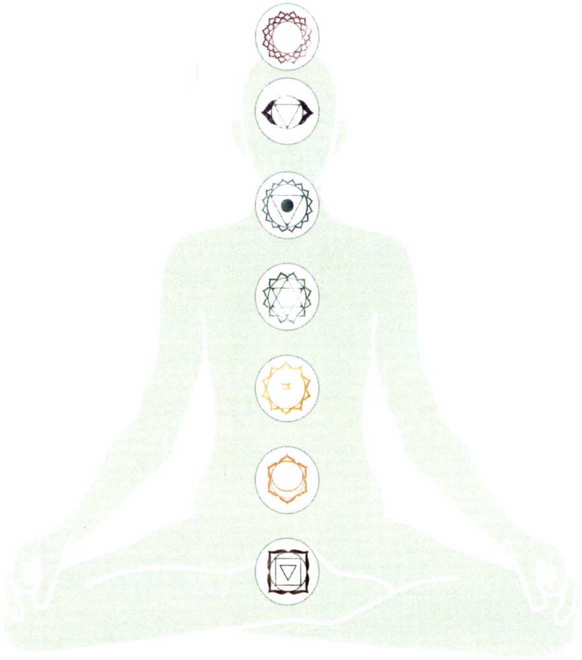

There are seven main chakras or energy centers of the body located along the spinal column. These chakras are like spirals of energy, each one relating to the others. They feed universal energy to all the body systems and functions. Each chakra vibrates at a specific vibrational frequency and resonates with a specific color, sound, life lesson and emotional thought. When these centers are balanced, one's life becomes more balanced, both physically and emotionally.

The Crown Chakra

The crown chakra, the Sahasrara (meaning "thousand-fold"), is formed in the body every day of our lives during adulthood. It is located at the top of the head. Its elements are cosmos, space, ether; its color is violet or bright white; association is with the brain. It's here for integration and dis-integration, for living and learning, knowledge and gnosis, understanding and inner-standing, intellect and intelligence. It's where the head meets the heart, and they begin to work together. The main obstacle is attachments to things, feelings, stories, outcomes. The mantra is *I know/gno*. The sound associated with the crown chakra is Agum Satym Om.

The Third Eye Chakra

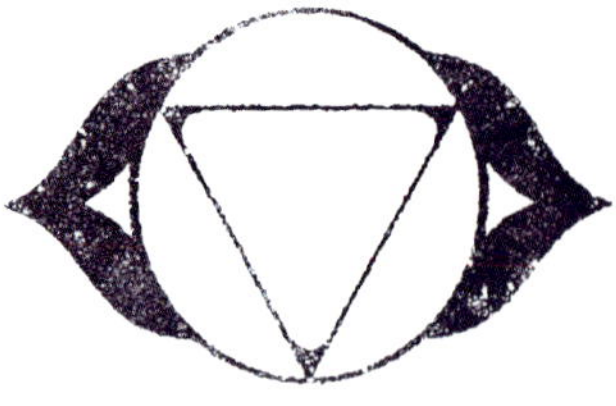

The Third Eye, Ajna, is formed in the body during adolescence. It is located in between the brow bones. Its element is light; its color is indigo; association is with the eyes. It's here for clairvoyance, intuition, for seeing the world inside just as clearly as we see the world outside. It is the last chakra in the body where the solar and lunar energies come together in a state of balance. The main obstacle is illusions. The mantra is *I see*. The sound associated with the third eye chakra is the primordial sound of the universe, OM, three syllables A-U-M (pronounced A-A-A-O-O-M)

The Throat Chakra

The throat chakra, the Vishuddhi, is formed in the body between the ages of eight and twelve. It is located at the throat region. Its element is sound; its color is a bright blue; association is with the lungs and the throat. It's here as your powerhouse, for the truth, for speaking things into existence. The main obstacle is lies and miscommunication. The mantra is *I speak*. The sound associated with this chakra is *hun* or *han* (pronounced HUNG).

The Heart Chakra

The heart chakra, the Anahata (literally translates to "unstruck"), is formed in the body between the ages of four and seven. It is located at the center of the chest. Its element is air; its color is a bright green; association is with the heart. It's here for balance, for compassion, and for unconditional love, first and foremost, for the self. The main obstacle is grief. The mantra is *I love*. The sound associated with the heart chakra is *yun* or *yan* (pronounced YUNG).

The Solar Plexus Chakra

The solar plexus chakra, the Manipura, is formed in the body between eighteen months and four years of age. It is located in the region of the navel. Its element is fire; its color is yellow; association is with the stomach, liver, and small intestine. It's here for sound physical health, specifically gut health. It's also here for empowerment and a strong sense of self. It's the home of integrity, where we burn old stories down and let them rise up in forgiveness. The main obstacle is shame. The mantra is *I can*. The sound associated with this chakra is *run* or *ram* (pronounced RUNG).

The Sacral Chakra

The sacral chakra, the Svadhishthana, literally translates to "the sweetness" and is formed in the body between six months and two years of age. It is located at the base of the spine and in the genital region. Its element is water; its color is orange; association is with the uterus, testes, prostate, and large intestine. It's here for Divine Feminine and Divine Masculine, for creativity, for sensuality and sexuality. The main obstacle is guilt. The mantra is *I feel.* The sound associated is *vun* or *vam* (pronounced VUNG).

The Root Chakra

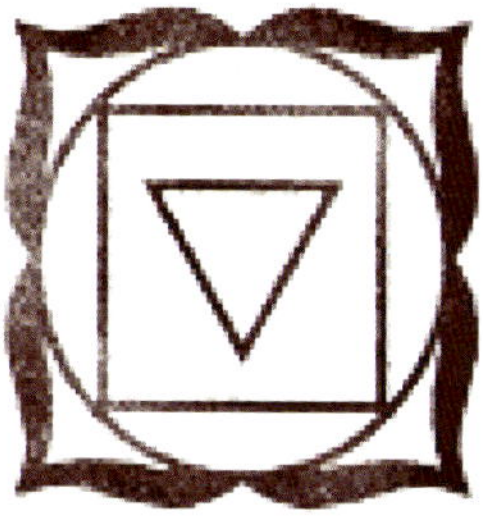

The root chakra, the Muladhara, is formed in the body between conception and one year out of the womb. It is located in the perineum region between the genitals and anus. Its element is earth; its color is red; association is with the kidneys and the bladder. It's here for survival and community, for tribe and for grounding. It is shown visually as a four-petal lotus with a square and a downward-facing triangle representing Divine Feminine Energy inside it. Inside the triangle is a black lingam symbolizing Divine Masculine Energy. Coiled three-and-a-half times around the lingam is a golden serpent, which represents the Kundalini life force energy. The main obstacle is fear. The mantra is *I have a right to be here.* The sound associated with the root chakra is *lam* or *lam* (pronounced LUNG).

The Kundalini

The Kundalini represents the life force energy. It is equally present in each and every one of us, although oftentimes it remains dormant in most people for the entirety of their lives. Its symbol is a golden serpent coiled three-and-a-half times at the base of the spine. Under the guidance of an adept, with the student's practice, patience, presence and awareness, the kundalini rises from her slumber, uncoiling and piercing each of the seven chakras from root to crown on the way up, leading to the flowering of consciousness.

THANK YOU. . .

THANK YOU. . .

THANK YOU. . .

THANK YOU. . .

THANK YOU. . .

THANK YOU. . .

THANK YOU!

There is no way I could have written this book without the support of so many. It took me a decade to write this and human spirits from around the world to complete it. So over the next few pages, you can scan the Flowcodes to meet my teachers, healers, mentors and guides that I write about throughout each chapter of the book.

I'd like to especially thank:

my family for their healing and their unwavering support . . .

I'd like to thank YOU for reading . . .

and finally, I want to show gratitude to my Self . . .

for doing the work and loving the work . . .

...*Now On To The Next One.*

For the full acknowledgement, scan the Flowcode above.

Dear Readers,

I believe Flowcode is an amazing alternative to using a footnote. Since 2020, I have done some great work with Flowcode, which has been described by the founder as "the Tesla of QR codes." Over the next few pages, you'll be able to scan the custom Flowcodes for each of my chapters and deep dive into the stories and posts I told throughout as well as meet my Teachers, Guides and Healers. This is one of my favorite parts of the book as it takes you on another journey and gives you the resources to look into . . . as you begin your Treasure Hunt.

Happy Trails,

Wholeheartedly,

Holly

FLOWCODE

PRIVACY.FLOWCODE.COM

HOW TO SCAN:

Open the camera on your phone

Aim it at the Flowcode

Tap the banner that appears

1.

The Dreamer

2.

The Parents

3.

The Matriarchy

4.

The Words

5.

The Body

6.

The Home

7.

The Internet

8.

The Mother

9.
The Exchange

10.
The Shadow

11.
The Heart

12.
The Truth

13.

The Light

14.

The Knowing

15.

The Warrior

16.

To See is to Be Free

17.

Whatever We Resist, Persists

18.

Wholeheartedly

19.

This Shit Happens For You

20.

To Heal it, Is to Feel it

21.
The Innernet

22.
The Awakening

THE ONE YOU WANT TO FIND IS...

We're going on a treasure hunt...

The world marks the spot...

With a dash dash dash ---

And a dot dot dot . . .

And three great big question marks

- Who am I?

- Why am I here?

- And how is my relationship with my parents?

Begin again...

Do the work...

And when you love the work...

You'll exchange all that for your golden key...

Which unlocks your heart to Your Higher Self.

And life's greatest treasure, called the shiverees.

HOLLY RUTH FINIGAN

Holly Ruth Finigan is a writer, entrepreneur, and meditation advocate. She teaches people through her words and her multi-layered communication skills how to feel empowered through Self-love and healing relationships with parents. Holly always begins by letting people know that the first and most important relationship to heal is the one they have with their Self. Holly studied English/Journalism at the University of New Hampshire. She has written blogs and lived around the world, yet always comes home to the island of Nantucket. It was on this "Grey Lady" in 2012 that she founded her first company, *The Nantucket blACKbook*, a platform for teaching brands and businesses to rely on advocacy over advertising for successful digital marketing. Holly is a free spirit and yet she is rigid about just two things in her life: daily gratitude lists and her meditation ritual. She considers every day she wakes up to be the best day of her life.

Wholeheartedly: *The One You Want To Find Is You* is her first book.